Frontier Community

FRONTIER COMMUNITY
KANSAS CITY TO 1870

A. THEODORE BROWN

University of Missouri Press

Columbia, Missouri

Copyright 1963 by

THE CURATORS OF THE

UNIVERSITY OF MISSOURI

*Library of Congress Catalog
Card Number 63-14768*
Manufactured in the United States of America

474
.K2B7

93990

To

Helen Norma Betts Brown

and

Andrew Hiram Brown

WITHDRAWN

EMORY AND HENRY LIBRARY

Preface

THIS HISTORY of Kansas City was begun by the late R. Richard Wohl, of the University of Chicago. The work was financed by a three-year grant from the Rockefeller Foundation which enabled Dr. Wohl to hire a staff of research associates, whose work he superintended until his untimely death in 1957. The scheme of the book had been worked out by then, and much of the research had been done. I was senior research associate on Dr. Wohl's staff, and I arranged to complete the research and to write the text. I believe the book reflects the emphases which Dr. Wohl intended to give it; at any rate, this has been my intention. Its good points—assuming it has some—must be credited largely to this imaginative scholar and excellent friend and teacher, unfortunately taken off in the midst of his work. Responsibility for its shortcomings is mine.

The fine work done by other staff members must be acknowledged: Elliot Rosen completed a preliminary study of early railroad plans in Kansas City, and Mildred C. Cox (who served also as our secretary) compiled a great deal more data on the town company and upon the histories of prominent families than it has been possible to incorporate in the present text. To Charles N. Glaab special mention is due; readers will note references to his work—and may, indeed, have read it in book form before this meets their notice.

The book was made possible, directly, by a number of agencies and individuals in Kansas City. James Anderson, who directs the Archives of the Native Sons of Kansas City, is in himself a one-man historical society, combining industry and perceptiveness with gracious hospitality; all serious work on Kansas City's history must begin with a visit to him. Richard B. Sealock, who conducts the Public Library with a view to the benefit of scholarship, inconvenienced himself on many occasions in order to help us; to him and his fine staff much gratitude is due. Community

Studies, Incorporated—a private research organization—provided office space and equipment, plus the advantage of associating with people from various disciplines who are closely acquainted with present-day Kansas City. I should like especially to mention Dr. W. D. Bryant, who directs this agency, and Dr. Martin Loeb, who was then associated with it. The University of Kansas City was very helpful to me in arranging and reducing my teaching schedules, and my colleagues in the Department of History and Government—especially E. J. Westermann (the chairman), John Dowgray, and Robert L. Branyan—kindly put up with a great deal in the work's interest. Mrs. Helen Branyan typed the final text and offered sensitive help in stylistic matters.

The Indiana State Historical Library in Indianapolis, the Missouri Historical Society in St. Louis, the Burton Historical Collections of the Detroit Public Library, the Kansas State Historical Society in Topeka, the Burlington Railroad, the Jackson County Court House (Independence, Missouri), and the Office of the City Clerk in Kansas City, all made valuable material available to us. Blake McKelvey and Richard C. Wade read most of the text and gave me the benefit of thoughtful criticism.

Another volume, again financed by the Rockefeller Foundation and this time sponsored by the University of Kansas City, is currently in preparation; it will carry the story from 1870 to the present day. Since footnote citations are in considerable detail, I have not included a bibliography; readers will find some discussion of the more easily available material in R. Richard Wohl and A. T. Brown, "The Usable Past: a Study of Historical Traditions in Kansas City," *Huntington Library Quarterly, XXIII* (May, 1960), 237-59.

A. THEODORE BROWN

Department of History and Government
University of Missouri at Kansas City
1963

CONTENTS

Illustrations

On the Rim of the
"Great American Desert"

THERE IS a building in downtown Kansas City, Missouri, above which was placed, a few years ago, an enormous painted statue of a Hereford bull. The building is on a high point known as Quality Hill, and a little to the north and west the land drops away almost precipitously—more gently to the east and south. At night the statue is illuminated, and it can be seen for many miles. When the bull was set in place, in 1955, there was some suggestion that at least a few Quality Hill residents were not entirely pleased, but the agitation was minor, and it subsided quickly. Now and then sarcastic remarks are passed about life in a "cow town," but the importance of livestock to the city blunts the point of such barbs. The great Hereford, after all, has a certain symbolic accuracy; if it could have been placed over the grain exchange it would call attention even more strikingly to what any townsman will concede: This city lives off its connections with the far-stretching plains country. As the City Plan Commission once put it, "the metropolitan area of Kansas City exists because of a very productive agricultural hinterland which is tied to it by a spiderweb of rail and truck lines."[1]

A short distance from the statue, just above the point of the bluffs, there is a small observation park in the center of which a plaque on a boulder commemorates the spot as Lewis and Clark Point. Those two explorers passed by the site of present-day Kansas City both ways on their expedition to and beyond the sources of the Missouri River. On the way upstream in June, 1804, they camped by the river, and William Clark noted in his journal that a few deer had been seen. Many months later, on

---

[1] *Agriculture: Greater Kansas City* (Kansas City: City Plan Commission, 1945), p. 3. A motion picture depicting Kansas City's development is entitled "Cow Town, U.S.A."

the way back to civilization, the expedition camped again at the same place. This time Clark climbed to the top of the bluffs, looked about him, and concluded that the situation would be excellent for a fort.[2]

The boulder and its marker in the park on Lewis and Clark Point are more satisfying aesthetically to a good many Kansas Citians than the big red bull is, but together they help to plot the course of Kansas City's history. Indeed, they do more, for in the wilderness notes of two brave explorers and the agricultural-industrial testimony of the statue there is suggested the crucial relationship between a city's growth, on the one hand, and notions about what its hinterland may be, on the other.

No fort was ever built on the location Clark indicated, but the site's prospects are still commanding. On a clear day one looks north across the Missouri River bordered by buildings and industrial development, past a broad area covered by warehouses and wholesale offices, to a thin line of trees on the far horizon. Part of this area is called North Kansas City; it is an independent municipality, now entirely surrounded by Kansas City. Bearing to the left, the observer's gaze passes over the large and busy Municipal Air Terminal, on the far side of which the Kansas River (sometimes called the Kaw) winds toward its junction with the Missouri, almost in the middle of that stream's "northward bend." Due south from the rivers' intersection runs the invisible line separating the states of Missouri and Kansas. As with North Kansas City, the logic of political boundaries could hardly be more effectively obscured, for there is no break in the urban panorama below Lewis and Clark Point. Still turning leftward, we see grain elevators, flour mills, stockyards, meat-packing establishments, a large railroad yard, and finally—out toward the southwest—the beginning of residential neighborhoods. Most of the last part of our scene is in Kansas City, Kansas. Officially, it is younger and smaller than Kansas City, Missouri, and quite separate politically; but neither place could exist as it is without the other, and the two form one metropolitan unit. At night the

2 R. G. Thwaites (ed.), *Original Journals of the Lewis and Clark Expedition* (New York: Dodd, Mead & Company, Inc., 1904), I, 58-59; V, 385.

view just sketched can rarely be surpassed; the lights of bridges, factories, office buildings, and railroad signals outline the energy and wealth of a driving urban community.

While the first fact concerning Kansas City's existence is that it rests directly on agricultural productivity, the second point to be made is that the community grew very rapidly. If not within the memory of a living man, then at most within that of his grandfather, Quality Hill and the land around it was almost untrammeled wilderness. As late as the 1840's there were only a few cabins near the river; according to one witness the area was blanketed by "the still solitude of the native forest, broken only by the snort of the startled deer . . . and mayhap the distant barking of the hunter's dog or the sharp report of his rifle."[3] Both the agricultural base and the quick tempo of growth were shaping influences in Kansas City's development, about which we shall have a good bit to say. It may be well, however, to begin by describing a rather interesting conflict of opinion over the nature of what became, in the course of time, Kansas City's hinterland.

It is well known that the development of the North American Great Plains was delayed by several obstacles which were peculiar to that region. Western settlers in the nineteenth century went as far as the edge of the tree belt, and there the great migration hesitated. In a sense, it jumped across both the Great Plains and the Rocky Mountains in the 1840's, and Oregon and California were settled before Kansas, Nebraska, western Iowa, and Minnesota. The land just west of the 98th meridian resisted assaults upon it for some time before farmers were finally able to bend it to their uses. The most comprehensive, so to speak, of the obstacles to settlement, coming partly as a result of all the others and partly as a result of early ignorance about the nature of the region, was not physical but mental: the idea, widely held

[3] Quoted in William Miller, *Early History of Kansas City* (Kansas City: Birdsall & Williams, 1881), p. 31.

by responsible people, that no development could ever take place on the Great Plains, that it was simply a stretch of useless territory for one to cross as quickly as possible, that it was, in short, a desert.[4]

Belief in the existence of a "Great American Desert," which was supposed to include most of the plains region, has had a long life in writings about this continent. It made its appearance, stamped with official and scientific approval, early in the last century. While Lewis and Clark did not use the word "desert," the existence of one could have been inferred from their sketchy descriptions of the country; no one expected them to find habitable country. More important were the later and better-equipped expeditions into the newly acquired West. Zebulon Pike, in 1810, compared the trans-Missouri region with "the sandy deserts of Africa," and ten years later Major Stephen H. Long reported that the area was "almost wholly unfit for cultivation, and of course uninhabitable by a people depending on agriculture for subsistence." To some extent this attitude toward the West influenced national policy. It is impossible to believe that, with a more accurate conception of what was at stake, political leaders would have been so lighthearted about setting aside most of the trans-Missouri country for Indian territory, as they did in the 1830's. All of the land immediately west of what became Kansas City—land from which the later city was to draw the wealth that made it grow—was guaranteed to various Indian tribes "as long as the grass shall grow and rivers flow," as the customary phrase in the treaties stated.

Once the desert notion received official sanction and even

---

[4] Walter P. Webb's classic, *The Great Plains* (Boston: Ginn and Company, 1931), describes the lack of water, building material, and fencing material, and the Indian barrier. On the desert idea, see R. C. Morris, "The Idea of a Great American Desert East of the Rocky Mountains," *Mississippi Valley Historical Review*, XIII (1926-27), 190-200. Changing attitudes toward the West are analyzed by Henry Nash Smith in *Virgin Land: The American West as Myth and Symbol* (Cambridge, Mass.: Harvard University Press, 1951), and more briefly in his article, "Rain Follows the Plow," *Huntington Library Quarterly*, X (1947), 169-94. For the relevance to Kansas City, see R. Richard Wohl, "Urbanism, Urbanity and the Historian," University of Kansas City *Quarterly Review* (Autumn, 1955), pp. 53-61. In the following paragraphs, quotations not footnoted otherwise are from Morris' article.

scientific currency—it is important to remember that Long's expedition had been elaborately fitted out with scientists and their tools—it spread widely. Travelers in the West were expected to write something about the desert when they got home. Their Eastern and European audiences awaited this sort of thing eagerly, and most of the writers were happy to supply it. Even men of the stature of Irving and Parkman did nothing to correct the established picture. In *The Oregon Trail*, for example, Parkman described the valley of the Platte River as

> a long, narrow, sandy plain [beyond which] lay a barren, trackless waste—"the Great American Desert"—extending for hundreds of miles to the Arkansas on the one side and the Missouri on the other.[5]

Perhaps the most ambitious exploration made by Americans in the nineteenth century was that connected with building a transcontinental railroad. During the 1850's, under the supervision of the Secretary of War, the Army sent out parties of men to determine which of five proposed routes would be the most satisfactory. These parties were well equipped, their work was well financed by the Government, and—partly because of sectional controversy over which route would be chosen—the explorations were possibly better publicized than any other government investigation before or since. The reports were published during the years 1855 to 1861, and public demand for them quickly outran the supply. These carefully printed and beautifully bound volumes contained exhaustive descriptions of the whole western country, along with detailed maps and full-color illustrations by some of the best artists in the United States. In other words, both the expeditions and the publication of their results were major government enterprises, and they contributed what one scholar has called "probably the most important single contemporary source of knowledge on western geography and history. . . ." Consequently, it is instructive to notice the editorial reaction of *The North American Review* to the whole enterprise:

[5] Francis Parkman, *The Oregon Trail* (3d ed.; Columbus, Ohio: J. Miller, 1857), p. 81; the same passage in the first edition is cited by Morris, *op. cit.*, pp. 195-96.

We may as well admit that Kansas and Nebraska, with the exception of the small strip of land upon their eastern borders, are perfect deserts, with a soil . . . of such nature as forever to unfit them for the purposes of agriculture. . . .

At about the same time, one United States senator argued against the admission of Kansas into the Union because, he said, "after we pass west of the Missouri River . . . there is no territory fit for settlements or habitation."[6] Travelers and writers of school geographies continued well into the 1870's to delimit an area—most of which is today within Kansas City's agricultural hinterland—and to call it "the Great American Desert."

Still, the impulses behind American expansion in the nineteenth century were ultimately too strong for the desert myth. It lay athwart the drive toward continental destiny for the United States, and as this drive gathered force in the years before the Civil War, those men who had expressed the desert myth replaced it with another, equally important from our point of view. Far from being a desert, said these men, the great West was "the Garden of the World." Here, in the American heartland, mankind would finally realize the dream of abundance for everyone, of untold wealth, of social freedom, and of every other imaginable variety of physical and spiritual well-being.

Among the proponents of this optimistic counterstatement perhaps the most colorful was William Gilpin. His active life brought him into association at various times with Andrew Jackson, Thomas Hart Benton, John C. Frémont, Andrew Doniphan, and Abraham Lincoln. All his many projects were closely connected with western development; at one time they included considerable land-buying in what has since become greater Kansas City. In a series of writings during the 1850's and 1860's, Gilpin set about to reshape the thinking of his contemporaries concerning the western country. The whole notion of a great American desert, he said, was "a radical misconception." Current ignorance about the trans-Missouri region was comparable to

6 Robert C. Taft, *Artists and Illustrators of the Old West* (New York: Charles Scribner's Sons, 1953), pp. 3-15, 5-6; J. L. Webster, "The West: Its Place in History," *Kansas Historical Collections*, XII (1911-12), 27.

European ignorance, before Columbus, about what lay on the far side of the Atlantic Ocean. "These Plains are not DESERTS . . ." Gilpin claimed; "they are . . . the Pastoral Garden of the World."[7] Other enthusiastic men, in public and private life, supported and elaborated Gilpin's thesis wholeheartedly. From this tension between two directly opposed beliefs as to the nature of the West, there arose a whole literature as the century wore on. What could be done with the area? What were its prospects?

It had been said that the climate was arid, west of the 100th meridian; it had been said that no trees grew there, that rivers were scarce, and so forth. With the passing years, however, more and more people were moving into this ambiguous West; more and more men were coming to have a direct stake in its growth. Land speculators, town developers, railroad builders, western state and local governments—all were heavily interested in replacing the unattractive image of the desert with something comporting more closely with Gilpin's optimism. Inevitably, more and more propagandistic efforts were turned in this direction.

Two answers to the charges of aridity and sterility were possible: to ignore them, or to try to convert them into advantages. A railroad land-advertising pamphlet, for example, simply stated that central Nebraska offered no special problems to the farmer but gave him the benefits of mild climate, plenty of timber, and a reliable supply of good water. "Broad prairies, dotted with well-cultivated and well-stocked farms, greet the eye . . ." the pamphlet went on, "and there is an absence of many diseases that render our lower lands so peculiarly unhealthy." Another writer, in response to the charge that Kansas was uncomfortably arid, suggested that this was a great boon for sufferers from respiratory ailments. "One good lung here is worth a pair in the damp heavy air of the older states," this man wrote; "western Kansas is pre-eminently the *Paradise* of the *Lungs*."[8]

---

[7] William Gilpin, *The Central Gold Region* (Philadelphia: Sower & Barnes; St. Louis: E. K. Woodward, 1860), p. 120; for a good essay on Gilpin see Smith, *op. cit.*, chap. iii.

[8] Bill Dadd (pseud.), *Great Transcontinental Railroad Guide* (Chicago: G. A. Crofutt & Co., 1869), p. 15; L. D. Burch, *Kansas As It Is* (Chicago: C. S. Burch & Co., 1878), p. 21.

A more important and more interesting approach to the problem of the West took the form of a scientific theory of climatic change. Indeed, the West had been dry and arid from time immemorial, but now cosmic readjustments were under way. Rainfall was beginning to increase; what had actually been a desert was now becoming a garden! The migration of human beings across the face of the earth had induced this profound change. As cultivators moved into this vast heartland area, they were slowly and portentously altering the climatic pattern of the planet.

In 1869 Cyrus Thomas, government geographer and scientist of high repute, had noted in a report that the basic difficulty confronting western settlement was the water supply. He found some evidence that the amount of rainfall in the region was increasing annually and leaped to the conclusion, which he gave as his "firm conviction," that as population grew so would the amount of rainfall. Other scientists agreed: Frederick V. Hayden (who was Thomas' superior officer in the government) believed that the planting of trees changed the air currents so as to produce more rain; Professor Samuel Aughey, at the University of Nebraska, attributed the happy development to the greater capacity of soil, when broken up by plows, to absorb moisture; according to another writer, "the effect of railroads and telegraphs is undoubtedly to cause more frequent showers, perhaps by promoting a more even distribution of the magnetic forces."[9] The significance of all these arguments was simply that wherever the American farmer went, a beneficent climate would go with him. The desert had, so to speak, met its masters; by 1881 a publicist of the West could note calmly that "the desert country, or American desert, reported . . . west of the 100th meridian, has no real existence."[10]

---

[9] James C. Malin, "The Agricultural Regionalism of the Trans-Mississippi West, as Delineated by Cyrus Thomas," *Agricultural History*, XXI (1948), 211; Smith, "Rain Follows the Plow," cited above; C. C. Hutchinson, *Resources of Kansas* (Topeka: By the author, 1871), p. 39.

[10] The last quotation is from C. D. Wilbur, *The Great Valleys and Prairies of Nebraska and the Northwest* (Omaha: *Daily Republican*, 1881), p. 146.

The purport of this debate over the prospects of the American West was not lost upon a number of men whose fortunes, around mid-century and after, were tied to the growth of Kansas City. Metropolitan centers do not flourish on the verges of deserts, but rather in or near productive hinterlands. The growth of this community—from a cluster of stores and warehouses in the 1840's, to a would-be railroad center in the 1850's, and finally (after the Civil War) to the status of regional metropolis—went in lock step, so to speak, with the history of the whole trans-Missouri West. The change in attitudes about the possibilities of that West is an appropriate frame in which to set the earlier phases of the city's history. This relationship, moreover, was always more or less understood on the townsite at the river's bend.

As early as 1858 a local booster named Charles Spalding brought out a slim volume called *Annals of the City of Kansas;* the Introduction reproduced four pages of Gilpin's panegyric to the Great Plains as "garden of the world." About a year later, the editor of Kansas City's first successful newspaper, Robert T. Van Horn, published a column entitled "The Desert Mirage—It Has Moved Again." Others joined in contradicting the desert myth. They described the "exceptional fertility" of Kansas City's western hinterland; as the city grew, they pointed out its ties with the Great Plains; local growth, they maintained, was "the direct and legitimate offspring of our national growth." By the beginning of the twentieth century, the secretary of the Manufacturers' Association felt he could afford some irony: "The 'Great American Desert,'" he wrote, " . . . has become the chief granary of this nation."[11] The garden-desert debate was in effect a debate over Kansas City's chances. Its various phases had some bearing on how the town's builders might calculate the future, and that, in turn, had a great deal of bearing on their actions.

11 James C. Malin, *Grassland Historical Studies* (Lawrence, Kansas: By the author, 1950), I, 139; R. T. Van Horn and W. H. Powell, "The New West—Its Outlets to the Ocean," in *History of Jackson County* (Kansas City: Birdsall & Williams, 1881), pp. 517-18; S. F. Howe, *The Commerce of Kansas City in 1886* (Kansas City: By the author, 1886), p. 7. The last quotation is from an undated clipping, around 1900, from the advertising section of *The North American Review*, in the Snyder Memorial Collection, University of Kansas City Library.

It is impossible to say when Kansas City was founded. The State of Missouri granted the municipal charter in 1853. The Jackson County Court had marked off the community for separate administration in 1850, and this date was chosen as the official "founding" date when the city fathers held a centennial in 1950. There had been a town company—a group of land speculators who surveyed streets and lots on the site—in 1838. But even before this, a succession of small communities had appeared in the area, associated with the fur trade, missionary projects, and Far Western commerce. Each of these played a part in shaping the future city, long before anyone dreamed that such a city was desirable or even possible. To interpret the history of Kansas City as a natural, cumulative process has some logic, but this interpretation obscures the uncertainties and the tentative nature of the city's beginnings.[12] To disentangle these beginnings, we must go back to 1821, when a fur-trade post was established near the juncture of the rivers. The first fact we note is that the impulse for the new settlement came from St. Louis.

Perhaps no American city was born under such favorable auspices as St. Louis, Missouri. It was located at the confluence of navigable water courses which drained over a million square miles of the continent, and it was built by a number of big businessmen ("big" for that time, which was 1764) who knew precisely what they were doing. These men were Franco-American fur-trade magnates. Their headquarters were in New Orleans, and their connections with the fur markets were world-wide. St. Louis was their inland substation from which agents with supplies and instructions could be dispatched and at which the profitable harvest of furs from hundreds of rivers and wandering Indian tribes could be gathered. They were not only operators of scope but also men with Old World ties and cultivation, urbane in every sense of the word. The family and the associates of Auguste Chouteau, who had superintended the building of St. Louis for the New Orleans company, were literate and well educated. The

---

[12] A similar picture of starts and false starts is given in Blake McKelvey, *Rochester: The Water Power City* (Cambridge, Mass.: Harvard University Press, 1945), pp. 3-71; see also Bayrd Still, *Milwaukee: The History of a City* (Madison: State Historical Society of Wisconsin, 1948), pp. 3-9.

Chouteaus' private library held many classical and modern works, the latter category including Voltaire and Rousseau, and there were other families in early St. Louis who exhibited the same kind of culture. St. Louis, in other words, was a *city* almost from the moment its first building went up, with all of the economic base, the capital, the social and cultural discipline implied in the notion of metropolitanism. On the margin of almost illimitable wilderness, it was a solid rampart of European urbanity and civilization.[13] It was to be about ninety years after the founding of St. Louis before any serious thoughts arose about the likelihood of an important American city farther west.

By 1820 St. Louis numbered something over four thousand inhabitants. Meanwhile, the great American Fur Company, which had earlier confined its activities to the northern regions, had in 1813 acquired control of the Missouri Fur Company, which was St. Louis' largest firm. The Chouteaus were now, for a time, to be part of the Astor enterprise, and during these years the American Fur Company seems to have embarked on a full-scale drive toward monopoly. The first objective was to eliminate the federal government from the fur business, and the second objective was to absorb or bankrupt the various independents.

The concern of government officials with Indian affairs had involved the fur trade in a curious and interesting way, and had led, very early in the nineteenth century, to the establishment of a government-sponsored community on the Missouri River about twenty miles from what is today the heart of downtown Kansas City. This was called Fort Osage, and it was part of a system of trading establishments or "factories" through which some optimists hoped that relations with the Indian tribes could be peaceably and progressively regulated. This system had begun during the 1790's, and over the years during which it operated, a total of twenty-eight Indian supply stores were set up at various times and on several frontiers. Indians were encouraged to bring their

---

13 Isaac Lippincott, "A Century and a Half of Fur Trade at St. Louis," *Washington University Studies*, III, Part 2 (1916), 235; H. M. Chittenden, *The American Fur Trade of the Far West* (New York: F. P. Harper, 1902), I, 3-4; John Francis McDermott, *Private Libraries in Creole St. Louis* (Baltimore: The Johns Hopkins Press, 1938), especially the Preface.

furs to these stores, where they might trade them for manufactured goods. The factors (the government employees who were in charge of the factories) were for the most part scrupulously fair, and a strong effort was made to keep liquor out of the whole factory system. Each store had a small fort located by it, and detachments of soldiers manned the forts. But the main purpose of the factory system was not military; it was hoped that the Indians might be—through perfectly fair means—lured into greater dependence upon the white man's goods. Along with this process, the Indian would be taught the skills and techniques necessary to produce those goods himself and would thereby be placed on the road toward ultimate and relatively painless absorption into nineteenth-century American society.

Fort Osage was built in 1808 on the right bank of the Missouri River. It soon became one of the largest of the factories, drawing upon a rich territory and managed by the competent factor, George C. Sibley. He and his wife, along with the little military group, entertained the parties of travelers who passed up and down the Missouri from time to time. In a good year the factory might take in more than $20,000, counting money, furs, and other Indian trade goods which the factor could accept. This was the first attempt of any kind at establishing a stable white community in the general area of the Missouri's great bend. Its existence, of course, presupposed conditions which, while they lasted, made it impossible for anything resembling a city to appear in that area.[14]

The fort, in fact, disappeared well before such urban prospects began to arise; it went out of existence along with the system of which it had been a part. Private traders, especially the American Fur Company, had never liked the idea of government

14 For the factory system see Edgar Bruce Wesley, *Guarding the Frontier: A Study of Frontier Defense from 1815 to 1825* (Minneapolis: University of Minnesota Press, 1935), pp. 31-54; Ora Peake, *A History of the United States Indian Factory System, 1795-1822* (Denver: Sage Books, 1954). James Anderson, historian for the Native Sons of Kansas City, has transcribed all the available documentary sources bearing on Fort Osage, some published and some unpublished; the transcripts are in two large notebooks at the Archives of the Native Sons of Kansas City, City Hall, Kansas City, Missouri. See Kate L. Gregg, "The History of Fort Osage," *Missouri Historical Review*, XXXIV (1940), 439-88.

competition. For years these interests carried on a campaign to abolish the factory system, and in 1822 they achieved this goal. Led by the new State of Missouri's junior senator, Thomas Hart Benton, General Lewis Cass, and others, Congress refused to continue the system of government trading posts. Within a few years after Fort Osage was abandoned, incoming settlers had taken from the empty structures any building materials which could be moved, and there was nothing but decaying foundations to mark the spot.[15]

The presence of settlers in western Missouri suggested that the days of the fur trade were about to be numbered—but not just yet. Into the area came the American Fur Company's agents, and one among them was François Chouteau, a nephew of the man who had planned the building of St. Louis. The younger Chouteau came up the river in 1819 or 1820, looking for good sites for small trading posts. He located several, returned to St. Louis, and in 1821 came back upstream almost to the mouth of the Kaw, to set up a somewhat more impressive station which would control the activities of the smaller ones. The first location of what might be called the Chouteaus' divisional headquarters was on the right bank of the river across from a point called Randolph Bluffs, between what are today the downtown centers of Kansas City and Independence. He brought about thirty employees with him, most of whom went on into the interior during the summer of 1821. A warehouse and a few cabins were built, and in the autumn François Chouteau brought his family upriver to the new post. Apparently, nothing outside of the normal fur-trade routine happened for about five years; then, in 1826, the Missouri River flooded and swept away the warehouse and the cabins. As quickly as he could, Chouteau resettled his little community three miles farther upstream on land which was later to become Guinotte's Addition in Kansas City.[16]

This was the first white settlement in the area of present-day Kansas City. Close to the Chouteau warehouse, the dwellings of the trappers and other functionaries made a small, scarcely no-

15 Gregg, pp. 486-88.
16 William Miller, in *History of Jackson County* (Kansas City: Birdsall & Williams, 1881), p. 378.

ticeable break in the wilderness. The community was, in fact, posited on continued existence of that wilderness and embodied no impulses toward growth. The land stretching away to the south, west, and north was the domain of Indian tribes, and in the land's extent and wildness lay its interest for the Chouteaus and their associates.

The population of their settlement varied with the seasons; much of it was transient, as French-Canadian or American trappers and scouts drifted in for a time and then drifted somewhere else. Late in 1833 Father Benedict Roux, a Catholic priest who had come from France to serve the faithful in the great West, found thriving communities at Liberty and Independence; there was very little to report from the mouth of the Kansas. "It is in Jackson County," he wrote, "that we have most of our Catholics; still their number there is very small. We have here only a dozen French families. . . ." Any possibility of erecting a church there rested almost entirely on the resources of the Chouteaus, who might also "levy on the purse . . . of Mr. Menard of Kaskaskia." However, the families did what they could, and in addition "a number of Americans declared to me their desire of co-operating in a work so advantageous, as they tell me, to the good of the locality." Father Roux was at least able to put together a congregation, and to start plans for the building of a church.

A few years later another priest sketched a little map of the area, noting the location of each house or cabin and the name of its inhabitant. One group of cabins on the map is gathered around Turkey Creek and another around the church which had by then been built. The names are mostly French: Chouteau, Rivard, Prudhomme, Laliberte, Clement, Philibert, and others. There are two Anglo-Saxon names on the map, the date of which is 1840-41: Andrew Dripps, who was an American Fur Company agent, and Thomas Smart, who kept a tavern and general store.[17]

[17] Chittenden, *op. cit.*, chap. vii; James Anderson, "The Roys and Rivards at 'Chouteau's'," *Bulletin of the Missouri Historical Society* (July, 1948), pp. 257-61; Gilbert J. Garraghan, *Catholic Beginnings in Kansas City, Missouri: An Historical Sketch* (Chicago: Loyola University Press, 1920), pp. 43-50, 55-58; "Plan de Westport, 1840-41," drawn by Father Nicholas Point; the original is in the Archives of the College de Sainte Marie, Montreal, and a photostatic copy is in the Archives of the Native Sons of Kansas City.

Even the almost self-subsistent fur-trade post radiated needs around which a few supplementary activities gathered. According to the later reminiscences of a lady who was born near the post in 1829,

> the Canadian-French were making more than a living feeding and rooming the hunters and trappers and selling garden products to the fur boats and to men passing in skiffs. . . . Nature had made a good landing place . . . and soldiers . . . would go to the Canadian squatters for potatoes, chickens and prairie birds and sometimes make contracts for a regular supply for the army. Money was passing hands and a few stores were doing good business. . . .

Now and then a nondescript family or two would come in from the Rockies and settle down nearby. Here and there could be found an early American settler, either awaiting or trying to escape the coming of nineteenth-century civilization. Still, the fur-trade community held no promise of development. It could not, for example, support a church until 1835; before that time, the French settlers gathered at the home of one or other of their number to hear Mass and to participate in the other services.[18]

The entry of Missouri into the Union in 1821 signaled some changes which would soon reach the western border of the new state. Exploration and fur trade, characteristically followed at some distance by land claimants and town boomers, drew political organization in their wake. Significantly, the great fur-trading interests felt no enthusiasm for the development. They preferred the old, authoritarian territorial structure under which their own enterprises had flourished and might be expected to continue to flourish. The Act of Congress of October 31, 1803, centralizing political power in the Louisiana Territory in the hands of the President, was popular with them. "These well-to-do French-

---

[18] See W. J. Dalton, *The Life of Father Bernard Donnelly* (Kansas City: Grimes-Joyce, 1921), pp. 62-69, 98; William Kuenhof, "Catholic Church Annals of Kansas City, 1800-1857," *Catholic Historical Review*, III (1917), 326-35.

men," writes one scholar, "petitioned Congress and through their representative, Chouteau, pleaded with Jefferson for just this kind of government."[19]

But the process of entering the Union could not be held back, although it was far from smooth. Born in a bitter conflict which foretold alike to Jefferson and John Quincy Adams the dissolution of the Union, Missouri experienced no sure and easy development from stage to stage and so to wealth. Crisis and doubt bestrode the course at frequent intervals, especially wherever the frontier happened to lie at any given moment, and there is much in Missouri's early history to help us understand that of her westernmost metropolis.

For one thing, nobody really knew what Missouri included— or, perhaps, what it implied. An early memorial to Congress favoring statehood, with boundaries making the Missouri River the center of the proposed commonwealth, remarked that

> the woodland districts are found towards the great rivers. The interior is composed of vast regions of naked and sterile plains, stretching to the Shining Mountains. The states must have large fronts upon the Mississippi to prevent themselves from being carried into these deserts.

Another appeal, this time from the territorial legislature in 1818, asked for a generous western extension of the proposed state boundary because fertile districts in that direction "are small, and are separate and detached from each other at great distances, by immense plains and barren tracts, which must for ages remain waste and uninhabited. . . ."[20]

This attitude, with its negative implications for western city-building, soon began to change. "Radiating from the earlier centers of settlement," writes William Switzler, "St. Louis being the chief or pivotal point from which emigration spread out like a great fan—the tide of population and colonization flowed along the valleys of our larger rivers and thence inland until it covered

---

[19] Floyd Calvin Shoemaker, *Missouri's Struggle for Statehood* (Jefferson City: Hugh Stephens, 1916), pp. 15, 22-23.

[20] *Ibid.*, pp. 43, 321-23.

the whole State".[21] Switzler's striking image enables us to see the filling-in of western Missouri in the 1820's and 1830's, until in 1837 it was clear that a garden had replaced the obsolete desert. "The impression is deeply fixed in the minds of connoisseurs in soil," states a gazetteer of Missouri which appeared in that year, "that the lands in Missouri increase in fertility as we travel westward from St. Charles, until the boundary of the State is reached." Jackson County was organized in 1826-27, at which time, continues the gazetteer,

> a rage for that quarter pervaded the whole emigrating world; and for several years, when movers with the most substantial equipment were questioned on the road as to their destination, they uniformly answered, "Up to the Blues."

Nor were these settlers wrong, or so it appeared: "The quality of the lands in Jackson has not been overrated. . . ." That county was

> happily situated, with a market close at hand for a large amount of its farming products. This market is made by the location of half-civilized emigrant Indians close on their borders, and by the wants of the half-starved tribe of Kansas Indians, who reside farther out. . . . The military post of Fort Leavenworth, on the same side of the Missouri river, and half a day's ride above, likewise swallows up a considerable amount of produce, particularly since the location of dragoons at that place.[22]

As settlement pressed upon the heels of the retreating fur trade, and as the whole character and role of the Indian in western economy changed radically, another set of events signaled what was occurring and where the future lay. The western boundary of Missouri as agreed upon in 1821 ran north and south through the present site of Kansas City. Both sides of the Missouri River, northwest of this site, were thereby left outside the

---

21 W. F. Switzler, *History of Missouri* (St. Louis: C. R. Burns, 1881), p. 285. Switzler points out that for a long time "permanent settlements for agricultural purposes were not contemplated" west of the Mississippi and south of St. Louis.

22 Alphonso Wetmore, *Gazetteer of the State of Missouri* (St. Louis: C. Keemle, 1837), pp. 92-93.

state; this marginal river land was reserved to the Indians, as specified in the Osage Treaty of 1808. This location of the boundary caused no discussion when the treaty was written, for the land in question was almost unknown except to the Indians. By the middle 1820's, however, the oncoming settlers had seen good farmland there, with the inevitable result. From 1825 on, violence on this frontier was endemic, the white settlers encroaching on Indian lands (across a boundary which, it must be pointed out, was for the most part invisible), and the Indians raiding toward the white settlements. On several occasions Missouri raised special militia companies to protect the settlers, and at other times the state appealed to Congress for aid. By 1830 there were at least three hundred families settled across the boundary line, and it was clear that the Indian title would have to be vacated. Missouri's politicians exerted themselves along the proper lines, Senator Lewis Fields Linn writing to Secretary of War Lewis Cass:

> At the time Missouri was admitted to the Union, a critical knowledge of the geography was not to be obtained, or this piece of land would not . . . have been left out of our limits. It is beautiful and fertile, and possessing water-power to an almost unlimited extent. . . . Already allured by its various advantages, and entertaining a confident belief that it will come under our jurisdiction, many families have crossed the line and commenced making farms.

Again the migrant American had forced his government's hand; the series of treaties, proclamations, and ratifications known collectively as the "Platte Purchase" was completed with the formal annexation of the triangle north and west of the mouth of the Kansas River to the State of Missouri on March 28, 1837.[23] A new expanse of land, directly across the river from Chouteau's post, was now open for exploitation.

In one or another way, Indians were involved in phases of Kansas City's history from the very beginning down through the Oklahoma statehood movement. Around 1830, as more and more

---

[23] I have used an unpublished M.A. thesis, "The Platte Purchase and its Significance in Frontier History," by Frederick E. Whitten, on file at the University of Kansas City Library; the Linn quotation is on p. 27.

tribes from east of the Mississippi were relocated by the federal government, increasing numbers of them settled in the area just west of the Missouri line. Along with the Indians came missionaries, some of whom set up impressive establishments near the junction of the two rivers, and some of whom stayed on after their dedicated but transitory religious enterprises had been swept away by the westward movement of Americans.

First to arrive were two circuit-riding Methodist brothers, Thomas and William Johnson.[24] They were Virginians who had come out to Missouri's Howard County in 1825, and when a group of Shawnees requested the services of missionaries, the Missouri Methodist Conference sent the Johnsons to begin work. Early in 1831, Thomas Johnson opened a log-cabin school for Indian children on the Kansas River about ten miles above its mouth. The Methodist mission grew quickly into a small community. By 1833 there were eight buildings, including dwelling house, school, kitchen, stable, workshop, and storehouses; forty children were attending school and thirty-eight acres of land were under cultivation. The mission's peak year was 1845, by which time it had several brick buildings, over a hundred young scholars, five hundred acres of land fenced in, more than a hundred head each of cattle and hogs, and an annual product of thousands of bushels of wheat, oats, and corn.

At almost the same time a prominent Baptist preacher arrived, bringing with him years of experience in the field as a missionary to the Indians. This was Isaac McCoy, and along with his sons and other associates he soon had a flourishing Baptist mission in operation.[25] McCoy had built important Indian missions

[24] See James Anderson, "The Methodist Shawnee Mission in Johnson County, Kansas, 1830-1862," *The Trail Guide*, I (Kansas City: The Westerners, January, 1956), 7-20.

[25] John F. Cady, *The Origin and Development of the Missionary Baptist Church in Indiana* (Franklin, Indiana: Franklin College, 1942), pp. 83-180; Emory J. Lyons, *Isaac McCoy: His Plan of and Work for Indian Colonization*, Kansas State College Studies, History Series, No. 1 (Fort Hays: Kansas State College, 1945), especially pp. 11-25. McCoy discussed his own work in two compositions: *Remarks on the Practicability of Indian Reform* (2d ed.; New York: Gray & Bunce, 1829), and *History of Baptist Indian Missions* (Washington: W. H. Morrison; New York: H. & S. Raynor, 1840).

in Indiana and Michigan before coming to Missouri, and in the course of his work he had come to two main conclusions. In the first place, he believed that in order to Christianize the Indians they must at the same time be "civilized," and by this he meant that they must be trained to enter into nineteenth-century European-American styles of living. They must be taught productive family farming, sewing, blacksmithing, storekeeping; they must be initiated into the arts of self-government on the American model. In the second place, McCoy reasoned that all this could be done only if the Indians were temporarily isolated from contacts with American frontiersmen. Hence he lobbied forcefully for the Indian Removal Act; painful and apparently cruel as its impact would be, the ultimate salvation of the Indians demanded it.

The land west of Missouri seemed to Isaac McCoy to offer an ideal field for his planned operations; the whites would not want it in the foreseeable future. Between Arkansas Territory, Missouri, and the north-south section of the Missouri River on the one side, and the Rocky Mountains on the other side, McCoy wrote, "is the proper place for the colony," thus subscribing to a variation of the desert theory of the trans-Missouri West. He came to Missouri in 1830, at the same time Thomas Johnson was looking for a place for his Methodist mission, and McCoy's own Baptist mission was soon under way on similar lines. Among his family was a son, John Calvin McCoy, who was shortly to lay out a townsite on the Missouri side of the line, and a fellow missionary named Johnston Lykins, who later became a key figure in the group of men who launched and guided the development of Kansas City. A Quaker mission was set up in 1834, and others followed under various sponsorships. Together, these agencies represented a considerable penetration of the wilderness by civilizing forces, but their continued existence depended on the continued isolation of the locale. In a few years the westward movement was to engulf all of them, and their lasting importance to our story lies in the people who were drawn into the area by the missionary impulse.

Other newcomers to the area in the late 1820's and early

1830's bore new impulses with them, and their activities and plans began to change its prospects. In 1828 a man named James Hyatt McGee came to Chouteau's landing; his career illustrates the kind of change that was taking place.[26] McGee's ancestors were among the Scotch-Irish immigrants who reached America in the eighteenth century. He was born in Virginia in 1786, and the family soon moved into Kentucky. In 1816 McGee owned a farm near Shelbyville, and for several years he and his wife and children stayed there. In 1827, for some unrecorded reason, they came west to Missouri; McGee left his family on a farm near Liberty, while for almost a year he searched the countryside for a permanent location.

Near the Chouteau post McGee bought some parcels of land which had been patented by some members of the French community; he also bought a gristmill which two of them had recently built. At about the same time, he made a trip back to Kentucky and returned to his newly chosen home with two slaves—the first, according to one account, in western Missouri.

At this time the local market was considerably enlarged as Congress passed the Indian Removal Act, and the relocated tribes began to occupy their reserved tracts west of the state line. McGee got a government contract to supply some of the Indians with flour from his mill. As the money began to come in, he added a distillery to his enterprises, bought more land, built a sawmill, and began lending money. When he died (1840), his estate included about one thousand acres of land for which he had paid, on the average, less than $2 an acre; at the division of the estate about ten years later, somewhat less than the thousand acres remained, and the remainder was appraised at almost $17,000. A new frontier was coming within the range of nineteenth-century geographical knowledge and business enterprise.

[26] H. L. Conard (ed.), *Encyclopedia of the History of Missouri* (New York: Southern History Company, 1901), IV, 260-61; J. W. Hodge (ed.), *The United States Biographical Dictionary and Portrait Gallery of Eminent and Self-Made Men,* Missouri Volume (New York, Chicago, St. Louis and Kansas City: United States Biographical Publishing Company, 1878), 316-17; R. Richard Wohl, "Three Generations of Business Enterprise in a Midwestern City: The McGees of Kansas City," *Journal of Economic History* (December, 1956), pp. 514-28.

The first substantial urban project on this frontier, however, was to fail. Along with entrepreneurs and missionaries, there came the Mormons who planned nothing less than to build the sacred city of Zion in Jackson County, Missouri. The literature commonly associates Zion with Independence, implying that the Mormons were engaged in operations some distance from the site of Kansas City. This was certainly not the Mormon conception. In their view, Independence, "which . . . embraced what is now Kansas City," was rather broadly defined. The inhabitants of Chouteau's post were powerfully exercised by the Mormon incursion. On June 17, 1834, Father Roux informed his bishop that "the little Catholic congregation" was in turmoil on this account, and that the Mormon trouble "will place certain obstacles for some time to come in the way of our designs."[27]

The background of these events, briefly stated, is this: In 1830-31, the young Mormon Church—founded by Joseph Smith, Jr., and concentrated in the area around Kirtland, Ohio—experienced a fever common enough in the United States at the time: It would realize salvation by moving west. Smith and a few other leaders settled upon Jackson County as the proper spot for Zion. Without being completely isolated, Jackson County and its seat, Independence, were on the extreme edge of settlement. Beyond them lay only the Indian country. Like other groups in the country at that time (Owenites, Fourierites, Rappists, and many more), they organized their migration as best they could, and economic development became inextricably entwined around religious doctrine.

The Kirtland church raised $3,000 from contributions, all of which was turned over to a bishop, Edward Partridge, who used it to buy the Jackson County land on which Zion was to be built. Partridge had no trouble acquiring the land; he bought from the United States, from the State of Missouri, and from individuals in and around Independence. In all, he purchased nearly two thou-

---

[27] Joseph Geddes, *The United Order Among the Mormons (Missouri Phase)* (Salt Lake City: Deseret Press, 1924), p. 17; Father Roux is quoted in Garraghan, *op. cit.*, p. 69.

sand acres of land, about half of which is today within the limits of Kansas City.[28]

The plans for the sacred city were carefully drawn. Two letters from the Mormon presidency, dated June 24 and 25, 1833, give an idea of the detail in which the elders envisioned their Zion. The plot was to be one mile square, divided into sub-squares, each containing ten acres. Within these smaller blocks, lots were to be laid out on two alternating plans: on the first, the lots were to run lengthwise north and south, on the second, they were to run east and west, and so on, throughout the master plot. In the center, a number of squares were reserved for public buildings: the bishop's storehouse, temples for the presidency and priesthood, schools, etc. "The whole plot is to contain from fifteen to twenty thousand people. . . ." Surrounding the residential area, small farms were to be laid out and worked by the residents of Zion. The planned streets were spacious, each lined by single-family residences set in lawns and gardens. No wooden buildings were permitted in the city. The Mormons planned a smoothly working metropolis on the edge of civilization; had they carried through their plan, it would have been more than a century ahead of its time.[29]

As a matter of history, they could not implement their plan in Jackson County. The migration got out of hand; hundreds of individuals packed up their goods and headed for Zion before arrangements had been made to receive them. This flood of settlers was not only contrary to the plans of the leaders, but it also disturbed the Gentiles who were already on the ground at Independence. These people, according to a contemporary renegade Mormon,

> saw their country filling up with emigrants, principally poor. They disliked their religion, and saw, also, that if left alone, they would in a short time become a majority, and of course, rule the county. The church kept increasing, and the old citizens became more and more dissatisfied. . . .

[28] Rollin J. Britton, "Mormon Land Titles—A Story of Jackson County Real Estate," *Annals of Kansas City* (Kansas City: Missouri Valley Historical Association, 1921-24), I, 145-53.

[29] Geddes, *op. cit.*, pp. 88-92.

There is other testimony to the same effect; the generally accepted statement is that by the summer of 1833 there were about
twelve hundred Mormons in Jackson County. They had set up a
general store, some mechanics' shops, and a newspaper press in
Independence.[30]

In July, 1833, several hundred citizens met in Independence
in order to decide upon ways and means of ridding the area of the
new immigrants; included were some of those who had only two
years earlier sold land to the newcomers. The meeting issued an
ultimatum to the Mormons: They were to vacate Jackson County
and guarantee that no more of their coreligionists would settle
there. The Mormon newspaper was to cease operations immediately, and the other businesses must prepare to close out. According to their manifesto, the Missourians felt themselves
justified "by every consideration of self-preservation, good society,
public morals, and the fair prospect (if not blasted in the germ)
that waits this young and beautiful country. . . ." As to religious
creeds, ". . . we have nothing to say. Vengeance belongs to God
alone!" The Mormons, loath to abandon their projects, tempor-
ized, whereupon the printing plant was burned to the ground by
the Missourians. At another conference a few days later, the
Mormons agreed to move out, and in return the Jackson County
leaders engaged to pay for the destroyed print shop.[31]

Months passed, and the Missourians saw no signs of preparations by the Mormons for the move. Violence broke out again in
October and continued sporadically. In the summer of 1834 the
Mormons yielded, at least temporarily; they crossed the river into
Clay County, where they were at first hospitably received. The
same pattern was repeated: The older settlers grew restive as the
incoming group discussed what they conceived the future to hold
for them. Threats and violence were then followed by another

[30] John Corrill, *A Brief History of the Church of Jesus Christ of Latter-Day
Saints* . . . (St. Louis: By the author, 1839), p. 19; James H. Hunt, *A History of
the Mormon War* . . . (St. Louis: Ustick and Davies, 1844), pp. 127-28.

[31] Hunt, *op. cit.*, pp. 128-32, is anti-Mormon; the same events from the Mor-
mon standpoint are covered in B. H. Roberts, *The Missouri Persecutions* (Salt
Lake City: Cannon & Sons, 1900), pp. 73-75, and in Joseph Fielding Smith,
Essentials in Church History (Salt Lake City: Deseret News Press, 1928), pp. 156-62.

move on the part of the Mormons. From Clay they went to Caldwell County, and from Caldwell into Carroll and Daviess counties. Ultimately, in the "Mormon War" of 1838-39, the unhappy
wanderers were expelled as an organized group from Missouri.

Why were these would-be city builders driven from the
Missouri frontier? Many explanations have been offered. It has
been held that their Jackson County newspaper, the *Evening and
Morning Star*, took ambiguous attitudes on the questions of slavery and free Negroes, although all it did was to print the laws of
the state on those subjects.[32] Another charge was that the Mormons intended to convert the Indians, who would then "through
rivers of blood . . . take possession of their ancient inheritance."
But as far as the evidence goes, the Indians meant to Joseph
Smith about what they meant to James Hyatt McGee and many
other Jackson Countians: a market to be supplied with grain and
other provisions in exchange for their annuity money.[33]

The question of possible political control in the hands of the
Mormons goes deeper, but it is quite likely that this question in
turn relates to another. The Jackson Countians referred to their
own bright prospects "if not blasted in the germ." In Daviess
County the Mormons began a town enterprise which they called
"Adam-ondi-Ahmen" (variously rendered), which grew rapidly,
dwarfing an already existing county seat named Gallatin. "This
stirred up the people of Daviess," said one contemporary witness,
". . . for they say that if this town was built up rapidly it would
injure Gallatin. . . ." Among a number of anti-Mormon petitions
to the governor of Missouri during the period, complaints like
the following occur:

> Most of us, sir, emigrated to these frontier counties before
> there were any settlements formed; we have had to encoun-
> ter . . . nearly all the difficulties incident to a new country—
> we have foregone the pleasures and the advantages of the
> old and well settled counties, which we have left in antici-
> pation of enjoying like blessings in these—but alas! our antici-

---

32 Roberts, *op. cit.*, pp. 78 ff.

33 Hunt, *op. cit.*, p. 134; Joseph Smith, *History of the Church of Jesus Christ
of Latter-Day Saints* (Salt Lake City: Deseret News Press, 1902), p. 279.

pations are blasted, and unless we can get rid of these . . . emissaries of the Prince of Darkness—we and our families are ruined.[34]

The Mormons were city builders at a time and place in which settlers were doing well to push up small towns. To them, the case was clearly one of mob violence versus a well-planned, decently conceived social organization. Jackson County's old settlers, as the Mormons saw them,

> lived in their log cabins without windows, and very frequently without floors other than the ground. . . . They were uneducated . . . and they had an utter contempt for the refinements of life. It is needless to add that they were narrow-minded, ferocious, and jealous of those who sought to obtain better homes, and who aspired to something better in life than had yet entered into the hearts of these people.[35]

These remarks denigrate the Jackson Countians unduly, but they also suggest that no metropolis could be imported into the Missouri frontier. A great deal of both cultural and economic growth was necessary before any urban enterprises could take root.

By the early 1830's, then, farmers, Indians, Indian missionaries, and Indian traders had come into Jackson County, Missouri. An overland trade with the Far Southwest had begun to grow, and its eastern terminus was moving up the Missouri River toward Independence, the county seat. To the north, across the river, farms were being staked out and towns were appearing; farther upstream, the military establishment first called Cantonment Leavenworth and later Fort Leavenworth was becoming a more important outpost with the passing years. The *voyageurs* and *coureurs de bois* who lived around the Chouteau station had

---

[34] Corrill, *op. cit.*, p. 28; General Assembly of Missouri, *Document Containing the Correspondence, Orders, &c., in Relation to the Disturbance with the Mormons* . . . (Fayette, Missouri: Boon's Lick Democrat, 1841), p. 19.

[35] Roberts, *op. cit.*, pp. 71-72.

still a few years in which to carry on their activities connected with the fur trade.

In 1825 a Major John Campbell was appointed to the Shawnee Agency just beyond the Missouri state line.[36] (Another John Campbell appears a few years later in the history of Kansas City; the two were not related in any way.) Major Campbell was a veteran of the Revolutionary War and a nephew of John Sevier, first governor of Tennessee; he had served as Indian agent at various locations for about twenty years. He soon became acquainted with Isaac McCoy and Johnston Lykins as they began to build the Baptist mission to the Shawnees. Lykins, upon his arrival, stayed temporarily in quarters provided by Campbell; among their other dealings, the two men worked together vaccinating the Indians against smallpox.[37]

Meanwhile, land was beginning to look like real estate. James McGee and others were coming into western Jackson County for the purpose of buying parcels of it, and those who were already on the ground also became aware of possibilities. The State of Missouri was selling some of its seminary lands about this time, and in 1833 one James Jennings bought the southwest quarter (160 acres) of Section 20, Township 49, Range 33, for $1.25 an acre. Jennings quickly sold his quarter-section to a Robert Johnson, who in turn sold it to Major John Campbell on August 9, 1834. Campbell was not averse to selling land, but first he had thirty acres of this parcel surveyed and made into a townsite plat, from which he intended to sell it, lot by lot. Campbell was slow in filing his plat, which was the earliest evidence of projected town promotion in the area of present-day Kansas City. The site was called Westport. The records do not tell who devised the name; it may have been Major Campbell.

On August 31 Campbell sold three quarter-acre lots to John Calvin McCoy—according to the deed, "in the town of Westport as appears on the town plat." This plat was probably Campbell's,

[36] Material on Campbell from the National Archives, and on his local land dealings from the records of the Jackson County Court, have been collected by Mrs. Adrienne Tinker Christopher, Kansas City, Missouri.

[37] Letters to Isaac McCoy in McCoy Letterbooks (Kansas State Historical Society, Topeka, Kansas), Vol. 20, January-December, 1833.

although he did not file it at the county courthouse until the following April. Shortly after he filed the plat, Campbell mortgaged his holdings and left for Washington, D.C., in order to clear up a controversy over the handling of some Indian matters in which he had been involved. He never returned; in 1836, while at the capital, he became ill and died.[38]

In the meantime, young McCoy had drawn up a Westport town plat of his own, which overlapped a small corner of Campbell's. He was actually two months ahead of Campbell in filing and was apparently a more systematic promoter. He had already built a general store; when his first efforts to sell "town lots" failed, he began offering them free to anyone who agreed to build in Westport.[39] One man constructed a harness-and-saddle shop on this kind of arrangement; another bought a brick building already in existence, in which he started a tavern. In 1836 William Chick, a prosperous Howard County farmer, moved in and bought McCoy's interest in the general store.

At the time about fifty people were living in Westport. At first slowly, but with accelerating tempo, the business of the place increased. In 1837 more establishments were opened, one by John Sutter of later California fame; a school was erected. Santa Fe traders began stopping at Westport, and, of course, quantities of Indian annuity money circulated. The town was becoming a western outpost of some consequence. Indians, Mexicans, American scouts like Jim Bridger and Kit Carson, and a variety of frontier opportunists gave it vitality and color.

The new town soon surpassed the little fur-trade station by the river, but changes were in the offing there as well. Pierre Roy had cut a road from near Westport down to a good natural landing place on the right bank, four miles to the north. McCoy widened this road in the early 1830's and had his trade goods unloaded from the steamboats at this point, not far from Chou-

[38] In addition to the McCoy items, see an article by Albert Doerschuck, "Did John Campbell Lay Out the Original Westport?" in *Kansas City Star*, July 12, 1925.

[39] For early Westport see Washington H. Chick, "The Vicissitudes of Pioneer Life," *Annals of Kansas City*, I (December, 1922), 207-18; Nellie McCoy Harris, "Memories of Old Westport," *ibid.* (October, 1924), 465-73; Louis O. Honig, *Westport: Gateway to the Early West* (n.p.: By the author, 1950).

teau's post. By 1838 it was time for the river landing to enter into the story on its own. Four years earlier, two of the French settlers had sold Father Roux forty acres of land (for six dollars), less than a mile from the river, on what was to become Kansas City's "Quality Hill." By September, 1835, a small church had been built on the plot; at first it was called "Chouteau's church," but only for a few years. New settlers were arriving, new lines of enterprise were opening, and the movement of men and merchandise was about to transform the community at the junction of the Missouri and the Kansas rivers.

CHAPTER 2

Tokens of Growth

AGAINST a background of settlement pushing westward up the Missouri River and successive waves of enterprise beating beyond it upon the western plains, the chain of circumstance which led to the establishment of Kansas City was forged. The first circumstance resulted, appropriately enough on the frontier, from a riot. For reasons which have long since vanished, a fight broke out one day in November, 1831, in the French community at the mouth of the Kansas. "It was a fierce brawl," one of the early settlers recalled many years later, and when it was over, "there were many wounds and much blood spilt, and Prudhomme lay on the ground still and dead." Gabriel Prudhomme left his wife with six living children and another unborn. He also left an estate which included 257 acres of land, patented ten months before his death; this land, in turn, included the natural rock landing on the south bank of the Missouri, immediately below the mouth of the Kansas.[1]

The Widow Prudhomme, along with another French-Canadian, administered the estate, and for several years nothing happened to call attention to its disposition. In 1835, however, John Calvin McCoy platted Westport; his interest in the rock landing only four miles away had antedated the filing of the plat. In 1836 the Platte Purchase was consummated, and some time before this

---

[1] "Life Tales of Early Days," *Kansas City Star*, June 6, 1898; *Vital Records of Jackson County, 1826-1876* (Kansas City: Kansas City Chapter, Daughters of the American Revolution, 1933), p. 91; where not otherwise indicated, the source material for this account of land transactions and town company organization is drawn from the records of the Jackson County Court and of the Jackson County Circuit Court. These records are available at Independence, Missouri. Particularly valuable for the earliest years are the records of the Circuit Court, Cause 3544, a suit brought by one of the Prudhomme daughters and her husband against the administration of the estate. Detailed citations will be supplied on request. The town company's history will be available with more detail and documentation in a forthcoming article by Mildred Cecile Cox.

Andrew Roy (called *Petit*) began operating a ferry from the landing to the attractive lands across the river. Prudhomme himself may have been engaged in the same business before he died; a ferry boat included in his estate was sold by the guardian of his minor heirs in 1839 for $85.[2] Interest was beginning to concentrate on this spot on the Missouri's "great bend."

Prudhomme's children were growing up, and late in 1836 his eldest daughter married Prosper Mercier. The following June, Mr. and Mrs. Mercier asked the county court for a partition of the estate. Meanwhile, the court had provided the minor Prudhomme heirs with a series of guardians, and in August, 1837, while the Merciers' petition was under consideration, it named James Hyatt McGee to that position. The court then accepted the petition and commissioned William Miles Chick, Peter Boothe, and Samuel Johnson to submit a report on the Prudhomme estate, on the basis of which intelligent action might be taken. The three commissioners reported that, due to the nature of the land in question, the proposed division could be made only with "great and manifest injury and loss" to the heirs. The land fronted on the river; it was "principally broken and only materially valuable for a ferry across the river and a warehouse." This meant that the land would have to be sold in one piece, the widow and heirs drawing their allotted compensation from the proceeds. Accordingly, the court ordered public sale of the 257 acres for July 7, 1838.

The sale was duly advertised in the *Missouri Republican* of St. Louis, and in what was probably the newspaper then published nearest to the site, the Liberty (Missouri) *Far West*. The land, according to the advertisement, was "one and a half miles below the mouth of the Kansas River and also one of the best Steamboat Landings on the River." There were warehouse and townsite

---

[2] On Roy's ferry, see William Miller, *Early History of Kansas City* (Kansas City: Birdsall & Williams, 1881), p. 395; some data on the administration of the estate are in an abstract record, *Old Town (Now City) of Kansas* (Privately printed [1889]), p. 27. This record, which is available at the Archives of the Native Sons of Kansas City, City Hall, Kansas City, Missouri, and in photostat at the Kansas City Public Library, will be cited hereafter as *Old Town*.

possibilities, and, all in all, "those wishing to invest capital advantageously in landed estate" would "do well to call and examine the premises."[3]

When the day came, the crier of the sale was none other than James H. McGee, guardian of the younger Prudhommes. At least twenty-one people attended, including two of the commissioners; the daughter of one of them (Boothe) was soon to marry Fry P. McGee, son of James. Another of McGee's sons, Mobillon, was at the sale with Fry. A number of prominent Jackson Countians appeared: Smart, Owens, Gilliss, Ragan, Noland, and others.[4] Exactly what happened at the sale is not clear, but the land was knocked down to one Abraham Fonda for his bid of $1,800. Early records indicate that Fonda was at least occasionally indebted to James McGee.[5]

This last circumstance may help explain Fonda's interest in the Prudhomme farm. At any rate, it suddenly appeared that many of those present at the sale felt they had been defrauded; the sale, it was charged, had been conducted in a highly irregular manner, and a group of complainants asked the court to set it aside and order a resale. McGee, they said, was an interested party. He had conspired with Fonda to close on the $1,800 bid, with a view to getting an interest in the property from that worthy later on. Since other parties might have made higher bids, the Prudhomme children had been cheated of several hundred dollars—and, it might be added, some well-placed settlers had seen an opportunity to acquire some good land cheaply evaporate before their eyes.[6]

McGee denied these charges. Peter Boothe, one of the com-

---

[3] *Old Town*, p. 14.

[4] In subsequent litigation (see below), testimony describing the sale was gathered from twenty-one witnesses, including those whose names are given here. It has not been thought worth while to point out the instances in which the present account differs from the versions in existing written histories; none of them agree with the court records on which this text is based.

[5] See the records of McGee's estate, Office of the Clerk, Probate Court, Jackson County, Drawer M-2.

[6] *Old Town*, pp. 17-19; William Chick, one of the original commissioners, was among the complainants.

missioners, had accepted his offer to cry the sale, in order to save expenses for the estate. The bid of $1,800 must be regarded as fair, "no one else appearing to bid more." During the sale, McGee said, two men belonging to "the Company" had intimated to him their suspicions that Fonda's agent was actually bidding in McGee's interest; he had denied it then, and denied it again now. (This interesting reference to a company in existence at the time of the July sale stands alone, and nothing more is known about it.) Then McGee seemed to give his whole case away: It had indeed been agreed, he said, that in case Fonda's bid was successful, McGee might have "an interest," but he hastily added that this understanding was not in any sense binding. Fonda's agent, whose name was Clarke, said in his affidavit that he was the one who reached the understanding with McGee, but he had not considered it binding because McGee had not specified an acceptable price "or anything about the purchase at all." And Fonda himself deposed that after the sale, when he could not meet the requirement of purchaser's bond, Fry McGee had been among those offering their names as securities![7]

The controversy was brief, if heated, and the court ordered another sale for November 14—understandably, since McGee had actually admitted most of the charge against him, namely, a prior interest in the land being sold. This time, George W. Tate, a Westport justice of the peace, conducted the sale. Near the ferry landing there was a fenced-in lot, used to corral livestock being sent across the river. "A few rails laid across one corner of the worn fence," as McCoy recalled the second sale,

> soon improvised a rostrum and Squire Tate . . . mounted the perch, and after carefully adjusting his spectacles and taking a fresh chew of tobacco with a deliberateness eminently suited to the occasion, proceeded to announce the sale.[8]

At the second sale, the successful bid was $4,220, and it came from a town company made up of fourteen men and including

[7] *Ibid.*, pp. 17-23.

[8] McCoy Scrapbook, Archives of the Native Sons of Kansas City, City Hall, Kansas City, Missouri, p. 39; this article, "Tales of an Old Timer," was printed in the *Kansas City Daily Journal*, March 19, 1880.

some of the most prominent names in the area; their bond for payment in one year, with interest at 10 per cent, was immediately accepted.[9]

According to McCoy, the company had been organized "in about fifteen minutes" by William L. Sublette. Sublette was the only member of the company who was not at the time a local resident; he was a partner in the far-flung fur-trading activities of Sublette and Campbell of St. Louis. His family history illustrates the changing stages in western history:[10] Distantly related on his mother's side to George Rogers Clark, Sublette as a young man had answered General Ashley's call in 1823 for "enterprising young men" to accompany expeditions into the Rocky Mountains. Three years later, with two partners, he bought Ashley's interest and traded for furs on his own account. A little later he joined with Campbell, and the two continued to press the American Fur Company with hard competition until their partnership dissolved in 1842—the same year the rival company went bankrupt. Fellow westerners testified to Sublette's competence in dangerous enterprises among the Indians, crediting him with founding the

---

[9] The company of fourteen were: William L. Sublette, Moses G. Wilson, James Smart, William Collins, John C. McCoy, William M. Chick, Russell Hicks, Fry P. McGee, Abraham Fonda, Jacob Ragan, George Tate, William Gilliss, Oliver Caldwell, Samuel C. Owens.

[10] Data for the brief accounts of the Town Company members which follow have been taken from so many and such varied sources that specific documentation is impractical. The best starting place is a file of biographical cards, each of which lists the sources for all the data on it, collected by James Anderson and available at the Archives of the Native Sons. McCoy's reminiscences as collected in the Scrapbook already mentioned are essential; in the same Archives, there are also "Kansas City" and "Chick Family" scrapbooks, which bring together a mass of newspaper stories. The D.A.R. volume, *Vital Records of Jackson County, 1826-1876,* is good for data on births, marriages, and deaths, and also contains some pioneer recollections. The Missouri Valley Historical Society, during its brief existence, published two volumes called *Annals of Kansas City* (Kansas City: 1921-24) which include several good reminiscent articles. To these may be added the biographical sketches in the published histories of Kansas City by William H. Miller and Theodore S. Case (1881 and 1888, respectively). Good manuscript data are to be found in the Sublette Papers and the Campbell Papers at the Missouri Historical Society in St. Louis; see also the published "Correspondence of Robert Campbell" in the society's bulletin, *Glimpses of the Past,* VIII (1941), Nos. 1-6. Other good manuscript material is in the Isaac McCoy Letterbooks, Kansas Historical Society, Topeka, Kansas.

post that later became Fort Laramie. He and Campbell had stores at various places along the Missouri, and Sublette carried on much business at A. G. Boone's store in Westport. What his interest in the town company may imply is impossible to determine; he was not involved in its subsequent career before his death in 1845 and may simply have been acting as a friend of the Prudhommes. Sublette's share in the company soon passed to Campbell, who seems to have sent his nephew, John, to look after affairs at the mouth of the Kansas; when John Campbell died in 1900, he was reported to be the richest man in Kansas City.

William Miles Chick was a Virginian who moved west to Missouri in 1822, at the age of 28. He had farmed near Glasgow until the flood of 1826, and then for ten years more in Howard County. In 1836 he came to Westport, where McCoy sold him the general store, and subsequently, he married Chick's daughter. Chick's interest in the townsite was more active than Sublette's. During the 1840's, he became known as "the first citizen" of Kansas and lavished an easy Virginian hospitality on all of the principal visitors: Frémont, Benton, Parkman, and others. Three of his sons grew up and throve with the rising town and helped give it a biographical continuity extending into the twentieth century.

William Gilliss was about the same age as Chick. Born in Maryland, he had lived through a tempestuous youth, running away to sea at the age of fourteen and later serving in General Harrison's Indian campaigns. He made money in Cincinnati by building homes on land owned by Harrison, and from there he went into the Indian trade; an 1820 reference has him supplying the emigrant Delawares with four hundred pounds of beef at Kaskaskia. In the twenties he crossed over into Missouri to pursue his trading activities, in the course of which he married a Delaware woman who bore him two daughters. In 1831 he left his Indian wife and her tribe, bought some land south of the Missouri and not far from the state line, set up a trading post, and developed his holdings. Within two years Gilliss owned at least a thousand acres of land in Jackson County. He was probably the wealthiest of the local members of the town company and continued to be active in business as the town changed into Kansas City. In 1867, two years before his death, he was chosen, as "the oldest resident," to drive the last spike in a newly completed railroad.

Of the other company members, McCoy and Fry McGee, like Chick and Gilliss, either were continuously involved in the building of the future city or else represented family interests so involved. Their careers are all similar: Beginning with mercantile operations, mostly Indian trade, they bought land and strove to increase its value at each successive stage in the region's history. The other nine shareholders soon drop out of the story. Jacob Ragan and George Tate were both prominent in Westport, along with Chick, McCoy, and the McGees. Samuel C. Owens was the principal merchant in Independence at the time and may have had a nascent interest in Kansas; if so, his death in the Mexican War prevented its fruition. Russell Hicks was an Independence farmer-lawyer, who apparently lost interest in the town company, as did James Smart. James's brother, Thomas Smart, however, became a big landholder in Kansas and profited heavily as the place grew. Of Moses Wilson, Oliver Caldwell, and William Collins very little is known, save that they were active citizens of eastern Jackson County. Lastly, Abraham Fonda held a share in the company. Fonda flits in and out of the early records in a baffling and intriguing manner. We know almost nothing of him, but McCoy claimed that it was Fonda who first mentioned the possibility of an important city where the Missouri and Kansas rivers join; this is close to incredible, unless James McGee had been talking expansively with Fonda during their negotiations before the first sale of the Prudhomme farm.

Just why Squire Tate's prior interest should not have prejudiced the second sale as much as had McGee's the earlier one does not appear in the records, but it is clear that the company was so constituted as to conciliate interests which might otherwise have collided with one another. The Westport members, excepting Ragan and Tate, maintained their interest in the townsite and did what building there was in the early years. The Independence members turned their attention elsewhere and do not figure in the later story. They may have been included among the shareholders to mitigate a feeling of rivalry which could have led them to try to cause trouble, legal and otherwise. Six of the fourteen company members had been among those protesting the July sale. It appears that James McGee, land-hungry and reaching out for good chances, had simply reached too far; now, there was something for everyone.

Exactly what lay at the confluence of the rivers, or what the shareholders in the Town of Kansas Company thought they held, remained obscure for some time. Metropolitan development could hardly have figured among their goals; businesslike and practical, these men seem not to have looked beyond such possibilities as a warehouse, a ferry, or the casual and characteristic speculative gains which might or might not arise from a quick townsite venture like the one just described. According to the only written reminiscence by any of the participants, John C. McCoy, the members of the company, "a few men with no capital . . . bought the land because it had a good steamboat landing and was the most suitable starting point for the . . . caravans to New Mexico. The idea that any one of them would live to see a city built up among those precipitous hills and impassable gorges . . . never entered into their calculation." The shareholders, McCoy wrote, "were not disposed to risk much in the experiment, and did very little to push the town." Had any of them ventured to predict "the results now patent to all," he continued, the enthusiast would have been laughed to scorn and his prophecies marked down as "the idle vaporings of a demented intellect."[11]

Early in 1839 some of the company (no more than eight, according to McCoy) met in a log cabin near the river. It was

---

[11] *Kansas City Daily Journal*, March 18, 1882; undated *Journal* clippings in McCoy Scrapbook, p. 7; *Journal*, February 5, 1885.

"an unpretending edifice of John Barleycorn," and the men may
have felt a need for fresh air, for they adjourned to continue their
meeting outside the place. They discussed clearing some of their
land and commissioned their secretary, McCoy, to survey it and
lay out lots for them. It was agreed to build a company warehouse and to improve the landing. Finally, the "town" was given
a name. It might have been "Port Fonda"—McCoy always regretted that it was not—but Fonda was not popular with the other
proprietors. After rejecting such scornful suggestions as "Rabbitt-
ville" and "Possumtrot," the company settled on "Kansas," taking
the name of the nearby river. "I did not like the name then,"
wrote McCoy, "and have no great admiration for it now. . . ."
For at least fifteen years he could have had little to complain of,
for no one (outside the possible exceptions of the company members) ever referred to a Kansas City until after 1854; during these
years, the place had no impressive status as an urban enterprise,
its future was doubtful, and it was called simply the town of
Kansas.[12]

Eighty-six lots were staked out, and early in May, 1839, the
company held a sale. Backwoodsmen and traders came in, apparently more to watch the proceedings than anything else; cheap
whiskey was plentiful, and a good many of the bystanders seem
to have enjoyed it. Nevertheless, only nine lots were sold; about
$900 was pledged in all by six buyers. Jacob Ragan took three
lots, McCoy took two, William Evans (son-in-law of James
McGee) took two more, and McGee himself took one. The
proprietors decided to put up their common warehouse on one of
Evans' lots, and commissioned him to run it.[13] But money was
scarce; it was several years before the lots sold in 1839 were paid
for. A year passed; the date on which the proprietors had con-
tracted to pay for their purchases passed, and no money changed
hands. Consequently, no deed was issued, and the company

---

[12] McCoy Scrapbook, pp. 39, 40, 55, 86.

[13] Manuscript Records of the Town Company, Archives of the Native Sons,
supplemented by McCoy's descriptions cited in previous notes. A typed transcript of the Town Company's records, prepared by Mildred Cecile Cox, may be
consulted at the Archives.

could not give a good title. Was the Town Company of Kansas nothing more than another of the countless paper speculations crosshatching the American landscape with imaginary lines in the nineteenth century?

It began to look that way. Those connected with the company and with the land it had bought seemed suddenly to be much more interested in suing one another than in any other economic potential the site might have. William Miller's *Early History of Kansas City*, which appeared in 1881, informs us that disagreements among the proprietors delayed town development for several years. McCoy supports Miller, noting that shortly after the first sale of lots "the habit of disagreeing had become chronic," and existing court records bear out the statement.

In April, 1840, Mr. and Mrs. Mercier successfully petitioned the county court to order its commissioners to sue the proprietors. Five months later the commissioners won judgment and proceeded to try to collect from the company members, so that the money might be distributed among Prudhomme's heirs. As soon as Prosper Mercier seemed in the way of getting some money, William Chick sued him. Shortly thereafter he also sued Gabriel Prudhomme, Jr. Chick had bought McCoy's Westport store in 1836. The store was not immediately profitable; this along with the expenses of his other enterprises, made him short of cash. He began a number of suits between 1840 and 1842, by the end of which time he in turn had been sued several times and was held liable for over $1,500.

Along with Chick, Fry and Eleanor McGee (James's son and widow) were suing Mercier and the junior Prudhomme. Both Chick and the McGees won judgments in the first instance, but they never collected the money. Prosper Mercier had now abandoned his wife, and the court ruled that she was not liable for any of the drunken ne'er-do-well's debts. These suits would not concern us beyond their mention except that in the case of Gabriel Prudhomme, Jr., Chick was suing on a note and the McGees on an alleged oral contract. This obligation was supposed to come to $1,200—far more than McGee normally loaned on written security. Again, no security for the McGee claim against Prosper Mercier has come to light. If, shortly after James McGee became the Prudhommes' guardian, he did lend the son and son-in-law some money on oral agreements alone, we might suspect that his interest in the Prudhomme farm antedated his guardianship and that the latter was conceived by McGee to subserve the former. This fits temptingly with the allegations made against him in reference to the first sale of the Prudhomme land.

In April, 1841, the court had ordered the commissioners of the original estate to make over a deed to the town company, but in the welter of litigation this could not be done. The affairs of the company were in hopeless confusion, the two surviving commissioners reporting not only that the land had not been entirely paid for, but also that they found themselves unable to determine just how much had been paid! Shortly thereafter, another concern of the town company entered the courts when Oliver Caldwell sued to revoke McCoy's ferry license. This suit was ultimately dismissed, but it was not the last which involved McCoy's ferryboat privileges.

Finally, however, the tangled web began to unravel. In the spring of 1843 the court made permanent its restraint on diversion of Mrs. Mercier's share of the proceeds; in August it accepted what appears to have been the final report by the commissioners on the Prudhomme farm. All, or nearly all, of the purchase money had been paid in; the sum could now be distributed among the heirs. By this time, only one of the court's commissioners was alive, and on August 17, 1843, he executed and filed a deed for the old farm to the town company.

There had already been one sale of lots under company auspices; a warehouse had been built, and John C. McCoy was running the ferryboat. Aside from this, nothing had been done to "push the experiment," and when the Missouri flooded in 1844 the warehouse went downstream. The shares of the original fourteen shareholders had been worth just over $300 each; within ten years after the company's formation, several of the fourteen had disposed of their shares, often for less than that amount. Squire Tate tired first and sold his share to William Evans in March, 1843, for $34. Since Tate's obligations were transferred along with his share, this figure should indicate a net profit of some kind. A few months later William Chick's share, along with some lots which he owned, were sold by the sheriff for $57 in satisfaction of some judgments against Chick. Between 1843 and 1845, other men sold their company holdings for between $250 and $600.

A number of unresolved problems prevent hard and fast conclusions as to what was being realized in these transactions: What kinds of currency were in use? How much money did men like Richard Rees and Russell Hicks (both of them sold out) make in the way of attorneys' fees? How much money actually was realized from the 1839 sale of nine lots, and exactly where did it go? Still, it does seem clear that no one was making great gains on town company shares, at least before the second sale of lots, yet to be described. The whole operation was a small one, secondary in the minds of those who were involved, with here and there, perhaps, a nice little handful of money to be picked up. The difficulties of William Chick, losing property which sold for $57 against obligations of more than $1,500, supply a clue to the circumstances surrounding important business activities in the area. The period, at least until 1843, was one of depression over the nation. The correspondence between Sublette and Campbell is full of references to the scarcity of cash in western Missouri; another large firm was at about that time instructing its Westport agent not to put out a single dollar in cash for any purpose whatever, and again as late as 1845, the same agent wrote to the home office that there was "no money in this country to be had from drafts. . . ."[14]

Nevertheless, in the transferring of shares of company ownership, a sort of "shaking down" process may have been going on. The following chart compares the ownership at the time of the

---

14 Campbell correspondence, *op. cit.*; W. G. and G. W. Ewing Papers, Indiana State Historical Library, Indianapolis; the Ewings to J. Clymer, February 14, 1841; Clymer to the Ewings, Westport, March 21, 1845.

1838 sale of the Prudhomme farm with the situation in 1848, along with the number of shares held by each man:

SHARES HELD IN THE TOWN COMPANY OF KANSAS, 1838-1848

1838	No. of Shares	1848	No. of Shares
William Sublette	1	Robert Campbell	4
Moses G. Wilson	1		
James Smart	1		
William Collins	1		
John C. McCoy	1	John C. McCoy	2
William M. Chick	1		
Fry P. McGee	1	Fry P. McGee	2
Russell Hicks	1		
Abraham Fonda	1	Henry Jobe	1
Jacob Ragan	1	Jacob Ragan	1
George Tate	1	William B. Evans	1
William Gilliss	1	William Gilliss	3
Oliver Caldwell	1		
Samuel C. Owens	1		
	14		14

The slow concentration of interest might of itself have encouraged development of the townsite, but two accompanying features should be specified. In the first place, the four shares in the hands of Robert Campbell indicate the presence of a serious business interest, backed by one of the most substantial fortunes in St. Louis. In the second place, all of the Independence interest had disappeared by 1848; the thread of interest ran from Kansas to Westport. In the intervening period, events of major importance had been bringing with them possibilities, at least, which were big with Kansas City's future: The Indian trade continued to grow, the emigrant trails to Oregon and California opened, and the troubles with Mexico focused attention on the Southwest and may have diverted more capital into the trade with that area.

It was time for the town company to straighten out its affairs so the members could take care of more important matters. William Gilliss suggested this forcibly in a letter to Sublette early in

1845. Kansas, wrote Gilliss, "is about making a commencement to be a considerable of a little Town, and all that has prevented it from being larger is that the shareholders cannot make deeds . . . for the reason that some live in St. Louis. . . ." He recommended the appointment of an agent who could act for the St. Louis interest. There were opportunities which Kansas should be in a position to take:

> It is generally understood (and credit can be given to it) that all the Mountain Companies intend stopping and landing their goods here this season, as there is no other landing above Independence. It is also rumored that as soon as Saml. C. Owens returns from the Spanish Country he intends building a very large warehouse, and by that means it will draw the Santa Fe traders here. . . . You will please make an appointment soon, for we wish to have a sale of lots in the Spring as there are several who wish to build.[15]

For some reason, it was not until more than a year after Gilliss' letter and two and a half years after the company held a clear title to its purchase that another sale of lots was held. Early in 1846 McCoy made up a new plat, which was filed April 30, the day of the sale. Prospects had improved since 1839, and the second sale proceeded briskly despite bad weather. Ninety-seven lots were sold for a total of $6,783.62, at prices from $22 up to $341 each.[16] Those which fronted on or near the rock landing at the foot of what is now Main Street, brought the highest bids. Ravines and creeks laced the bluffs around the narrowing rock shelf, and bids on lots to the east of the main part of the levee abruptly dropped to as low as $30. Even more depressed were the bids on lots platted on the angular, ragged bluffs which rose precipitously behind the wedge-shaped landing. Although topographical irregularities explain to some extent the slow bidding for lots in certain locations, it is more significant that the buyers

---

15 Westport, January 20, 1845, Sublette Papers.

16 See William E. Connelly (ed.), "Journal of Governor William Walker," Nebraska Historical Society, *Proceedings and Collections*, 2d Series, III (1899), 177. Cited hereafter as "Journal of Governor William Walker." Data on the sales in this and succeeding paragraphs are from the manuscript Records of the Town Company.

had an extremely limited concept of the townsite's potentialities. The heaviest investors were Gilliss and McCoy—$673 and $559, respectively—and each was especially interested in river-front lots. One W. D. Priddy bought the largest number of lots at prices from $22 to $65. Priddy must have sold his lots or his sales contracts almost immediately; he leaves our story at this point. Fry McGee obligated himself to pay $194 for four lots, two just in back of the landing—one well to the east and the other to the west—and two close together at the top of the hill. Benoist Troost bought five lots well back from the river, and P. M. Chouteau bid in four.

More important than subsequent sales or indeed than the internal negotiations of the company itself is the fact that as 1847 progressed, the holders began the process of breaking up their collectivity. In May the company made P. M. Chouteau its treasurer and handed him about $8,000 in notes to be collected or negotiated. In July they agreed to complete the survey of their land and to divide between them the unsold lots along with the notes then held. By the beginning of 1848, aside from a couple of reserved areas, only $77 in notes and two lots remained to be divided. As late as March, 1850, an accounting revealed a balance of $55 in Chouteau's hands for his use as the company's attorney, but the company had effectively ceased to exist.[17]

McCoy sold his remaining interest in the reserved holdings in 1856 for $140; the following year, Jacob Ragan disposed of his remaining interest for $350. During 1858 there was a sudden boom in Kansas City real estate, and these circulating interests began to carry higher figures. Joseph C. Ranson, by the onset of the Civil War, had bought up 8/14 of the total interest in one reserved section for an outlay of over $2,000. The war forced him into bankruptcy, and half his interest was sold by the marshal; Ranson sold the last 4/14 in 1880 for $500.

At the same time, private land transactions outside the company produced startling results for those who bought and sold at

17 Interests in the reserved plots, always calculated in fourteenths, continued to circulate; suits to clarify rights and debts based on them were still in the courts as late as 1912.

the proper times. Much of the story which we have yet to tell is prefigured in the outline of one parcel's course: In the division of unsold company holdings, 1847-48, Robert Campbell was awarded a block called "Land No. 29," then valued at $30; in 1867 Campbell conveyed a little less than half of Land No. 29 to Charles Kearney for $7,000; three years later, Kearney sold it to one Helena Beck for $18,000; she, in her turn, sold half of what she had bought to another party in 1885, for $26,000.

The town company had served as bridge between two epochs: from the French fur-trading community into nineteenth-century America. While the aims of the company shareholders were limited, the possibilities were not, once the ground had become real estate. Between Prudhomme's farm in the 1830's and Kansas City in the 1850's there lies the story of the Town Company of Kansas which picked up a chunk of potentially valuable land, fissured it into individual holdings which were nearly worthless unless made ancillary to some form of business enterprise, and then went quietly out of existence.

It has already been suggested that the rise and fall of the Rocky Mountain fur trade provided one of the initiating impulses in Kansas City's prehistory. While it flourished, this trade drew into the area men who, while not consciously intending to build cities, were not likely to miss a good bet. Their characteristic activities, their needs—as these changed—outlined the desirability of town growth on the western fringe of civilization. This was not, indeed, necessarily the case. The fur trade by its nature inhibited any such town growth west of St. Louis. But as the trade declined, some of these men were left in the region with their money, their ambitions, and the westward bent of their interest and knowledge.

The Kansas City branch of the Chouteau family is one good illustration of this kind of continuity through successive stages of trans-Mississippi business history. The life of François Chouteau was almost coterminous with the fur-trade epoch. He had

selected the site of the future city for his upriver agency; as the
site exchanged its original function for a new one in 1838, he
died. His eldest son, Pierre, was just approaching maturity at the
time; he had been brought to the trading station when still an
infant. He reappears in the mid-forties as attorney and collector
for the town company. As the town grew, Pierre engaged in local
real estate and mercantile operations and became the captain of
a Missouri River steamboat. His mother, Berenice, survived in
Kansas City until 1880, by which time she had become the local
grande dame.

Another illustration is found in the Ewing brothers, William
G. and George W. Their father had founded a substantial fortune
trading in furs in Pennsylvania and Ohio. In 1822 he went to
Fort Wayne, Indiana, where he and his sons scoured the Maumee-
Wabash area for the profitable skins. Following his death in
1826, the firm of W. G. and G. W. Ewing continued to operate.
After a few years of buying goods from the American Fur Company and selling furs to it, the Ewings made independent arrangements with a New York house and went into the field
against Ramsay Crooks.[18]

But these were increasingly difficult years in the fur business.
The panic of 1837, the ensuing depression, and the competition of
independent traders kept the pressure of enterprise high. In
May, 1838, Crooks wrote to his Detroit agent, William Brewster,
on the subject of one of the independents, "You have our full
permission to put him down in any way you please, only do it ef-
fectually. . . ." Brewster apparently succeeded in this case, but
the Ewings were another matter. They inveigled a capable and
trusted western agent, George Hunt, away from Crooks and sent
him west to push competition, among other places, on the Missouri River. Crooks and Brewster reacted characteristically to
this threat: "Achieve so decided a victory this season as will
discourage our opponents completely," wrote Crooks. "Kill them
in your own way."[19]

18 Paul C. Phillips, "The Fur Trade in the Maumee-Wabash Country,"
Indiana University Studies, XII (1925), 106.

19 *Ibid.,* pp. 110-11; Ewing Papers, the Ewings to Hunt, January 4, 1839.

There were limits to the advantages of this sort of conduct, however, and with money scarce and European prices falling, it was almost inevitable that the two companies should try to make common cause. Arrangements were mooted in 1838-39, and again in 1840-41, but they broke down, partly because the Ewings, once having gone into the Missouri River country, would not give it up. Still, economic conditions and the effects of cutthroat competition took their toll, and the American Fur Company went bankrupt during the 1842-43 season. The Ewings, now confronting the independents alone, owed their eastern correspondents $150,000 and in order to stay in business had mortgaged their entire establishment.[20]

Why stay on in the fur business? The independents (Brewster and the Chouteaus among them) were powerful in some cases and always bothersome; prices did not recover, and by the spring of 1846 the Ewings still owed $145,000. The end was in sight for one line of enterprise, and the brothers had already considered what to do. They had stores and warehouses at various western stations, including Westport and (by 1840) the town of Kansas; they had business connections and experience in dealing with Indians; they had strong New York backing which was probably as interested in their solvency as they were. With these assets, and much to lose, the Ewings extricated themselves from a languishing enterprise and shifted their resources into other, rising lines. The shift from the fur trade carried its own implications for townsite possibilities.

As early as the 1839-40 season, George Ewing had written to his brother that supplying the Indians with goods might be more profitable than trading for furs "*in future.*" In 1841 Hunt was instructed to move to Council Bluffs and concentrate on the exchange of goods for annuity money.[21] The Ewing brothers moved into the field of general Indian trade, with a sideline business in Indian claims. Frequently, a man might have a claim against a

---

[20] Phillips, *op. cit.*, pp. 111-16.

[21] *Ibid.*, p. 118; the Ewing Papers, after 1848, contain many items bearing on the pork operations.

tribe for some service rendered or goods supplied. These claims could involve costly and drawn-out lobbying or litigation which most frontiersmen were unlikely to want to pursue. For a commission, the Ewings—with many claims of their own and good connections in the government—would represent such claims. Thus, in 1851 A. B. H. McGee and a partner appointed the Ewings as attorneys to collect a claim against the Sac and Fox tribe, allowing a 25 per cent commission. One Sac and Fox debt owing to McGee two years later came to $4,353; at the same time the tribe was asking the government to pay its creditors, in all, $15,000.[22] Of the two businesses, the first was more important to the story of town growth, and it is worth noting that the Ewings were not moving into an unoccupied field.

The movement of the Indian tribes, complete with their government annuities and other benefices, to the lands just west of the Missouri state line, took place between the years 1832 and 1840. By 1840 the territory from the Platte River south to what is now the Oklahoma border was blocked into tribal allotments. Into these allotted lands, 90,000 Indians moved, with claims on the government amounting almost to $27,000,000.[23] As the Indian trade grew, steamboats appeared on the Missouri River to convey the goods, and the importance of Gabriel Prudhomme's farm became clearer. In 1839 Thomas Smart set up what was probably the first general trading post near the landing. The Chouteaus, of course, already had the establishment which had served their fur trade; in 1840 the Ewings built their own warehouse near the Chouteaus'. In 1843 William M. Chick erected one for himself—of the warehouses by the landing, his was the only one to escape the flood of 1844. Meanwhile, other traders were moving in: An early writer lists one Anthony Richters, a firm by the name of Cahn and Block, and A. Canville, all arriving around 1840. The Indians brought in ponies, pelts, and annuity monies; in exchange, they bought powder and lead, food, clothes,

---

[22] Ewing Papers, power of attorney, October 18, 1851; Indian Agent John R. Chennault to Commissioner of Indian Affairs, January 7, 1853.

[23] Miller, *History*, p. 387.

saddles, and "a little bad whiskey."[24] In 1844 Hiram Northrup brought in the largest stock of goods yet seen in Westport or Kansas and significantly began a jobbing business with Indian traders all over the area. By 1858 Richters at least had also converted his business to wholesaling. This development, always important in the growth of a commercial center, impressed Alexander Majors so strongly that in his memoirs he stated that although a town company had been organized in 1838, "very little was done toward founding a city until some eight years later, when a new company was organized by H. M. Northrup. . . ." There was actually no connection between Northrup's business and the town company, and Majors' date differs by two years from that given by Miller. Nevertheless, Majors' memory did catch the significance of the beginning of wholesaling. In 1845 one of James McGee's sons began making brick on his farm near Westport.[25]

This new trade with the Indians, while it never reached breath-taking proportions even for the 1840's, was still substantial enough to attract attention. The Ewings' Westport agent, who was now one Joseph Clymer, wrote them early in 1841 that in a few weeks he would deposit $10,000 to their account, exclusive of a consignment of good furs. W. G. Ewing urged his brother to send plenty of goods west in 1843—forty to fifty thousand dollars' worth. A Ewing memorandum for 1849 notes that $8,000 in silver and $6,500 in gold is in transit down the Missouri River for the firm's St. Louis office. The elder Ewing, enjoying the pleasant prospect of a thriving Indian business, suggested to his brother that an able man at Westport "could make us $100,000, the next five or six years."[26]

In 1849 G. W. Ewing bought $15,000 worth of trade goods in

[24] *Ibid.*, pp. 388, 401, 406; Charles C. Spalding, *Annals of the City of Kansas and the Great Western Plains* (Kansas City: Van Horn & Abeel, 1858), pp. 19-20. Cited hereafter as Spalding, *Annals.*

[25] Alexander Majors, *Seventy Years on the Frontier* (Chicago and New York: Rand McNally & Company, 1893), p. 254; cited hereafter as Majors, *Seventy Years.* Miller, *History*, p. 406.

[26] Ewing Papers, Clymer to the Ewings, Westport, March 12, 1841; W. G. to G. W. Ewing, May 2, 1843; memorandum dated October 14, 1849; W. G. to G. W. Ewing, December 10, 1851.

New York, to be consigned to Westport. His agent there, now a W. D. Harris, suggested that buttons of all kinds, combs, boots and shoes, and scarlet yarn were the best items to send. Before this, in 1842, during the course of a treaty negotiation in Iowa, the Ewings had presented a bill for $90,000, representing less than two years' business with the Sac and Fox tribe. The claim was scaled down to $66,000 by government investigators who observed that "profit should not be turned to plunder."[27] Their total outlay in the Indian trade for the 1847-48 season was represented by them as amounting to over $100,000, distributed among six western posts. Single payments to Indian tribes by the government could run high: In 1847, the Sacs and Foxes each received $36,000, of which the Ewings immediately extracted $21,000 and the Chouteaus $9,000.[28]

If the Indian business was profitable—at least to some of those engaged in it—it was also rough. The Ewings, according to one scholar, "were in trouble from the beginning of their business careers." In Indiana, General John Tipton had found it advisable once to confiscate their entire stock of goods.[29] At the 1842 treaty negotiation, they had presented a suspiciously high claim. In 1843 an observer for the Army at the Sac-Fox payment reported that antipathy between the Ewings and the Chouteaus "has for a long time kept the traders and Indians about here in ceaseless turmoil. . . ." At the time, however, they got together in order to keep prices high. (W. G. Ewing had argued the desirability of an accommodation with the Chouteaus: "We can do it," he wrote his brother, "if we prosecute our business with energy the next two years. It will drive them to terms, and place us in easy and comfortable circumstances.")[30] In 1848 the Indian Superintendent at St. Louis revoked the Ewings' license on what appeared to be good evidence that they or their agents had interfered with the

---

[27] Ewing Papers, Harris to G. W. Ewing, Westport, March 4, 1849; memorandum dated July 5, 1849. On the Iowa treaty and claim, see U.S., Congress, Senate, *Senate Executive Document No. 70*, 30th Cong., 1st Sess., 1847-1848, pp. 35-36.

[28] *Ibid.*, pp. 5, 75.

[29] Phillips, *op. cit.*, p. 106.

[30] *Senate Executive Document No. 70*, pp. 28-29; Ewing Papers, April 8, 1843.

United States mail at Westport so as to prevent some "reform" instructions from reaching the Indian agent at the Sac and Fox station. The Ewings protested, of course, but their case is not convincing. (They denied, among other things, that any agent named Harris had ever been in their employ, which comports ill with G. W. Ewing's letter to his elder brother, April 27, 1847: "William Harris promises well, and will, I think, prove a good assistant.")[31] They were not unrepresentative. The same investigation made it clear that other large operators in and around Westport, including the Chouteaus, knew very well what the Ewings were doing and made no effort to stop them. William Gilliss had been singled out as early as 1826 and on several later occasions for trading with the Indians without a license. In the early 1840's Elijah Milton McGee, later to be a mayor of Kansas City, was fined $800 for selling liquor to the Indians.[32]

Conflicts between traders and missionaries (who were also traders on occasion) broke out from time to time. W. D. Harris reported indignantly to his employers in 1849 that the "hypocrite missionary" Johnston Lykins should be expelled from the territory. John Calvin McCoy, he went on, was a tool of Lykins' and had been bribed to slander the Ewings at Washington. This controversy had arisen because of some allegations by Lykins concerning the ethics of a financial transaction between the Ewings and Indians in 1846. It could have been a case of missionary idealism versus pecuniary greed, but W. G. Ewing thought not. "This old rascal [Lykins]," he wrote to G. W., "has got his son trading below the mission where the Oregon road crosses the Kaw river. . . ."[33]

---

31 *Senate Executive Document No. 70*, p. 6; Ewing Papers, April 27, 1847.

32 On Gilliss, see the Richard Graham Papers, Missouri Historical Society, St. Louis, for December 9, 1826, December 3, 1828, and November 2, 1830. On McGee, see Records of the United States District Court (Missouri), Book A, p. 34; these records are preserved at the General Services Administration, National Archives, Old Records Branch, Kansas City, Missouri.

33 Ewing Papers, Harris to G. W. Ewing, Westport, November 24, December 6, 1849; deposition of Johnston Lykins dated July 11, 1850, at the Westport store of Simpson and Hunter; W. G. to G. W. Ewing, Westport, December 15, 1850.

The Indian trade succeeded to the fur trade, and in doing so it jacked up the townsite potential of the western border at least by a few degrees. It stimulated the Missouri River steamboat business and localized some of it at the town company's rock landing. It brought moneyed men such as the Ewings and Hiram Northrup into the area, while it offered those already on the ground, such as the McCoys and the McGees, a means of extending their commitment to the locale. As late as 1857 a Kansas City editorial pointed happily to the annuity money as among the guarantees which the young city had against the effects of depression. But by that time Indian money was only one item, and not the largest, in a list of profit sources. The Indian trade alone could hardly have created an urban center. Colorful, risky, with enormous profit margins for successful ventures, violently competitive, it could serve only to widen the narrow opportunities marked out by the fur trade. Its long-range significance lies in the role it played in converting the great West from a vast and mysterious Unknown into an equally vast and much less mysterious field for investment.

Another line of business was growing up at about the same time, which at first supplemented the Indian trade and later came to surpass it. This was the Santa Fe trade, the famous "commerce of the prairies." As long as Spain held Mexico (including, of course, the entire American Southwest), there was very little contact between the two regions. With the Mexican Revolution, however, the picture changed. Trade began to grow, and the Mexican War seemed to have fulfilled some kind of destiny by bringing the two regions under one government. From the beginning the Missouri River was the major eastern contact point for whatever connections had been attempted. When regular trade began in 1822, a series of towns along the river served successively as its outfitting points. The location of the outfitting point moved westward as time passed, as far as the Missouri's course ran west-to-east, and the steamboats moved farther and farther upstream. The outfitting point stayed close to the extreme fringe of settlement: Franklin, Boonville, Lexington, Independence, and finally Westport and Kansas.[34]

While the Santa Fe trade's eastern terminus moved westward, the trade itself grew and took on an increasingly complex business structure. By the time it had reached Independence, its annual average value came to about $200,000. Carried on originally by small-scale individual enterprisers, by 1843 the trade involved at least 170 men each year, only about twenty of whom were proprietors. The rate of profit was still high, running well over 20 per cent, although it had fallen somewhat. Mexico offered specie in quantities which were an important part of Missouri's circulating media, mules, and pelts in exchange for cotton, leather, woolen goods, and such luxury items as velvet and silk.[35]

This was not an enormous business by New York or Philadelphia standards even at the time, but it was attractive on the frontier. When its eastern terminus located in a community, the local merchants might engage in it directly, or they might supply the traders with goods; sometimes they acted as agents for the traders, buying goods in the East on commission. A Lexington merchant sold nearly $10,000 worth of goods in the Santa Fe trade in May, 1830, at an advance of 25 per cent over Philadelphia prices.[36] Like the Indian trade, this enterprise offered a field for moderately well-to-do men in the West, seeking chances for rapid accumulation. It brought business into the area, and business promoted town growth.

By the 1830's Independence was drawing most of the commerce of the prairies. According to one traveler, in 1832 it was

34 F. F. Stephens, in "Missouri and the Santa Fe Trade," *Missouri Historical Review*, X (1916), 238, says that for ten years after 1822 the average annual increase in volume was 40 per cent. See also R. L. Duffus, *The Santa Fe Trail* (New York: Longmans, Green & Company, 1930); Josiah Gregg, *The Commerce of the Prairies* (New York: H. G. Langley, 1844). There are good modern editions of this classic.

35 Stephens, "Missouri and the Santa Fe Trade," Part II, *Missouri Historical Review*, XI (1917), 295, 297, 302, revising Gregg's figures. Walker Wyman, "Freighting: A Big Business on the Santa Fe Trail," *Kansas Historical Quarterly*, I (1931), 17-27.

36 See Lewis Atherton, "Business Techniques in the Santa Fe Trade," *Missouri Historical Review*, XXXIV (1940), 335-41; Ralph P. Bieber, "Letters of James and Robert Aull," *Missouri Historical Society Bulletin*, V (1928), 267-310.

like most western towns, "full of promise" but actually unprepossessing, made up of "a ragged congeries" of log buildings. Nevertheless, he added, "the fortune made here already . . . by a bold Yankee shopkeeper who had sold sixty thousand dollars' worth of goods in three years, was a matter of equal notoriety, surprise, and envy."[37] But this was only the beginning. When Josiah Gregg published his *Commerce of the Prairies* in 1844, he described Independence as still the chief "port of embarkation" for western travel of any kind. In the years from 1830 to 1836, Jackson County's population grew from 2,823 to 4,522, and Independence was the only considerable place in the county.[38]

Independence had some drawbacks as a commercial center, however, and in the later 1840's Santa Fe business moved increasingly through Westport and the town of Kansas. By assembling their outfits in either place, the caravans could avoid eighteen miles over bad roads from Independence, including some inconvenient creek crossings, and through a countryside which was being divided into farms. Westport had the additional advantage of its proximity to the prairies, with plenty of grassland where teams could be herded.[39]

The presence at Westport of men already engaged in the Indian trade added business attractions to those of geography; commerce with the Indians and commerce with Santa Fe were never far apart. The Sublettes, for example, had engaged in the latter enterprise at an early date. E. C. McCarty, who stayed on to become one of early Kansas City's most prominent commission merchants, had been in both the Santa Fe and Indian trades. As early as 1834 Bent and St. Vrain landed some goods for Mexico at Chouteau's warehouse.[40] The Ewings were not backward in

[37] Charles Joseph Latrobe, *The Rambler in North America* (London: Seeley and Burnside, 1836), I, 128.

[38] See R. G. Thwaites (ed.), *Early Western Travels*, XIX (Cleveland: A. H. Clark, 1905), 189; Alphonso Wetmore, *Gazetteer of the State of Missouri* (St. Louis: C. Keemle, 1837), pp. 92-99, 267.

[39] Miller, *History*, pp. 392, 406-7; W. R. Bernard, "Westport and the Santa Fe Trade," *Kansas Historical Collections*, IX (1905-1906), 557.

[40] Spalding, *Annals*, pp. 31-33; Missouri Historical Society (St. Louis), *Indian Mss.*, contract for McCarty and others to supply the emigrating Creek Indians, dated March 28, 1837.

this regard, and early in 1850 they bid successfully for a contract to carry government freight to Santa Fe. It was, Harris wrote from Westport, "a splendid operation"; the Independence people had been beaten, and the Ewings' success would make for a good opening the following year. "Or," continued Harris, "you might freight out to San Tafee on your own account. There is a might pretty opening now at San Tafee. . . ."[41]

Managerial elements in the shifting of the Santa Fe trade from Independence are reflected further in W. R. Bernard's claim that he had caused the shift all by himself. Bernard had come to Westport in 1847 and engaged in merchandising with A. G. Boone, one of that town's leading men (and one who, it may be added, had earlier been active in the Indian trade). Some time around 1849, a wealthy Mexican trader named Chavez was on his way to Independence from the West, carrying $100,000 in silver. Along his route he fell into company with the well-known scout, F. X. Aubrey, who persuaded him to stop at Westport. There he found that Bernard could ship the money to St. Louis for him; not only that, but the Mexican trade could find all the accommodations it needed at Westport—credit, goods, connections with the East—without traveling the additional distance to Independence. This, according to Bernard, "together with the advantage of a natural route, carried the trade to Westport, to the injury of Independence."[42]

A similar claim was later made for William Chick, namely, that by convincing Bent and St. Vrain in 1845 to do business in Kansas and by offering them warehousing facilities, Chick had begun the process of diverting the Santa Fe trade. Certainly the twenty-five large wagons from the Southwest which were unloaded at Chick's warehouse that year (it was more than the warehouse could hold, and 5,000 buffalo hides had to be stacked on the levee pending their shipment downstream) provided a windfall for Kansas and may indeed have signalized what Chick's son was to call "the turning point of the great overland trade to

---

41 Ewing Papers, February 14, 1850; Harris mentioned also that a new warehouse for the Ewings had been completed.

42 Bernard, *op. cit.*, p. 557.

this city." Stories of this kind, however, indicate chiefly that a combination of business enterprise with locational advantages was building up Kansas during the 1840's.[43]

Although the shift in one sense went first to Westport and then to Kansas, the two towns represented two phases of the same movement. As Westport's outfitting business expanded, so did activity around the river landing. Since most of the local profit was to be made in the transfer of goods from one holder to another rather than in their shipment across plains and mountains, the warehouses and business offices tended to gravitate toward the place where the goods were landed. The experience of Bent and St. Vrain makes this clear. When, in the 1830's, the steamboat terminus moved to Independence and the caravans began herding their teams near Westport, competition broke out for the available grass. Some of the traders staked out "ranches" of their own, and Bent and St. Vrain fenced off an area south and slightly west of Westport. Hitherto, they had done most of their business through Independence, but the establishment and location of their new ranch made it much more convenient for them to do their transshipping at Kansas, and the business now went there.[44]

According to E. C. McCarty, the first train to leave directly from Kansas City for the Southwest was assembled in 1847. By 1850 enough business had already moved to the river front that six hundred wagons left from there for the western trip. Alexander Majors recalled that he began running trains from Kansas in 1850, one consisting of ten wagons drawn by 130 oxen. "There are a great many Santa Feans now in Kansas," according to a newspaper in 1851, ". . . busily preparing to set out on their journey across the plains. Those now here will leave in a few days, and we are glad to find that they are so numerous and so well armed as to rob the trip of most of its dangers."[45]

While the Indian trade was setting up connections between

[43] See the reminiscences of J. S. Chick, typescript in "Early Settlers" folder, Archives of the Native Sons of Kansas City.

[44] David Lavender, *Bent's Fort* (New York: Doubleday & Company, Inc., 1954), p. 209.

[45] E. C. McCarty is quoted in Spalding, *Annals*, p. 33; Majors, *Seventy Years*, p. 128; *Kansas Public Ledger*, clipped in the *Liberty Tribune*, May 9, 1851.

the town and the immediately surrounding hinterland, the great commerce of the plains drew the town's interest across that hinterland in one great leap into an entirely different region, where another kind of business was to be done. Like the Indian trade, this business was probably not large enough to power the growth of a metropolitan center; in both cases, Kansas and its older double star, Westport, were essentially meeting points between the highly developed East and a western empire which grew ever more attractive. The two towns, even as they grew, functioned not so much as initiators, but rather as agents for drives which developed independently and beyond the range of their influence.

The same pattern appears again in the third kind of business which offered itself to the Missouri border. This was the outfitting of emigrants. Again, the settlement at the mouth of the Kansas River appears as a child of manifest destiny. In the 1830's American settlers began to supplant trappers in the Oregon country. Dramatic missionary enterprises called attention to the area, and soon a great migration in that direction had set in: 100 settlers in 1842, 900 in 1843, 1,200 in 1844. At first, most of them took the circuitous sea route to get there, but as time passed the choice fell heavily in favor of the overland route from Independence. Hall J. Kelley had already proposed a railroad to the Columbia from "the bank of the Missouri near the mouth of the Kansas. . . ." Between 1840 and 1850, Oregon's population grew from 150 to 13,500. California had begun to attract American settlers as early as 1841; progress in this quarter was slow, with only about 700 Americans there by 1846, but then came the Mexican War and American acquisition, followed by the gold rush. There were more than 100,000 Americans in California by 1850. Again, the chief route for the migration began near the northward bend of the Missouri River.[46]

There was Army outfitting to be done. For example, when

[46] Dorothy O. Johansen and Charles W. Gates, *Empire of the Columbia* (New York: Harper and Brothers, 1957), pp. 203-64; F. W. Powell (ed.), *Hall J. Kelley on Oregon* (Princeton: Princeton University Press, 1932), p. 198; John W. Caughey, *California* (New York: Prentice-Hall, Inc., 1953), pp. 200-255. A good introduction to this whole stage in the westward movement is Bernard De Voto's *Year of Decision, 1846* (Boston: Little, Brown & Company, 1943).

Colonel Andrew Doniphan led his Missouri volunteers to the Mexican War, Westport participated in that business.[47] The civilian outfitting trade was more important because it was more stable, and Independence, Westport, and Kansas all participated in this operation. Several other little towns arose on the Missouri border in response to the series of opportunities: Parkville, Weston, and St. Joseph. Even into the early 1850's, however, nothing indicated very firmly which, if any, of these places would succeed in organizing all of these more or less chaotic enterprises for its own special benefit.

Independence and St. Joseph are mentioned more frequently in the surviving documents, at least up to 1850; thereafter, until late in the decade, it is safe to say that more Americans had heard of Westport than of Kansas. Independence, as one member of Thomas Farnham's Oregon party in 1839 recalled, "was then the very frontier of civilization." A few years later Rufus B. Sage coupled Westport and Independence in a similar description: "Situated as they are, at the utmost verge of civilization, and upon the direct route to Oregon and regions adjacent, they must retain and command, as the starting points for emigrants and traders, that importance already assumed by general consent." Independence boasted two thousand people; Westport, however, Sage simply called "a small town in the same county. . . ."[48]

"The emigrants are gathering numerously at Independence," according to the *Liberty Tribune* in April, 1846, where the reference is clearly to a trade already well set up. A year later, the same paper clipped the *St. Joseph Gazette* to the effect that the spring migration through Independence had amounted to 433 wagons, while that through St. Joseph was upward of 800. "Averaging five persons to each wagon, and you have 6,500 persons,

---

[47] Spalding, *Annals*, p. 18; the allegation that the Mexican War gave Westport its effective start is clearly wrong, but indicates the importance of the Army's business to an already established community.

[48] L. R. and Ann Hafen (eds.), *To the Rockies and Oregon, 1839-1842* (Glendale, California: A. H. Clark, 1955), pp. 125, 155; and *Rufus B. Sage, His Letters and Papers, 1836-1847* (Glendale: A. H. Clark, 1956), pp. 117-19. The quotations from Sage are from his *Scenes in the Rocky Mountains* (Philadelphia: Carey & Hart, 1846).

large and small, now on their way to Oregon and California."[49]
The standard terms in which the river towns conducted their
rivalry appear in another St. Joseph item which describes a throng
of emigrants passing through the place. According to conversa-
tions with them, the editor wrote that all were eminently satisfied
at finding plenty of equipment at good prices for sale in St.
Joseph. "This being a producing country," he concluded, "our
market is well supplied with bacon, flour, etc. . . ."[50]

This must have been small pickings compared with what
followed. Gold was discovered in California in January, 1848,
and as reports filtered eastward, an army of migrants began to
crowd the river boats to Independence. Between April and September, 1849, 2,400 gold hunters left for California from the
western border of Missouri. "Never since we have had any ac-
quaintance with this place," said the *Western Expositor* of Independence in May, "has Independence presented a more businesslike appearance. . . . From morning till night the streets are
crowded with people from all parts of the United States, all waiting for the rising of grass before they launch themselves out on
the almost boundless plains . . . it is next thing to an impossibility
to drive a carriage through our principal streets."[51]

Again, Independence benefited more directly than the other
towns near the bend in the river. Kansas citizens indeed participated in the gold-rush business: the ubiquitous Ewings were
happy to hear from Westport in 1850 that "all the noise here is
people getting ready for California—mules and other stock is
high." They had already been careful to lay in a supply of goods,
and they had especially instructed their Westport agent to advise
them in good time of the prospects for an emigration business.[52]
Still, the younger settlement's participation was marginal. A St.

[49] *Liberty Tribune*, April 18, 1846; June 19, 1847.

[50] *St. Joseph Adventure*, clipped in *Liberty Tribune*, May 12, 1848; discussion arguing in similar terms for Parkville as the most advantageous outfitting
point is in the *Tribune* for April 9, 1852.

[51] Quotation from Ralph P. Bieber (ed.), *Southern Trails to California in
1849* (Glendale: A. H. Clark, 1947), p. 360.

[52] Ewing Papers, Richard Pearson to G. W. Ewing, Westport, January 30,
1850; memorandum dated Westport, October 12, 1849.

Joseph writer, certainly painting the rosiest picture for his own town, summed up the 1850 emigration as follows: 32,000 had left from St. Joseph, 6,000 from Weston, and 10,000 divided between Independence, Parkville, and Kansas. Emigrant letters mention Independence and St. Joseph most frequently, then Westport, while Kansas is rarely referred to. Charles Spalding, Kansas City's professional booster in the later fifties, notes simply that the town "derived no extravagant benefit" from either the Mexican War or the gold rush.[53]

The importance of the emigrant trade for Kansas was not so much in the goods which were bought and sold there. Rather it lay in the whole area's growth, which ultimately gave rise to the future city. Rufus Sage, in the 1846 account already quoted, in which he did not mention Kansas, revealed what was happening when he observed that "the country in this vicinity is beginning to be generally settled by thrifty farmers," and tied this in with the emigrant business.[54] The businesses described so far began the process of developing a locale; meanwhile, Kansas grew by accretion, veiling itself, so to speak, behind the mantle of Westport. In the 1840's and early 1850's it is a mistake to see the two as rivals. The situation is more accurately described with St. Joseph, Independence, and the little Westport-Kansas complex acting out the roles of three major competitors—Weston and Parkville being for the most part on the fringes of the struggle.

The relationship of Kansas to Westport is shown in a curious controversy over the early names which were applied to the river settlement. "Kansas City is a colony," wrote John C. McCoy, "originally sent out by Westport to her steamboat landing. . . ." During the doldrums following the town company's organization, it was, according to McCoy, "simply Westport Landing. . . ." There is no evidence that the town of Kansas, once it developed momentum, was ever called "Westport Landing," but McCoy's memory for the common usage of merchants and travelers to the

---

[53] *Jefferson Inquirer*, June 15, 1850; Walker Wyman (ed.), *California Emigrant Letters* (New York: Bookman, 1952); Spalding, *Annals*, p. 18.

[54] Hafen, *Sage Letters*, p. 119.

site itself is probably accurate and reflects the relationship between the two places within a context of town rivalry.[55]

Traders and emigrants found Kansas increasingly adequate to their needs. In 1847, according to the *Liberty Tribune*, the town was "improving with a rapidity unprecedented in the history of western towns. The general impression, we believe, is that it will eventually become the starting point for traders and emigrants, owing to its being on the river." Early in the following year the *Tribune* again described Kansas as "flourishing" and gaining both business and population; "some of the heaviest Santa Fe traders now start from that point." The editor went on to praise John Calvin McCoy's competence as a ferryman and noted that the inhabitants of Clay County, across the river from Kansas, carried large stocks of bacon, beef, and other produce there for sale. "We have no doubt," he wrote, "Kansas will very soon be the chief point of trade between Lexington and St. Joseph." (There is independent evidence that McCoy's ferry was earning about $700 a year.) In 1850 a correspondent signing himself "Kansas" —probably a local resident boosting his investment—portrayed the settlement's advantages for California migrants in a letter to the *Missouri Republican*. The steamboat landing, he said, was "perhaps the best on the Missouri river"; in fact, the entire river front constituted a "natural wharf," where any kind of vessel might discharge or pick up freight safely. "The town contains," continued this writer,

> four immense warehouses; several grist and saw mills; blacksmith and wagon-makers' shops; grocery and provision stores, and a magnificent and commodious hotel, the "Troost House," containing over one hundred apartments. In the immediate vicinity are well stocked farms, from which every

[55] See Louis O. Honig, *Westport, Gateway to the Early West* ([Kansas City]: By the author [1950]), pp. 111-13; Henry C. Haskell, Jr., and Richard G. Fowler, *City of the Future . . . 1850-1950* (Kansas City: Frank Glenn [1950]), p. 27; McCoy Scrapbook, p. 86, "The First Letter" [republished posthumously], *Kansas City Daily Journal*, September [3?], 1889.

desirable variety of the best stock, as well as produce, can be obtained at prices as low as in any other part of Western Missouri. An excellent road leads from the river through the flourishing town of Westport, to the open prairie. . . . Wagons, mules, cattle, ponies, saddles, harness, grain, provisions, groceries—everything, in fact, necessary to the trip and the comfort of the immigrants, can be obtained at Westport as well as at Kansas.[56]

What government there was, the county supplied. There was, in fact, very little government, but public authority nevertheless played an essential role. Townships were established for police and other administrative purposes, justices of the peace were elected, school taxes and merchants' and peddlers' licenses were collected. Aside from private litigation and probate matters, however, the Jackson County Court spent most of its time in the 1830's and 1840's dealing with roads and—to a lesser extent—bridges over the creeks and runs. Road districts were set up, lines specified, and overseers named to supervise the clearing and other necessary work. Frequently this kind of public enterprise, supported by tax funds, was undertaken at the request of inhabitants who petitioned for the building of particular roads. The names of McGee, McCoy, and others with whom we are familiar occur often in the court's records in connection with these roads. In 1839, even before their title was clear, some of the shareholders in the town company, along with other inhabitants, "in consequence of the projected creation of the new town of Kanzas . . . and deeming it essentially necessary that a free and open communication ought to exist between the Town of Kanzas and West Port," asked for a road between the two points. Satisfied of its public utility, the court sanctioned the proposal and appointed Thomas Smart overseer for the new road.[57]

Gradually, in this way, the ground of Jackson County came

[56] *Liberty Tribune*, November 5, 1847; April 7, 1848; on the ferry see the suit against McCoy, 29 *Missouri Reports*, p. 356; *Missouri Republican*, April 12, 1850. A photostat of this article is in the Archives of the Native Sons.

[57] Material for the paragraph comes from a study of the Records of the Jackson County Court in the office of the Clerk of the County Court, Independence, Missouri. For the Westport-Kansas road, see Record 3, pp. 144, 250, 255 (August 21, 1839; July 6, 7, 1840).

to be crosshatched with roads along which people and goods could move. The roads led to and from the pockets of settlement; isolated groups and farms were drawn into vital connection with one another and the great highway offered by the river.

Gradually, too, the enterprises near the rock landing began to look like a town in fact as well as in name. The town company filed its plats for land sale purposes in 1839, 1846, and 1847. These give us what might be a map of Kansas, except that the projection describes only a town which might come to exist—not one which already existed. The streets were so far no more than ink on paper; between the 1839 and 1846 plats they changed not only names but directions. The carefully numbered lots were only places where, it might be, going concerns and busy families would come to locate. These plats, nevertheless, especially by 1847 and taken in conjunction with the earliest actual drawings of the town, give a reasonably accurate over-all view of events. The town settlement embraced—even hugged—the rock landing near the foot of Main Street, then straggled away toward the south, over the hills.

The warehouses and stores went up, the McGees and others made brick, the ferryboats crossed and recrossed the river. Each accretion to the trading community broadened the need for services: doctors might find practice, druggists might find customers, clergymen could expect congregations. A visitor with business in Westport wrote to a friend in 1848 that "Kansas on the Mo River" already had four brickyards and one steam mill in operation; in all, there were about two hundred families. He listed ten stores, three taverns, and a livery stable in the town. About a year later the same writer estimated the population of Kansas at seven hundred.[58]

Signs were not wanting that a new stage in community development was at hand. In 1850, for example, the inhabitants of

58 Receipt of these letters, along with details, is specified in the diary of Ellis G. Evans. His correspondent was one Abner Calloway, writing July 28 and October 5, 1848, and early in June, 1849. The second letter, according to Evans' diary, mentioned 500 "families," which is almost impossible and must be a slip for "persons." These citations were kindly supplied by Dr. J. Neal Primm from a typescript of the Evans diary, which he had been able to examine.

Kansas petitioned successfully for town organization which would bring them certain services (notably police) otherwise spread out over an entire township. The settlement now became known officially as "the Town of Kansas," and provisions for it as such were made by the county court. Trustees, responsible to that court, were appointed by it to supervise the town's affairs. The first group of trustees whom the court named included some of the most active movers at Kansas, but of the five named, four— McCoy, Pierre M. Chouteau, Hiram Northrup, and one Robert Kirkham—failed to qualify, and new trustees had to be named. The reason for their failure to qualify may be that these men had no especial desire to serve as trustees, being occupied in other pursuits. The new trustees, William Gilliss and Benoist Troost among them, set about improving the wharf and some of the streets leading to it.[59]

Another important sign of growth was the appearance of a hotel. William Gilliss and Benoist Troost built it on the river front probably in 1849. It had forty-six apartments, which were advertised as roomy and modern.[60] The hotel business was especially important in hopeful western towns. In lobbies and saloons wealthy outsiders could form their impressions, favorable or otherwise, of local businessmen and opportunities. Later on, as Kansas became Kansas City, the demand for more hotel space was constantly and loudly expressed.

At about the same time (in 1851), the first newspaper appeared. Here was another enterprise like hotel-keeping, the success of which directly concerned the ambitions of everyone interested in the town. Robert V. Kennedy moved from Independence and began to publish the *Kansas Public Ledger*. Much attention was given in the *Ledger* to the Oregon and California

---

[59] County Court Record 8, p. 101 (February 4, 1850); M. J. Payne, "Early Municipal Government, City of Kansas," in Howard Conard (ed.), *Encyclopedia of the History of Missouri* (New York: Southern History Company, 1901), I, 616-17.

[60] *Kansas Public Ledger*, July 4, 1851; the *Missouri Republican* story quoted above must have exaggerated in attributing one hundred apartments to this hotel. There was another hotel in the town by mid-1851: the "Kansas," Benjamin Threlkeld, proprietor, which was advertised in the same issue of the *Ledger*.

migrations; emigrants were advised as to the best routes, and the paper maintained agents on the West Coast as well as in the eastern cities. The role of Kansas as "entrepôt" for the trade of the Far West was stressed, as was its convenience as a market for farmers in the immediately surrounding area. The editor took up the cudgels of town rivalry with a will, scorning the efforts of Independence papers to stigmatize the town of Kansas. He painted a scene of lively activity near the landing: mills, hammers, and trowels were hard at work. "We expect to astonish the natives of some of our neighboring *cities* (!) with a recital of what her *natural advantages* alone are just *beginning* to do for Kansas."[61]

Men attached to the Indian missions were moving in and participating in building the new town. Along with the McCoys there came Johnston Lykins, for example, to work among the Shawnees in the Baptist interest. A native Virginian, Lykins was on the Missouri border as early as 1830, helping to set up Baptist missions; he seemed particularly interested in linguistics and supplied the tribes with a written alphabet so that they could read his translations of the Bible and other material. Lykins was closely connected with the McCoys and married John Calvin's sister, Delilah. He had already (by 1840) bought from one of the French-Canadian settlers sixteen acres of land on which he soon put up a brick warehouse. In 1848 he removed from the Baptist mission and settled in Kansas. That Lykins' activities attracted the unfavorable attention of the Ewings has already been shown. They regarded him as a hypocrite, not so much interested in the improvement of the Indians as in his own fortunes. "I am told," wrote George Ewing, "that he has accumulated a large property and that he has money—that he has educated his children quite expensively and made valuable improvements on his land, etc. . . ."[62] The allegation proves

<hr>

[61] See "Journal of Governor William Walker," entry dated March 22, 1851; issues of the *Kansas Public Ledger* for April 25, July 4, and August 29, 1851, are available at the Kansas City Public Library.

[62] Ewing Papers, to Rev. S. Dyer, Secretary of Baptist Missions, August 31, 1850. Where not otherwise indicated, data on the missionaries have been taken from a file of biographical cards at the Archives of the Native Sons.

nothing more than that Lykins found the shift from primarily philanthropic to primarily business activities no more difficult than McCoy had found it. Like McCoy, he continued to be prominent in Kansas City's affairs until after the Civil War.

At the Methodist mission, William Johnson died in 1842, and his surviving brother, Thomas, found that he needed more help. In 1848 he brought in Nathan Scarritt from Howard County, who was to conduct, of all things, the classical studies department of the mission school! It will surprise no one to learn that by this time the school did not limit itself to advanced Indian scholars, but also educated the children of some of the white settlers by the landing. Scarritt soon had land holdings at Kansas, and the family interest has survived, as has that of the McGees, into the present day.

Obviously, the role of the Indian missions in Kansas City's prehistory was an important one. If the French community did not promise well for future growth either in its structure or in its characteristic personnel, the same cannot be said of the missions. Here were men who had been born and raised in the middle of nineteenth-century America's expanding culture. Well-educated and imaginative men, they had no intention of leaving "civilization" forever behind them. If the traders—McGee, Gilliss, Northrup, Chick—brought the main impulse to growth, the missionary men were willing and able to help shape it and even, it may be, to give it a more impressive intellectual rationale than the purely mercantile group could have done.

There were still, however, major obstacles in the town's way. In the first place, there was its appearance. Immediately behind the buildings on the river towered high bluffs which seemed to pen the little settlement effectively on the bank. Ravines leading back to the south had been somewhat improved into roads by 1850, but without much more labor of cutting and grading, the blithely platted Main, Delaware, Walnut, and Market streets must remain evidence only of someone's overenthusiastic dream. Who would buy a lot, no matter what number it carried on the plat, if it was actually situated on a seventy-degree slope? This unattractive feature of the site drew the notice of people who passed through the town. "The turbid river and mud bluffs," wrote one, "destroy the pleasing effects generally attendant on northern rivers." To John Calvin McCoy, it seemed in retrospect that "nature . . . exhausted her resources in a grand effort to thwart the schemes of city builders. . . ." Not only were the town founders faced with topographical difficulties, but, continued McCoy, these difficulties were for many years "seized upon by our neighboring villages to wound our sensibilities and lacerate our feelings, thus adding insult to injury by applying to our protege the low humiliating sobriquet of 'Gully Town.' "[63]

Not only the terrain, but in some respects the social landscape as well might have appeared unpromising around 1850. What struck many travelers apparently was the rather motley appearance of the human material. Francis Parkman noted simply that he had left his baggage with William Chick, "whose log house was the substitute for a tavern," and had gone to Westport to purchase supplies for his Oregon trip. His only impression of the landing was the presence of some Indians, a few mountain men, and "thirty or forty dark, slavish-looking Spaniards, gazing stupidly out from beneath their broad hats. . . ."[64]

Liquor circulated freely in the rough little community; the county court granted many dramshop licenses for Kansas. Nathan Scarritt, appalled by "sinks of dissipation" which he saw around him, asked the editor of the Ledger to support a drive for temperance and morality in general in order to improve the appearance of the town. Fifty years later, Alexander Majors remembered this aspect of his life in Kansas very well. "Prohibition," as he put it, "was an unknown element in social science." On at least one occasion, a gala social affair planned by responsible town leaders broke up in a drunken spree. A contemporary neighbor, William Walker (half-blood and chief of the Wyandot nation), noted in his diary in 1851 that the proprietors of the Union Hotel had for some reason been unable to interest their wives in cele-

[63] Lewis H. Garrard, *Wah-to-Yah and the Taos Trail*, ed. Ralph P. Bieber (Glendale: A. H. Clark, 1938), p. 52. Garrard made his trip in 1846 and published his book in 1850; McCoy Scrapbook, p. 39.

[64] Francis Parkman, *The Oregon Trail* (Boston: Little, Brown & Company, 1898), pp. 5-6.

brating Washington's birthday with a nice party. "It appears to have been a failure," Walker wrote:

> . . . the Landlord and Managers got drunk, most royally so, in order to be avenged on the refractory ladies. The Landlord, to show his indignation, made a perfect mash of the supper table and all the good things that were placed thereon. Even the "saur kraut" was not spared. . . .[65]

It would not do to exaggerate these rough features of town society; there were also influences of a different kind. A Catholic congregation had been organized for some time by 1850, as already mentioned. The Methodists were not much later; in 1845 they organized a regular society which seems to have met at the house of William Chick. Both Lewis Garrard and Francis Parkman acknowledged the gracious hospitality of Chick, "the principal man" of Kansas. Benoist Troost drew a more pleasant picture of social life around the Union Hotel than Walker's diary affords; the younger set in Kansas congregated affably in the hotel's two saloons.[66] But the presence of two churches and one published boost by a deeply interested party should not blind us to what must have been, by and large, a dreary social scene in the town of Kansas. Independence and Westport were far ahead of it in amenities.

Nor were these lacks the only obstacles to growth. In 1849 the dread cholera struck in western Missouri. All the border towns suffered; according to William Walker, the disease reached Kansas late in March and did not abate until May. It recurred during the summer of 1850, and again the following year. The *Ledger* repeatedly assured its readers, "for the benefit of strangers, who are liable to be imposed upon by false rumors," that Kansas was healthy, but other contemporary witnesses differed. In June, 1849, one man writing from Kansas reported that twenty-four had died there in thirty-six hours. According to Charles Spalding, who wrote his *Annals of the City of Kansas* only a few years after the epidemics had apparently ceased, the mortality had been

---

[65] See "Journal of Governor William Walker," entry dated February 26, 1851.
[66] *Kansas Public Ledger,* April 25, 1851.

enormous. Fear had driven others away from the town, "and the loneliness of a deserted village still more"; at the end of 1851, he wrote, the town's population was not over three hundred.[67]

All in all, there was no reason to suppose that Kansas was a success in the very early 1850's. Perhaps a half-dozen important business houses clustered around the rock landing in surroundings far different than those to be found at St. Louis or Cincinnati. Some people moved away. If Hiram Northrup or William Gilliss or the Chicks had moved, the town would almost certainly have lapsed into a torpor. The *Ledger* was not a success. Kennedy left after publishing several issues, and publication was continued by two other men. Local firms were continually urged to support the enterprise with their advertising, and some did; nevertheless, it failed in 1851, and Kansas had no organ to represent its general interest. The failure of the *Ledger* makes us wonder how strong the putative general interest in building a community was at the time.[68]

In fact, however, great new possibilities were in the offing in 1853. The rapid rise of the Pacific Coast settlements placed the building of a transcontinental railroad prominently on the national agenda. Partly in connection with this and partly independent of it, a demand grew in 1852 and 1853 that the territory west of Missouri and Iowa be thrown open to American settlement. These two momentous developments caught the town of Kansas, picked it up, and ultimately made a city out of it.

Western railroads had been projected in the early 1840's by

[67] See "Journal of Governor William Walker," entries dated March 29 and May 3, 1849; July 6, 1850; and various dates in July, 1851. See also the *Kansas Public Ledger* for July 4 and August 29, 1851; *Liberty Tribune,* July 11, 1851; Evans diary, cited in note 58, for June 9, 1849; Spalding, *Annals,* pp. 18-19.

[68] Eleven local businessmen advertised in the *Kansas Public Ledger* for July 4, 1851, including one tailor and one doctor; twelve advertised in the issue of August 29, 1851. Ten merchants' licenses in Kansas are mentioned in the County Court Records for 1849, and eight for 1850. Of the merchants listed as having paid fees November 3, 1850, Hiram Northrup paid $28 out of a total of $72 collected. In both the *Ledger* and the records of county merchants' licenses, it is abundantly clear that Independence was far ahead of Kansas as a business center.

such men as Asa Whitney and Stephen A. Douglas, but it took the gold rush and California's admission to the Union to make a real issue out of a project that had seemed more or less visionary. However, sectional antipathies had become strong enough to prevent any one scheme for western rail connections from passing through Congress. As North and South and conflicting interests within both major sections checkmated one another's efforts, some of the western states tried to put themselves in favorable positions for such time as a transcontinental connection could be decided upon. They chartered corporations to build west as far as possible; they granted all kinds of state aid to the railroads and brought what pressure they could on Congress for federal land grants to help their projected roads.[69]

Missouri was very active in these ways and quickly worked out a comprehensive railroad plan to penetrate every section of the state. Two of these roads were to cross the state from east to west: the Pacific Railroad of Missouri (the title of which made its intentions obvious), and the Hannibal and St. Joseph; both had federal land grants in addition to aid from the state. Work began on both railroads early in the 1850's, and as they fitted into the widely agitated question of the transcontinental connection, they brought another increment of national attention to the western Missouri border. In 1851 the *Ledger* clipped a news item about a "stupendous" railroad projected between Baltimore and Kansas.[70]

Meanwhile, Missouri's great Jacksonian senator, Thomas Hart Benton, had taken up the issue of a transcontinental railroad. He adopted the "central" or 39th parallel route as his own—it was the one most likely to benefit St. Louis—and spoke over all the state and elsewhere in its favor. Of Missouri's two westward creeping railroads, Benton's oratory was on the side of the Pacific, the western terminus of which had been left uncertain. (The Jackson County Court had already notified the Pacific Railroad,

---

[69] See Robert R. Russel, *Improvement of Communication with the Pacific Coast as an Issue in American Politics, 1783-1864* (Cedar Rapids, Iowa: Torch Press, 1948).

[70] *Kansas Public Ledger*, April 25, 1851; clipping from the *Chester* (Illinois) *Herald*.

September 3, 1850, that unless it built through that county it could expect no official subscriptions to its stock from Jackson.) In March, 1853, Benton issued a manifesto in the form of a letter to the Missouri voters in which he quoted his son-in-law, John C. Frémont, and the well-known "mountain-man," Antoine Leroux, as favoring the central route. The latter had said that on "being asked by Col. Benton . . . the best way from Missouri to California, I answer: Start as the people now do, going to New Mexico, from the frontier of the State, at Kansas or Independence. . . ."[71]

About the first of May, Benton started on a speaking tour up the Missouri River on behalf of his railroad project. He spoke at Kansas and Westport on May 6 and at Independence the following day. His audiences were reported to be large, and in all three places he laid heavy stress on the desirability of the 39th parallel route. Benton was a national figure, and when he spoke, his words were often printed in eastern newspapers; in the present instance, the New York *Illustrated News* quoted several of his remarks "in a recent speech delivered at Kansas."[72]

The importance of this kind of publicity and what might follow it was clear. References to Kansas now began to appear more frequently in the press. The *Lexington* (Missouri) *Express* remarked dourly in August that while it had no reason to like either Kansas or the whole of Jackson County, "yet we hesitate not to say that nature has designated that spot as the terminus of the Missouri road and the commencement of the National Road to the Pacific." And Kansas finally appeared on a map: that of the proposed central railroad route to California drawn by Gwinn Harris Heap, illustrating the report of an expedition he had ac-

---

[71] L. R. and Ann Hafen (eds.), *Central Route to the Pacific* (Glendale: A. H. Clark, 1957), p. 35.

[72] *Jefferson Inquirer*, May 6, 14, 28, and July 2, 1853; *Glasgow Weekly Times*, May 12, 1853. Hafen, *Central Route to the Pacific*, gives the published version of Benton's speeches from the *Inquirer* on pp. 56-71. Contrary to a widely cherished tradition in Kansas City historiography, it contains no prophecy of a "great metropolis" arising "where these rocky bluffs meet. . . ."

companied and Benton had backed. It was published in 1854.[73]

But any transcontinental railroad would have to cross a large expanse of territory which was still reserved to the Indians. It became urgent that the country west of Missouri be organized as a territory and opened up for settlers. This country was, or included, "the Great American Desert," but that myth was not popular in the West. The *Missouri Republican* had noticed that the Mormons in Utah were adding their voice to the cry for a transcontinental railroad. "A new State will be proposed," said the *Republican,* and in Kansas the *Ledger* eagerly copied the item, "immediately west of . . . Missouri. . . . This would include the 'future Eden of America,' a body of land as fine as the sun shines upon." A letter from Kansas in May, 1853, to the *Missouri Democrat* praised alike Thomas Hart Benton and the fertility of the valley of the Kansas River. William Gilpin had been agitating for the opening of this country for some time. "The maritime tyrants," he now wrote, "have always defined it to be a desert, and not worth selling." Already several border newspapers had commented on local interest in organizing the territory just west of Missouri. The *Ledger* published an elaborate argument in favor of the project in 1851; a public meeting in Parkville the following year petitioned Congress to the same effect. Border settlers were beginning to meet without benefit of federal sanction to elect "delegates" to Congress, and at the 1852-53 session, Representative Willard P. Hall, from western Missouri, introduced his territorial bill into that body.[74]

During these years of tentative business beginnings and early town organization at Kansas, the image of the West was obviously in rapid transition. This change was woven into the politics of American expansion and should not be attributed to any one man. Nevertheless, for present purposes, Gilpin himself is a central figure. His call for the organization of Nebraska Territory stemmed logically from interests which had grown by the 1850's

[73] *Jefferson Inquirer,* August 20, 1853; Heap's map is in Hafen, *Central Route to the Pacific.*

[74] *Kansas Public Ledger,* April 25, 1851; *Jefferson Inquirer,* June 18, November 12, 1853; James C. Malin, *The Nebraska Question, 1852-1854* (Lawrence, Kansas: By the author, 1953), pp. 77-81.

to define his whole purpose.[75] Born into a well-to-do Pennsylvania family, given the best formal education which private tutors could supply, and launched upon the study of law at an early age, Gilpin was restless and unsatisfied. He sought a military career, which brought him to Missouri as a recruiting officer. Almost immediately Gilpin caught the germ of western enthusiasm which never left him. He wrote to his sister in 1836 that all he had previously read about the West was distorted and misleading; words could hardly convey the fabulous natural wealth which was waiting to be exploited. "The part of the Valley which lies on the Mississippi River and West of it," he went on, "must one day surpass aught now existing or which has existed . . . indeed, one who has not seen the valley of the Mississippi can hardly be said to have been in America—he knows not what a *Heart* and *Sinews* she has."[76]

His association with senators Benton and Linn involved him in state politics as a journalist and occasionally as secretary to the General Assembly. After holding this post briefly, Gilpin moved to Independence, where his home was to be until 1861. Actually, Independence was only a base of operations for him. In 1843 he went west with Frémont and participated in Oregon's early struggle for organization. In 1846 he was in Washington, lobbying strenuously for the establishment of a Missouri-to-Oregon mail service. In this connection he began to develop the more or less formal theory of continental destiny which has preserved his name in history.

It was wrong, said Gilpin, to imagine the trans-Missouri West as a barren waste which separated poles of civilization on either

[75] On Gilpin, see H. H. Bancroft, *History of the Life of William Gilpin* (San Francisco: The History Company, 1889), which, however, is not entirely reliable. It may be supplemented with William E. Connelly, "Characters and Incidents of the Plains," *Kansas Historical Collections*, X (1907-1908), 111-19; James Willard's articles on Gilpin in the *Dictionary of American Biography, sub nomine*; Bernard De Voto's "Geopolitics with the Dew on It," *Harper's Magazine*, CLXXXVIII (March, 1944), 313-23; and Henry Nash Smith, *Virgin Land* (Cambridge, Mass.: Harvard University Press, 1951), pp. 35-43.

[76] To Miss Elizabeth Gilpin, October 4, 1836, Gilpin Papers, Missouri Historical Society, St. Louis. There are several other letters in this fascinating little collection which elaborate the same theme.

side of it. On the contrary, Oregon and New England were but the maritime wings of a great central heartland, into which a "vast army of pioneers" was already sweeping with tidal force. When this contention was read on the floor of Congress, according to the official reporter, "the Senate was from time to time convulsed with laughter, and the galleries absolutely rolled with amusement." But Gilpin was undeterred, and after serving in the Mexican War, he returned to Independence and continued to write and speak on his favorite theme. It is quite natural that Gilpin should have been drawn into the movement for territorial organization across the state line. According to one source, he not only participated in a meeting held on the site of Kansas which drew up a provisional constitution for the territory, but actually drafted the document.[77]

As he agitated, so he theorized. In the fall of 1853 one of Gilpin's published speeches assured hearers and readers that those great emporia which are the world's urban centers grow up regularly along the navigable rivers about three hundred miles apart. In the course of inevitable western development, Gilpin went on, Independence could not fail to become one of these centers. Its future growth was written in the same cosmic script which had already produced St. Louis; the two places "stand out upon the face of the continent like eyes in the human head."[78] Within a very few years he had moved his prediction about seven miles to the west, because Kansas City had eclipsed Independence. The Kansas Citians happily picked up his theory and built their own publicity around it, offering to the world the spectacle of a city whose future was guaranteed alike by nature and destiny.

The city grew as the trans-Missouri West entered into the mainstream of American history. It did so by making itself into

[77] U.S., *Congressional Globe*, 29th Cong., 1st Sess., May 18, 1846, pp. 831-32; William E. Connelly, *Doniphan's Expedition* (Topeka, Kansas: By the author, 1907), p. 151 n.

[78] "The City of Independence," in *Western Journal and Civilian*, XI (October, 1853); a mimeographed transcript, used here, is in the Kansas City Public Library.

an instrument serving that entry. Tentatively at first, and then more rapidly, the "desert" receded before the advance of exploration, business, and finally, settlement. Three times in the 1840's John Charles Frémont passed through the town on his way toward the mountains. Recalling his early expeditions, Frémont gratefully acknowledged assistance from the fur trappers, the wild, romantic mountainmen, whose whole way of life had to disappear before the little town could become a city. The Chouteaus in particular were helpful to Frémont, whose whole effort was part of a drive, crystallizing in the forties, to shape the continental impulse known as "manifest destiny." This aspect of the Frémont expeditions is more important than the fact that he outfitted at Kansas and Westport. On his first trip, in 1842, he found a settlement at the mouth of the Kansas River, "where a few houses were the nucleus of a future town, but then called 'Chouteau's,' or Kansas Landing." On the second trip, the next year, he stayed twelve days at "the little town of Kansas," completing his preparations; it was still a "little town" when he returned from the West in 1844.[79] Frémont's fourth trip, in 1853, was explicitly a search for a practicable railroad route close to the 39th parallel.

Curiously, the Ewing brothers, whose business acuity has already been noted, did not anticipate a bright future in land speculation in the town that was to become the metropolis of the mid-Missouri Valley. There is no evidence that either of them, or both, ever held more than a half lot in Kansas, where their warehouse must have been, on the levee. W. G. Ewing indeed knew that city property in the West was a good investment and regretted that he and his brother had parted with some of their St. Louis real estate. But what he had in mind was San Francisco. "Just let our western business pass into other hands, and it will soon 'fizzle out' and can be closed," he wrote. Then they could

---

[79] J. C. Frémont, *Memoirs of My Life* (Chicago and New York: Belford, Clarke and Co., 1887), pp. 32, 73, 409; on the subject of the Frémont expeditions and their significance, see Allan Nevins, *Frémont, Pathmarker of the West* (New York: Longmans, Green & Company, 1955), chaps. vi-xiv.

move to California.[80] For once, the Ewings had called the wrong turn.

Their mistake, in view of the general sharpness and speed of their economic perceptions, is more than ironically interesting. It shows that a well-placed man, carrying a good record for adaptability, could fail to predict what was just about to happen at the great bend of the Missouri River. That the Ewings did not foresee a great future for Kansas is of some importance, in view of the prominent role which imputed prophecy came to play in subsequent written histories of Kansas City. It is understandable that the city's early boosters should argue, as they did, that nature itself had laid out an urban destiny for the site in which they were interested. This, if true, would support allegations that far-seeing men had been able to predict and to prophesy the future before any concrete manifestations of it had appeared. The city's history, then, would amount to a continual fulfillment of these early prophecies, and it is in this vein that it came to be written. Spalding in 1858, Miller in 1881, Case in 1888, Whitney in 1908, and most of those who followed them built their narratives around the complementary themes of natural advantages and accurate predictions of Kansas City's growth.[81]

The key prophecy, so to speak, was imputed to Senator Benton. Once in 1845 and again in 1853, so the story runs, Benton visited Kansas and portrayed its future growth in characteristically eloquent terms.[82] Gilpin, Frémont, and even Josiah Gregg, the Santa Fe merchant, are frequently drawn in to reinforce Benton's view. But these men seemingly epitomized the optimism of local residents. Writing in 1927, one historian of Kansas City remarked casually that when a man, in the early nineteenth century, took "a perspective view" of the Missouri's

[80] Ewing Papers, W. G. to G. W. Ewing, December 13, 1851; also, W. G. to G. W. Ewing, undated, but probably 1851 or later.

[81] Detailed citations are in "The Usable Past: A Study of Historical Traditions in Kansas City," by R. Richard Wohl and A. T. Brown, *Huntington Library Quarterly*, XXIII (May, 1960), 237-59. A fascinating review of "Prophets Who Foresaw a Great Kansas City," by Robert M. Snyder, Jr., is in the *Kansas City Star Sunday Magazine*, April 5, 1926.

[82] The earliest reference is in Spalding, *Annals*, p. 16.

great bend, "the paramount thought immediately suggested a city within the radius of a few miles from the mouth of the Kaw at no distant day."[83] The tradition of prophecy was not confined to the written history, but took a prominent place in what may be called the city's "self-consciousness" as it developed after the Civil War. Shortly after the turn of the century, Kansas City's best-known surviving figure from the 1850's said in a memorial address:

> To be the commercial metropolis of this [western] empire was the ambition of Kansas City, and its fulfillment, then a dream, a prophecy, has become an actual realization.
>
> To foresee and realize the possibilities of Kansas City as a site for the inevitable metropolis of this embryo empire required an intelligent comprehension of its natural advantages, and a practical idea of the agencies necessary to develop them. . . .[84]

The image which was thus built up of a prophetic as well as ambitious group of men, foreseeing the future and capitalizing on it, raises some larger questions in the philosophy of history generally. Here, it will suffice to point out that the image to an important extent misrepresents what Kansas City must have looked like and "felt like" in the years before 1854. It is easy to mention the fact that a similar body of prophecy can be dredged from the histories of many other towns in the area: St. Joseph, Atchison, Quindaro, Leavenworth, and others. More interesting, and more important, is the very slender basis of the documentation which has supported the whole concept of early prophecy. In considering the key prophecy, for example, the most striking fact about Benton's prediction is that it has never been found in any of his writings. He might, of course, have added some impromptu remarks to his formally prepared speech. Some early settlers—much later—claimed that they remembered Benton's words and that these did include the prophecy in question. John

[83] Charles Deatherage, *Early History of Greater Kansas City* (Kansas City: By the author, 1927), p. 324.

[84] Robert T. Van Horn, Address Honoring Milton J. Payne (manuscript, n.d.), Van Horn Papers, Archives of the Native Sons of Kansas City.

C. McCoy, on the other hand, doubted that the prophecy had ever been made, and he, too, was present at the time.[85]

The question of prophetic founders in early Kansas City cannot be disposed of quite so easily as this. Some men, following business opportunities, did indeed "predict" that events would take a certain course. Others thought they saw their opportunities elsewhere, and thus "predicted" another course. Lykins, Gilliss, the McGees, Northrup, and the Chicks, sank what resources they had in the river settlement, and later history ratified their choices. But it is a mistake to suppose that the option was obvious. In 1843 Audubon convinced himself that St. Joseph had a brighter future than any place near Kansas. The Ewings, in 1850 and 1851, saw no reason to invest at the landing. In 1858 the founder of what later became one of Kansas City's best-known department stores (Rothschild's) removed to Leavenworth, apparently dissatisfied at the prospects which two years at Kansas had offered. Horace Greeley, in 1859, was sure that Wyandotte was the coming metropolis. As late as 1867, another editor, Albert D. Richardson, favored Leavenworth's potential over Kansas City's. An early territorial official of Kansas recalled having expanded to a visiting eastern capitalist on the likelihood of a railroad center developing at Kawsmouth. "My dear sir," was the reply,

> I beg of you, for your sake, and that of your promising town, you will never again make your last observation to anyone else. I can excuse your enthusiasm, but others may not. Your steamboats are here, you will have a good town, perhaps a respectable city, but never in your day or your children's, will a railroad reach, much less go to the west of you.[86]

The case of one quite literal prophecy is illustrative: "Thus saith the Lord," wrote Joseph Smith, "if you will receive wisdom, here is wisdom. Behold the place called Independence. . . ." But the Mormons were driven away by force of arms.

[85] McCoy Scrapbook, article in the *Kansas City Daily Journal,* November 18, 1883.

[86] McCoy Scrapbook, pp. 114-15, undated clippings.

Some men acted on one set of assumptions and some on others. Such is the weight of historical success, pressing heavily on all our interpretations, that it is difficult to recreate in our minds the problematic, ambiguous, hazardous prospects which awaited any important course of action at Kansas in the year 1853. Nevertheless, whatever sophistication is afforded by data such as these ought to be in mind when we read the account of the city's first municipal organization, written many years later by a participant. "Just at this juncture," that is, in 1853, wrote Milton J. Payne,

> a movement looking toward statehood was inaugurated among the civilized Indians of the Indian country . . . who sent delegates to a convention which met in Wyandott. . . . This convention resolved to organize the Indian country into a Territory, which they named Nebraska, and elected William Walker . . . provisional governor. . . . This action was the harbinger of the greater civilization, and of the unparalleled development of the country in the trans-Missouri States. The far-sighted men of the town of Kansas at once saw that their future needs required city organization. They consequently applied to the General Assembly, and on February 22, 1853, obtained a charter for the city of Kansas.[87]

The city's first formal historian, William Miller, attributed municipal government to a much less auspicious, almost accidental, set of circumstances. It was discovered, late in 1852, through an arrest which proved to be without authority, that the local police force, minimal though it was, had been operating beyond the geographical limit of its commission. "This led," Miller writes, "to a movement looking to municipal organization."[88] Why the police authority could not have been extended by a simple appeal to the county court for new commissions is not indicated, and one is left with the impression that the ambitions described by Payne did have something to do with the whole proposition.

[87] Milton J. Payne, "City of Kansas, Early Municipal Government," in Conard, *Encyclopedia*, II, 616.

[88] Miller, *History*, p. 413.

At any rate, Payne's account of prophetic town-founders serves to reinforce the main point of this presentation of the city's early years. Indian trade, commerce of the prairies, and emigrant outfitting had made it possible to set up a town on the border; the opening of Kansas and of Nebraska were to convert the town into a city. Additional turning points were to be reached and passed; in fact, Kansas' major crises were still in the future. But as railroad and settler drove into the wilderness and tamed it, the town attached its hopes as tightly to them as it could. One of the early acts of the new city council was payment of expenses incurred in entertaining Thomas Hart Benton when the senator stopped over at the landing and called loudly for the railroads.

CHAPTER 3

The Pitfalls of Politics

ON March 28, 1853, the citizens of the City of Kansas voted into effect the charter offered by the state legislature, and on April 18 they chose an administration. In this first election, William Gregory defeated Benoist Troost for mayor, 36 to 27. Councilmen were named at large; there were eight candidates of whom the six receiving the greatest number of votes were elected. Thompson McDaniel, Tilman H. West, Milton Payne, and Johnston Lykins polled from 55 to 62 votes each, while W. G. Barkley and W. J. Jarboe won 39 and 38 votes, respectively. The only other elective post, that of city marshal, went to one M. B. Hedges. It is clear from the names of the city officials during the pre-Civil War period that the profession of municipal politics had not begun to be distinguished from the other enterprises identified with the growing community. For example, William Gregory, the first mayor, had been farming in the area since his arrival from Kentucky in 1844, and at about the time of his election he began operating a grocery store on the levee. Of the first two city treasurers, P. M. Chouteau and Hiram Northrup, Chouteau had been a warehouseman, a merchant, and later was agent for members of the old town company, handling the sale of city lots and parcels of land. Northrup, during this period as earlier, was a merchant.[1]

Its legislative authors did not create an original charter for Kansas City; rather, after substituting the name of the one city for the other, they freely plagiarized the charter previously granted to St. Joseph. In the prewar period the charter was

[1] Ordinance Record Book A, pp. 14-15; this manuscript record is in the office of the City Clerk, Kansas City, Missouri, and will be cited hereafter as *ORB*. When no other citation is given, data on city government are taken from this record and from Milton Payne's article, "City of Kansas: Early Municipal Government of," in H. L. Conard (ed.), *Encyclopedia of the History of Missouri* (New York: Southern History Company, 1901), I, 616-27. No figures have been found for the charter election.

amended several times, often by the simple expedient of pasting in provisions from the St. Louis charter. The resulting document delimited boundaries, defined political eligibilities and mechanisms, and provided the ordinary taxing and police powers. Boundaries were extended in 1857 and again in 1859. A brief experiment with a bicameral council was abandoned.[2] The mayor and city council soon exercised their power to create new offices. In 1854 and 1855 the offices of wharfmaster, city engineer, wharf register, sexton, and collector of special taxes were created, and the functions of each were provided for by a number of pertinent ordinances. This nascent trend toward special municipal services represents the principal concerns of the city administration: developing the levee and making internal improvements.

Enjoying a broad range of powers, the local government was potentially a powerful social and economic engine, but actually its operations were quite limited. In some matters the local solons may have imitated consciously the official proceedings and codes of other cities. In any event, their acts are strikingly analogous to those of their municipal brethren elsewhere.[3] One leading objective was to get as inexpensive a government as possible. The city fathers continually experimented with the amounts and sources of officials' salaries. An example is the fluctuation, 1855-64, in the salary of the city engineer, an especially important man in Kansas City, as will be seen. In 1855, when the office was created, it was stipulated that the engineer would receive "the usual rates for surveying, etc., for all work done in the City." Toward the end of the decade a spectacular effort was made to pay him $1,000 a year. In 1862 his annual salary sank to $200; in 1864 it was doubled to $400 per year. The mayor, in the meantime, experienced the same uncertainty of income as his salary

[2] To the sources in note 1 may be added *Revised Ordinances of the City of Kansas . . . 1859-1860, with the Various Charters of the City* (Kansas City: By order of the Council, printed at the *Enquirer* Book and Job Rooms, 1860), and another edition of the same printed in the *Journal* in 1864. Some of these data are incorporated in Roy Ellis, *A Civic History of Kansas City, Missouri* (Springfield, Missouri: By the author, 1930).

[3] The characteristic growth of early midwestern city government is described by Bayrd Still, "Patterns of Mid-Nineteenth Century Urbanization in the Middle West," *Mississippi Valley Historical Review*, XXVIII (1941-42), 187-206.

rose from $500 in 1856 to $800 in 1859 and fell to $600 in 1864—a year of adjustment in which the mayor lost $200 and the city engineer gained the identical amount. Several city officials, such as the attorney, wharfmaster, and the collector, were compensated from established fees for their various services or from a regular percentage of the funds handled by them.

The attitude of the local officials toward municipal affairs is evidenced by the numerous council meetings in which no quorum sat. In some cases it was difficult to find men willing to accept the various offices. Resignations and no-quorum days were frequent during 1853 and 1854, and the council tried to work out a procedure to penalize its absentee members. On June 8, 1853, Thompson McDaniel's seat was declared vacant because of absenteeism. W. G. Barkley's seat was similarly vacated on the 24th—on which day, also, the marshal resigned. In February, 1854, Gregory resigned as mayor, and the council named Lykins to act in his place. Two men elected to the council in 1855 refused to serve. At this election, in which Lykins was chosen mayor in his own right, the voters' indifference was expressed by nonattendance at the polls. The highest number of votes cast for any candidate was 40, a 27 per cent decrease from the showing for McDaniel the previous year. All this while, the mayor and council had no regular meeting place, although periodically individuals were officially requested or committees were named to find suitable accommodations.[4]

The city government was a small operation indeed, if gauged by the amount of money collected and dispensed by the city treasury. Kansas City received $7.22 from the old (county-administered) Town of Kansas. In the city's first fiscal year, a little less than $300 in taxes was collected. But the growth of the city is reflected brightly enough in the treasurer's accounts in the following years. As a source of income in this early period, wharfage fees were at least as good as taxes. Levee revenue totaled $200 by April, 1854, and an additional $300 was collected between then and November of the same year. By April, 1856, the city

[4] Proceedings of council meetings through most of 1859 are included in ORB.

government was turning over about $1,000 annually. Thereafter the figure steadily grew, except during the lean Civil War years.

By this time, also, such civic concerns as street grading, social control and the like, as well as railroad bond issues, had broadened the field of municipal operations; however, during the first three years of its corporate existence, Kansas City did little more than rehearse its role as a municipality. It was in August, 1854, that the subject of aid for railroads came before the administration for the first time, and Councilman Troost and Mayor Lykins were appointed to offer right-of-way privileges to the management of the Pacific Railroad of Missouri. Along a different line, at an early stage in council proceedings, Lykins (then a councilman) had sponsored an ordinance abolishing the sale of liquor in the city. The measure was passed by the council, but as might be expected, this experiment in social legislation was short-lived. In November, 1855, Councilman Payne introduced an ordinance providing for dramshop licenses which passed by a 5-0 vote. Mayor Lykins, part of whose heart lay in the prohibition of sale of spirituous liquors, vetoed the measure, deploring the council's action by commenting that "strangers and citizens have with commendation noted the happy change in our city consequent upon the closure of all dram shops. . . ." Nevertheless, his veto was overridden unanimously, and the city reasserted its frontier character.[5]

Meanwhile, far from Kansas City, legislation of another kind was being enacted which was to remove at a single stroke any political or territorial limitations on the community's hopes for growth and prosperity. With three years of political maneuvering and frontier pressure behind it, the Kansas-Nebraska Act, creating two new territories from the old Indian Territory, was passed by Congress and went into effect May 30, 1854. Under the provisions of the Missouri Compromise, thirty-four years earlier, this land had been permanently closed to slavery. In the interim, however, the South had anxiously watched as it steadily dropped behind the North and the West in economic power and political influence. Only by including in the Kansas-Nebraska

5 *ORB*, pp. 53-54.

measure a provision repealing the old compromise was Stephen A. Douglas finally able to steer it through Congress. Now, with its passage, the North and South could race for the conquest of Kansas. Now the land which Pike and Long had described as "uninhabitable" was open to American settlement; the "Great American Desert" was to become an agricultural Eden—but only in an explosive political context.

There remained, of course, the problem of the lands which had been guaranteed "forever" to the various Indian tribes. But the Government, as usual, responded to the immediate needs of the settlers and the desires of land speculators by negotiating the relocation of the tribes or further reduction of their land allotments; the Kansas City press enthusiastically endorsed this policy.[6] Isaac McCoy's dream, the huge Indian territory which had played an important role in Kansas City's prehistory, now vanished as yet another level in regional development was reached. The agriculturalist could now exploit the enormous prairie opened to his plow, and the city man could collect his profit by channeling through his hands the two-way commerce in raw materials and industrial products.

But, would the pipeline of this rich trade go through Kansas City? This question was much more important to the city's future than any entertained in the city council. The possibilities it presented, in fact, brought a real city government into existence. Throughout its brief history Kansas City, with its Westport partnership, had waged an uphill battle with Independence and St. Joseph for supremacy as a commercial center. Now that Kansas and Nebraska territories were open to immigration, other and more powerful town enterprises—especially those of Leavenworth and Atchison—arose to reach after the same prize. The intensified town rivalry which followed was further complicated by the political questions which were suddenly raised. Conflict began not only among but within the border towns—a condition

---

[6] See James C. Malin, *Indian Policy and Westward Expansion* (Lawrence: The University of Kansas Press, 1921), and Paul Wallace Gates, *Fifty Million Acres: Conflicts over Kansas Land Policy, 1854-1890* (Ithaca: Cornell University Press, 1954).

of affairs which might well tear apart any community. While the
Act of Congress of May 30, 1854, held up tempting possibilities
of new growth, it also posed problems of real danger and made
necessary greater risks than any which Kansas City had yet experienced. To outmaneuver and outdo her urban rivals, Kansas
City had to attract capital and population from the East, but at
the same time, the struggle over slavery had to be sidetracked
or contained.

The old town company had served its purpose by going out
of business, yielding to individual enterprises which had grown to
a point where a real town was possible—indeed, it was not only
possible but highly desirable, if the pattern of growth was to
continue. Sometime between 1853 and 1855, a crucial point in
Kansas City's history was reached and passed at which individual
profit-making enterprises came to show signs of interdependence
and the need for limited collectivity. Individual interests, competitive as they might be and as they often were, shared a good
many needs and hopes from which a kind of general interest
derived. The individual landholders—Lykins, McGee, and the
rest—could raise the value of their personal holdings by diligently
improving them, but within a pattern of streets, hotels, and mis-
cellaneous trades and services, much more could be expected
from the increased activity at the river junction. The success of
individual enterprises was, of course, the primary concern of the
men engaged in them, but there was also a community interest.
A successful merchant, attracting customers and developing
sources of supply, contributed to the prosperity of others, up to a
point. A stage of enterprise in Kansas City would soon be
reached at which such institutions as banks and insurance agencies would be needed, and they in turn would represent a further
interweaving and centralization of enterprise.

In some instances, these shared interests were more compelling than those of any individual. This was most apparent in
the common need for public improvements, the attraction of immigrants, a local newspaper, increased river commerce, and later,
the building of railroads. As a means to these ends, local businessmen united informally to become a kind of board of directors,

an executive committee, to consult with one another and determine courses of action suitable to the requirements of the city. We observe at this point in Kansas City's story a kind of historical watershed, from which time the activities of various men with disparate interests suddenly begin to coalesce, and the new entity, a city, begins to develop an individuality of its own—to become, in fact, a distinct "urban enterprise."

Municipal organization, however improvised, was only one prerequisite to the realization of urban success—a newspaper was equally important. After the failure of the *Ledger*, Kansas City's first newspaper, nothing but word of mouth, some published accounts of western travel, and a few maps had let the rest of an uninterested world know that there was a town (now city) of Kansas. Without a newspaper, there was no way to erect a public platform, so to speak, which would advertise the city's merits abroad while it rallied and focused energies at home.

The town's business leaders were well aware of the need for this type of spokesman for their interests, and they discussed it among themselves. Finally, probably in the spring or early summer of 1854, in a formal meeting of a group of businessmen at the Gilliss House hotel, a company to back a paper was organized. William Gilliss, H. M. Northrup, Joseph Chick, Milton Payne, E. M. McGee, Robert Campbell, Benoist Troost, and others subscribed stock in the company. Not one of them was a journalist. Much of the spadework was deputed to Payne, who went to St. Louis to buy equipment for the printing plant. A journeyman printer, David K. Abeel, drifted into Kansas City at about that time, and the company promptly engaged him for the technical work. The editorial responsibility was delegated to a local lawyer named William A. Strong.

By late September, 1854, this curious amalgam of professional and amateur talent succeeded in putting out a weekly paper called the *Kansas City Enterprise*.[7] Events showed, however, that the businessmen were performing only what they con-

[7] William H. Miller, "History of Kansas City," in *History of Jackson County, Missouri* (Kansas City: [?], 1881), pp. 418-19; Theodore S. Case, *History of Kansas City, Missouri* (Syracuse: D. Mason, 1888), pp. 50-51.

sidered to be a necessary duty and that they were anxious to rid themselves of an unfamiliar job. It was not long until a committee was set up for the purpose of selling the *Enterprise* to anyone who would take it over and run it on a full-time basis. By midsummer of 1855, editor-lawyer Strong was in St. Louis (whether specifically to look for a buyer is not known), where he met a young man from Ohio—Robert Thompson Van Horn—a former newspaper editor who was now looking for opportunity in the new West. Strong outlined the proposition to Van Horn, and after a quick trip to Kansas City the latter agreed to buy the *Enterprise* for $500.

Van Horn returned to Ohio to wind up some personal affairs and by the end of October, 1855, was back in Kansas City. He paid $250 down on his purchase and arranged to pay a final installment of $250 one year later to complete the deal. He began at once to operate the paper. As the time on his contract to purchase expired, Van Horn presented the final payment to the company's representative. The *Enterprise* had become so successful in that short period of time, and Van Horn had so closely identified himself with the community's hopes for the future, that the paper's grateful owners refused to accept his money and presented him, instead, with a receipt for the full amount of his purchase. In the following years the most characteristic aspect of early Kansas City, its unquenchable thirst for growth—investment, building, population—came to be almost completely personified in this one man.

Van Horn was born in Pennsylvania in 1824. After boyhood on a farm, he became an apprentice printer and continued in this trade in various New York, Pennsylvania, and Ohio towns. Now and then he taught school and somewhere picked up enough training for occasional legal practice. At one time he worked on an Erie Canal boat. He won popularity wherever he went. While living in Pomeroy, Meigs County, Ohio, he encountered the problem of declining a nomination for the state legislature (as an enthusiastic Whig) without giving his would-be constituents the real reason—he was too young to meet the constitutional age requirement.

In Pomeroy, he took over the editorship of the *Telegraph,* a weekly paper, in which he made internal improvements, the virtues of Whig policy and candidates, and the interests of "the Great West" his editorial themes.[8] After a couple of years in Pomeroy, Van Horn sought more fertile fields. He went to Cincinnati, where he and some partners published an anti-Nebraska sheet called the *Union.* A disastrous fire ended this venture, and the participants scattered. Van Horn, now thirty years old, with a wife and two children depending upon him, found himself adrift again, with nothing but debts to show for his active career. His next job was on a Mississippi River steamboat, and with this new beginning he started to build once more a substantial life. Frequently, in his editorial days, he had written about the Great West with its shining future, and now a project consistent with those notions took shape in his mind. "I am again a loser," he wrote to his parents:

> . . . So much for that. I have inherited from one of you or perhaps both, a light heart and hopeful disposition. . . . I am again on the river, clerk of a steamboat, in which I will remain until fall. I get $50 a month, and by the first of October will be able to get clear of some little debts I am owing, and if I can financier so as to be able to raise a few hundred dollars, I am going out West, probably to Nebraska, where I hope in a few years to retrieve my fortunes and kick up a dust generally among the natives.[9]

So it was that Robert Van Horn happened to arrive in St. Louis at the same time Strong got there from Kansas City. Each had exactly what the other was seeking.

[8] The last two quotations are from the *Meigs County Telegraph,* a file of which is available at the Kansas City Public Library, for June 27 and April 25, 1850, respectively. Biographical accounts of Van Horn are in the histories of Kansas City by Miller, Case, and Whitney. There are small and valuable collections of Van Horn Papers in the Archives of the Native Sons of Kansas City, City Hall, Kansas City, Missouri, and in the library of the State Historical Society of Missouri, at Columbia, Missouri.

[9] June 15, 1854, Van Horn Papers, Archives of the Native Sons of Kansas City.

Van Horn arrived in a Kansas City which was just then enjoying the prospect of a classical boom. Immigration, new capital, and the development of a new hinterland were the conditions of its growth. While the young editor's newspaper plant in Cincinnati was burning to the ground, another sequence of events had got under way, this time in New England, which seemed to offer fulfillment of all these conditions of growth free of charge. Even while politicians were steering the Kansas-Nebraska bill through Congress, interested parties in the East were planning to capitalize on this newest western opportunity. The Massachusetts Emigrant Aid Company was chartered in April, 1854; it later became the New England Emigrant Aid Company. To some extent this company was the model for several other enterprises with ostensibly similar purposes which were later set up in other states.[10]

What were these purposes? Members of the New England Company defined them as both economic and political; different members stressed the two in different proportions. Some were primarily interested in land development and consequently, real-estate investment in Kansas. Closest to the hearts of others was the desire to preserve Kansas as a free territory, forever closed to the institution of slavery. The presumption must have been that economics and politics marched together. By mobilizing capital and directing it to the Kansas frontier, by building towns and surrounding them with hardy yeoman farmers, it was thought that slavery would be automatically excluded from the new territory. As one of the company's agents wrote to the trustees, "let capital be the pioneer." Eli Thayer, one of the company's chief movers, summed up the proposition in the phrase, "sawmills and liberty."[11] Unfortunately, this optimism in New England meant something entirely different on the Missouri border.

It is easy to see why part of the company's work was attractive to Kansas City. Amos Lawrence described it well in his

---

[10] Samuel A. Johnson's *Battle Cry of Freedom* (Lawrence: The University of Kansas Press, 1954), is an excellent history of the company.

[11] *Ibid.*, chap. i. See also Russell K. Hickman, "Speculative Activities of the Emigrant Aid Company," *Kansas Historical Quarterly*, I (1931-32), 240 n, 237.

testimony at the Congressional investigation of the border conflict which resulted from the "race" for Kansas between the North
and the South. "It is well known," Lawrence told Congressman
Howard's investigators,

> that one of the chief difficulties which the settlers in a new
> country have to contend with is the want of capital for the
> support of those undertakings to which the means of indi-
> viduals are inadequate. It has been one of the first objects
> of this company to supply this want by the erection of hotels,
> mills, and machinery; by favoring the establishment of
> schools and churches; and by doing all in its power to sur-
> round the settlers, even on their first arrival, with the com-
> forts of civilized and cultivated life. It was at the same time
> the belief of some of the originators of the company, that
> such investments of capital, while in the highest degree use-
> ful to the emigrants, would also in the end prove profitable
> to the company itself, as the population should increase, and
> the value of permanent property in the Territory be thereby
> enhanced. It must be apparent, therefore, that the whole plan
> of the company's operations is based on the idea of a *perma-
> nent settlement* of the Territory.[12]

The company was willing and able to back its plans with
cash. According to an account in 1857, of $127,000 spent by the
company, almost $14,000 had been spent in Kansas City. Most
of this sum was accounted for in the company's purchase of the
American Hotel, formerly the Gilliss House. After its acquisition,
the company leased the hotel to a succession of operators and,
finally, sold it to the last of the lessees, one of the Eldridge
brothers of Lawrence, Kansas Territory. It was always open to
the general public as well as to personnel of the Emigrant Aid
Company. Its importance to Kansas City is clear, in that during
the same period Van Horn was editorially urging the city fathers
to provide more hotel space for the growing settlement.[13]

While the New England organization fell far short of raising

[12] U.S., Congress, House, *Report of the Special Committee Appointed to Investigate the Troubles in Kansas,* 34th Cong., 1st Sess., H. Rept. 200, 1856, p. 878.
This document will be cited henceforth as *Howard Report.*

[13] Hickman, *op. cit.,* p. 255 n; *Howard Report,* pp. 884-85.

its authorized five million dollars and never sent more than about twelve hundred migrants into Kansas, its total western investment was impressive. One of its major efforts was to set up mills of different kinds. Along with direct investment went indirect effects which should not be ignored. One New York City man who had invested $6,000 in the company later stated that, in return, he had received much more than his original investment in his profits on goods he had sold in Kansas and Kansas City.[14] The activities of the company unquestionably stimulated interest in the territory.

All of this might have been an unmixed blessing to Kansas Citians had the economic development not taken place in a political inferno. The agitation of the forces wrestling for ascendancy in Kansas threw a roadblock across the city's path. During the time the emigrant aid companies were taking shape, other—proslavery—interests were making organized efforts to assure the entry of Kansas into the Union as a slave state. The resulting conflict over Kansas enlisted sympathies all over the South as well as in the North. Actually, however, it was in western Missouri—specifically, in the immediate vicinity of Kansas City—that most of the proslavery organization and agitation took place.

In Missouri, slavery was most profitable in the lands bordering the river, where hemp and tobacco were grown. To a noticeable degree the system was concentrated in those counties bordering the newly opened Kansas territory. During the border troubles in 1855, one Missourian wrote to an associate that "the excitement is confined chiefly to Platte, Clay and Jackson [counties]." Slaves in the counties of Platte, Clay, Ray, Lafayette, Saline, and Jackson constituted 23.5 per cent of the population as against 13 per cent for the state as a whole. There were, according to the 1860 census, 3,316 slaves divided among 736 slaveowners in Jackson County.[15] There was probably some hope that slavery would prove to be as profitable in Kansas as it was

14 Samuel A. Johnson, "The Emigrant Aid Company in Kansas," *Kansas Historical Quarterly*, I (1931-32), 434-35; Hickman, *op. cit.*, p. 247 n.

15 See Allan Nevins, *Ordeal of the Union* (New York: Charles Scribner's Sons, 1947), II, 302; Harrison Trexler, *Slavery in Missouri* (Baltimore: The Johns Hopkins Press, 1914), pp. 17, 199.

in Missouri. Even without such a hope, however, the prospect of a free Kansas, immediately to the west, was disquieting to Missouri's slaveowners, for Missouri, then, would be surrounded on three sides by free territory and would provide an excellent field for the operations of the Underground Railroad.[16]

It was not their disposition toward slavery alone, however, which drew the interested attention of Missourians to Kansas Territory. Land speculation was already under way before the Kansas-Nebraska Act went into effect. One eastern paper carried reports from St. Joseph according to which camps and tents dotted the prairies. Thousands of persons waited legal permission to cross the line; many had already done so and were locating claims and staking out farms.[17]

A proprietary interest in Kansas lands and proslavery sentiment combined to shape the attitude of western Missourians toward Kansas. Here was economic opportunity in lands as familiar to western Missourians as their own, which New Englanders threatened to take from them. The potential of the New England Emigrant Aid Company was frightening: Its corporate charter, its five million dollars (never minding that the sum was never raised), Free State politics—everything, in fact, fit into a local picture of rapacious Eastern imperialism. Missourians, with some small aid from certain other Southern states, organized to thwart the "imperialists." On June 3, 1854, Westport citizens met and committed themselves as a society to "protect" slavery in Kansas. They called upon others to rally immediately "that we may avail ourselves of the great advantages which the contiguity of the new Territory at once gives to us. . . ." Two days later another group, meeting in Independence, urged "action, that we may meet and repel the wave of fanaticism which threatens to break up our border."[18] Numerous secret societies appeared, dedicated to the cause of slavery in Kansas. Later, a member of

[16] James C. Malin, "The Pro-Slavery Background of the Kansas Struggle," *Mississippi Valley Historical Review*, X (1923), 285-305.

[17] Quoted in Nevins, *op. cit.*, 309 n.

[18] *Ibid.*, pp. 309-10, quoting the *National Intelligencer*; the Independence item was clipped from an Independence paper called *The Agrarian*. Compare the local reaction to the Mormon incursion, above, chap. ii.

one of these "orders" was to tell the Howard Committee that the first proslavery "lodge" he had heard of was located in Westport.[19]

The means by which its adherents served the cause of slavery soon became notorious, locally and abroad. At the first election held in the new territory, Missourians swarmed over the polling places to turn in a thumping majority for their proslavery candidate for delegate to Congress. Legally, only residents of the territory were to have voted in this election, or (in view of the short time which had passed since its opening) perhaps men who had made known their intent to reside there permanently. The restrictions on voting eligibility were brushed aside by the Missourians, many of whom came from Westport and Independence to vote in Kansas' first election.

In their testimony before the Howard Committee in 1856 and in other public utterances as well, the Missourians emphasized the defensive character of their action, sturdily holding to their "rights." "They said they had a right to vote here," noted one witness, "that this country belonged to Missouri, and they would vote." One of the election judges said in his testimony that he "had a long talk with Mr. [Henry F.] Younger [of Westport] during the day"; that Mr. Younger had said

> he had a right to vote there, as he had a claim. . . . Mr. Younger said the Missourians had as much right to vote here as the Yankeees had, of whom some four boat loads had landed a few days before, at Kansas City. . . .[20]

In many cases it was impossible to distinguish between a Missourian who intended to live on a Kansas claim and one who went across the line only to cast a fraudulent ballot. Many witnesses told the investigating committee that they had worked "claims" from time to time in Kansas and that such considerations gave western Missourians a proprietary interest in the new country. According to one account by a Free State writer,

> Scarcely a merchant or store-keeper's clerk—in fact scarcely anyone about Westport and Independence—but had a "claim

[19] *Howard Report*, p. 904.
[20] *Ibid.*, p. 232.

staked out" . . . [which] rest[ed] on a bowie-knife and re-
volver basis.[21]

Opposition to the Free State interests was frenzied in Westport and Independence. The *Westport Frontier News* rallied partisans for the March, 1855, election in Kansas with the outcry:

> Freemen of the South, pioneers of the West, . . . this is the
> twelfth hour of the night—birds of darkness are on the wing
> —the day will soon dawn—the battle will soon commence.
> Arouse and fight a good fight! Let the eagle of victory perch
> upon your banners. Steady, men! Forward!

The Missourians' activities and intentions were well known
on the border, and some uneasiness was communicated to federal
authorities. "There is a plan in Westport, Mo.," wrote Kansas'
Governor John Geary to President Pierce, "to invade the Territory with about 1000 men, to take possession of the 'Shawnee
Reserve' about the 20th of Feb." And, Geary noted, "there has
almost from the first been a combination here (. . . having their
headquarters at Westport) to defeat my policy. . . ." It is understandable that Westport soon became known as "one of the most
violent border towns."[22]

What of Kansas City in this turmoil? Most of its leaders in
the 1850's were from Southern states. Of thirty-nine men who
were actively engaged in representative businesses and whose
records are available for documentation, thirty-one had come
from south of the Ohio River. Many were slaveowners: L. C. Cary
was assessed for eight slaves in 1857, T. M. James for three, the
firm of Gilham and McDaniel for nine, that of Northrup and
Chick for two, and so on.[23] Undoubtedly slaves represented a
considerable investment in Kansas City proper, but the most

---

[21] William Phillips, *The Conquest of Kansas* (Boston: Phillips, Lansom &
Co., 1856), cited in Gates, *Fifty Million Acres*, p. 53.

[22] Quoted in Charles Robinson, *The Kansas Conflict* (New York: Harper and
Brothers, 1892), pp. 102-3; P. O. Ray (ed.), "Some Papers of Franklin Pierce, 1852-
1862," *American Historical Review*, X (1904-5), 126, 353; Phillips, *op. cit.*, p. 116.

[23] Data from biographical card file, Archives of the Native Sons of Kansas
City, and from manuscript 1857 Tax List, in possession of Miss Frances Berenice
Ford.

important effect of the local agitation upon Kansas Citians was probably not so much economic as cultural. Geographically bracketed by Westport and Independence, Kansas City, too, was at least sympathetically proslavery. Southern-minded though the city may have been, however, its opportunities were Western, and there lay the crucial influence in the conduct of its citizens. The border troubles posed a much knottier problem for Kansas City than for other nearby communities.[24]

There were Kansas Citians who were as vitally interested in Kansas land claims as were Westport citizens. The Lykins family had claims near Lawrence, Kansas, where Johnston's son, William, was deputy postmaster and the owner of a log building. A visitor to this structure shortly before the March election recalled having heard unusual activity in an unoccupied part of Lykins' building and upon inquiry, learned that young Lykins was storing bacon, corn, and other provisions for the use of the Missourians who were expected in great numbers on election day. With his son operating a commissary for the "border ruffians," it is not surprising that Dr. Johnston Lykins, at a meeting of a squatter association, publicly argued his own contention that he had a right to vote in Kansas. The Free State candidate attempted to refute Lykins, denying that resident Missourians could claim franchise in Kansas. "This produced very great excitement," the candidate himself later recalled. "A man by the name of McGee . . . made gestures with his fist toward me and cried out 'Beware what you are doing!' "[25]

The McGee brothers were actively concerned with Kansas land. Fry had worked a claim on Wakarusa Creek where, among other business operations, he sold timber to other claimants. At the November, 1854, election Fry's house was the polling place for the district. Allen B. H. McGee also staked and, perhaps,

[24] Elmer L. Craik, "Southern Interest in Territorial Kansas, 1854-1858," *Kansas Historical Collections*, XV (1919-22), 385.

[25] *Howard Report*, pp. 134-37, 158-59, 950.

worked a Kansas land claim. It should be noted, however, that witnesses before the Howard Committee sometimes confused one or another McGee with his brothers. One witness detailed questionable acts which he attributed to a McGee and specifically ascribed them to Allen:

> He pretended to live [there] at that time. I suppose he did. . . . He had a house two miles west of where I lived. . . . Mr. McGee kept a kind of family grocery store there, with plenty of provisions to sell at enormous rates. He kept a kind of hotel there for a few days.[26]

The claims of Allen and Fry McGee became headquarters for groups of proslavery Missourians, just as did that of William Lykins. At the March, 1855, election Mobillon McGee was elected to the "bogus" (slave-state) territorial legislature. He had polled heavily in Fry McGee's district where, disgruntled Free State men recalled, armed crowds of Missourians had come to vote for Fry's brother. On the day of election one Free Stater had seen, he said, "quite a procession . . . with flags flying, [come] from towards the 'Wakarusa,' I think from where Mr. McGee lives; I saw two McGees in the party." Another remembered that Allen had "brought his company" to the polls. When an armed troop—the "Border Mounted Riflemen"—was organized in Westport, A. B. H. McGee was commissioned lieutenant, and James H. McGee, the youngest of the brothers, served the squadron as corporal.[27]

Milton (E. M.) McGee was as active as his brothers. He rounded up Missourians to vote in Kansas elections and agitated vigorously in the proslavery interest. When Major Jefferson Buford arrived from South Carolina with his company, fully prepared to fight for a slave state, Milton McGee quartered the company free of charge on his property near Westport. When a Jackson County group organized to promote Kansas settlement by Southerners, Milton was selected to represent it on a tour through

26 *Ibid.*, pp. 11-12, 145-47.

27 *Ibid.*, pp. 251, 140, 144. For the "Riflemen," see *Kansas City Enterprise,* February 16, 1856. Hereafter cited as *Enterprise.*

93990   EMORY AND HENRY LIBRARY

the South. In 1856 a clamorous Free State publicist referred to "the famous, or infamous, Milt McGee, of Westport. . . ." Another Free Stater wrote that some members of his party had bought a wagon and oxen "of the since notorious McGee. . . ."[28]

For all his energy directed toward the establishment of slavery in Kansas, there are on record at least two instances of an appealing generosity shown by Milton McGee toward political foes. One Free State prisoner, held at McGee's home while his captors discussed his fate, turned to Milton as a brother Odd Fellow and escaped with nothing more damaging than a search of his person. McGee, in discussing the border conflict with his prisoner, said, "I am a border ruffian, and I am not ashamed of it." The Missourians, McGee asserted, would "wade in blood" to keep Kansas for slavery. At another time a migrant from Ohio had his horses and wagon commandeered for service with the Missourians. "With the friendly aid of a Mr. McGee, a pro-slavery man," he noted in his memoirs, one of his horses was ultimately returned to him.[29]

Only slightly less Southern in its ties of blood and background than its nearest neighbors, Kansas City had valuable economic prospects in the new territory which Westport and Independence did not seriously share. Kansas City saw Kansas Territory first, as a region through which trade flowed, and second, as a potential agricultural hinterland. Violent conflict could not serve either interest. At the height of the various crises in the conflict, Kansas City must not have presented a very attractive panorama to the prospective migrant or investor. Armed horsemen dashed to and fro; excited people crowded the streets and the roads around the city.[30] When Andrew Reeder, the former governor of Kansas who had taken a firm stand in favor of the Free State party, passed through Kansas City on his way east, he was threatened with assassination and had to hide in disguise at

28 *Howard Report,* pp. 549, 159; *Enterprise,* May 5, 1856; Phillips, *The Conflict of Kansas,* p. 357; John Doy, *The Thrilling Narrative of John Doy of Kansas* (Boston: Thayer & Eldridge, 1860), p. 7.

29 *Howard Report,* pp. 1113-14; Donald W. Stewart (ed.), "Memoirs of Watson Stewart, 1855-1860," *Kansas Historical Quarterly,* XVIII (1950), 388.

30 See the *Howard Report,* pp. 206, 547.

the American Hotel. When the Howard Committee arrived to conduct its investigations, the commandant at Fort Leavenworth felt impelled to offer the members a safe seat at the fort. T. H. Gladstone, an English journalist, arrived in Kansas City at a high point in the excitement and wrote that he could "never forget the appearance of the lawless mob that poured into the place. . . . The hotel in Kansas City where we were, was the next, they said, that should fall; the attack was being planned that night."[31]

Gladstone was a guest at the American Hotel, leased or owned at the time by the Eldridge brothers of Lawrence in favor of the Emigrant Aid Company. It was widely regarded as "a hot-bed of abolitionism" on the Missouri border. Mrs. Kersey Coates, wife of an important newcomer to Kansas City in 1856, described it in some detail at the time of her arrival. "Conspicuous on the levee," she wrote,

> . . . it is a large four-story-and-a-half brick building surmounted by a steeple containing a large bell whereby the signal is given for rising in the morning and for attendance at meals. . . . A long table was set, capable of holding fifty or sixty persons. The emigration at this time was so immense that often three times this number would obtain meals here. . . . Often the parlor floor would be literally covered with beds to accommodate the vast tide that was pouring in from the East. Their lodging-room was insufficient, though numbering some fifty or sixty private chambers, in addition to a long room containing some twenty beds for the accommodation of men.

Mrs. Coates and others supplemented the English reporter's testimony as to the frequent threats against the hotel.[32]

Here, of course, was a direct threat against a nuclear business interest in the city. But the general business situation was imperiled much more than is indicated by this threat alone. The *St. Louis Leader* published a letter from Independence in which

[31] Robinson, *The Kansas Conflict*, p. 416; *Howard Report*, pp. 112, 128; T. H. Gladstone, *The Englishman in Kansas* (New York: Miller & Co., 1856), pp. 40-42.

[32] Laura Coates Reed (ed.), *In Memoriam, Sarah Walter Chandler Coates* (Kansas City: Franklin-Hudson, n.d.), pp. 106-23; hereafter cited as *Coates Memorial*. Also, *Howard Report*, p. 1092.

it was said that Kansas City was almost blockaded by armed crowds: "The roads, especially around Westport, are becoming very dangerous." A Topeka merchant was arrested by proslavery men while on the way to Kansas City to purchase a stock of goods; a Kansas migrant said that "the unsettled condition of affairs in the territory prevented immigration"; his brother, in Kansas City to purchase supplies, found that even the influence of Milton McGee, who interceded in his behalf, was insufficient to allow him safe passage through the territory back to his claim. Editor Robert Van Horn, although disposed to put as bright a face as possible on events bearing on Kansas City's destiny, made no secret of the fact that the situation was bad. At one time in the building climax he admitted that "should this state of things continue . . . our business transactions must necessarily be checked somewhat." By March, 1856, a group of Lawrence businessmen had passed resolutions severing commercial relations with the Missouri towns in favor of Leavenworth merchants who did not approve of border-ruffianism.[33]

When the explosion came in May, 1856, with the proslavery attack on Lawrence and John Brown's Osawatomie massacre, it was close to disastrous for Kansas City. "Trade to and from the frontier towns of Missouri which amounts to thousands of dollars weekly is entirely cut off," wailed Van Horn. "The Territory is under a state of siege, and all intercourse suspended." This was the inauguration of "bleeding Kansas," a foretaste of the coming Civil War. All the ensuing summer armed bands marched, countermarched, and plundered.[34]

One grim possibility was that some of the other river towns would profit from Kansas City's time of trouble. New towns were springing up in Kansas, and the focus of urban rivalry was shifting from St. Joseph and Independence to Leavenworth. Jealously and anxiously Kansas City watched the new town, first settled in 1854, grow like a weed. Inevitably the border conflict would

---

[33] See *Enterprise,* clipping the *Leader,* September 13, 1856; *Howard Report,* p. 1115; "Memoirs of Watson Stewart," *op. cit.,* p. 390; *Enterprise,* December 8, 1855.

[34] *Enterprise,* August 23, 1856.

become intermingled with urban competition. A Lawrence, Kansas, editor urged on Kansas buyers the superior advantages of Leavenworth as a transshipping point, and because of the mobs in Kansas City, emphasized Leavenworth's probity. After the catastrophic summer of 1856, an alternative route into Kansas Territory was actually opened which ran overland from Iowa and avoided Kansas City entirely. In 1857 it was estimated that 20,000 migrants used the new route.[35]

Their precarious situation was pressed upon the Kansas City businessmen with ever-increasing force. Both the transit trade and the supply of capital from the East were threatened. A Free State migrant wrote from Kansas during the winter of 1856-57 that things might soon improve: "The merchants of Kansas City are very tired of the past state of things and will do what they can undoubtedly for quiet." According to the wife of Free State leader Charles Robinson, the Kansas City men did their best to assure Easterners that life and property were safe in the city and its hinterland.[36] But headlines spoke louder. As rumors spread, in 1856, about quantities of arms sent into Kansas by Free State backers, proslavery men began waylaying shipments into the territory. On March 22, seven men boarded a steamboat at the Kansas City levee, broke open some cases consigned to a local commission firm, found only a piano, and disappeared. In July an unidentified band captured a plains-bound wagon loaded by Northrup and Chick.

Reaction to these depredations was quick and vigorous. Van Horn, who had been trying to take a clear but nonaggressive proslavery position, suggested that future marauders "should be careful to bring their coffins with them, as there are a hundred men ready at a moment's call to attend to all such parties in the future." A correspondent to the *Enterprise* urged the city fathers to provide adequate security for business and warned that otherwise trade and migration would certainly be diverted from

35 *Enterprise*, January 12, 1856; Craik, *op. cit.*, p. 372.

36 "Letters of John and Sarah Everett . . . ," *Kansas Historical Quarterly*, VIII (1939), 3-34, 143-76, 279-310, 350-83. Our citation is from p. 154. Sara Robinson, *Kansas: Its Interior and Exterior Life* (Boston: Crosby, Nichols & Company, 1856), p. 293.

Kansas City. The business leaders called public meetings, passed resolutions condemning the "unlawful and sinister" acts, and assured all and sundry that property would be fully protected in Kansas City. A vigilante committee, "after the fashion of San Francisco," was projected toward the end of the period of disturbance. Whether or not it actually functioned has not been determined.[37]

The real concern for business interests appeared in steps taken locally to protect the American Hotel. At times, according to Mrs. Coates, guards were stationed around it. Van Horn, still proslavery, carefully referred to the American as "one of the best hotels on the border." Later he noticed a *St. Louis Intelligencer* story to the effect that the Emigrant Aid Company was thinking of moving its custom elsewhere, especially if the American should be mobbed. Van Horn emphasized the business character of the hotel and assured his readers that it was in no danger because of the politics of its owners. The situation was ultimately settled by sale of the hotel to proslavery proprietors. This solution to the problem gratified Van Horn, but he explained the matter to the credit of the Eldridges: "It was thought that the interest of the city demanded a change of proprietorship, in consequence of their supposed connection with the Emigrant Aid Society [sic], and they promptly complied with the wishes of our citizens. We recommend [the Eldridges] as good hotel keepers, against whom no *personal* objections can be urged."[38]

Enough has been said to show the position taken by the most prominent Kansas City businessmen during the border crisis: a resolute determination to protect property, to keep the lines of trade open, and to maintain a moderate "law and order" approach to events. Compared to mass meetings in other Missouri towns where Free State men, or abolitionists, were threatened with death or tar and feathers, meetings in Kansas City served an entirely different purpose. The city could not afford to have the

---

[37] *Enterprise,* March 29 and August 2, 1856.

[38] *Howard Report,* p. 1093; *Coates Memorial,* p. 123; Mrs. Robinson also mentions the guard, *op. cit.,* p. 276; *Enterprise,* December 8, 1855; January 19 and June 7, 1856.

reputation abroad of a wild, roaring center of riot, mob action, and banditti. It was damaging enough that by the end of 1855 Westport and Independence had attracted critical attention with their enthusiastic proslavery meetings and organizations. Kansas Citians met in an effort to counteract the unfavorable impressions which had been generated. The meetings themselves all followed a pattern which is not difficult to summarize.[39]

The leaders at these meetings were always the same men. Representing the city's business elite, they were, of course, predominately Southern and pro-Southern. The resolutions consistently recognized the danger to the area should "our" proslavery attitude be misunderstood as condoning violence. Invariably, these leaders pledged themselves to protect life and property against *any* threat of destruction, whatever the source might be. It was frequently asserted that disturbances stemmed less from conflict of political principles than from the efforts of urban rivals to destroy Kansas City's lead on its competitors. Invitations were publicly extended to law-abiding men and women to come and settle in Kansas. One instance of this commitment deserves quotation: "Resolved," pledged the Kansas Citians in December, 1855,

> That as slaveholders and pro-slavery men, we do not desire to excite animosity between the citizens of Missouri and the settlers of the Territories west of us, but to cultivate friendly relations . . . and that we invite our pro-slavery friends to settle upon the rich lands of Kansas, as the true policy and the only practicable and *legitimate* means of controlling her future institutions.[40]

The resolutions were characteristically concluded with the wholesome request that they be published as widely as possible, both locally and in the East, so that Kansas City's real sentiment would be known and understood.

Such utterances as these, when compared with what was

[39] For these meetings and the resolutions passed at them, see the *Enterprise* for December 15 and December 22, 1855; July 5, August 16, and September 20, 1856.

[40] *Enterprise*, December 22, 1855.

occurring in nearby towns, reveal some hard constructive thinking on the part of the Kansas Citians. Pulled one way by cultural
ties and another way by economic aims, with a promising urban
enterprise in the midst of a potentially hostile countryside as their
responsibility, they strove to work out a platform broad enough
to cover all their problems. The task could not have been an easy
one, and the results are important in the city's cultural history.
The relationship between urban rivalry and the border conflict,
for example, ran through all of Kansas City's thinking on the
subject. It was claimed that "our position as proslavery men" was
being used maliciously by the competitive Kansas towns to the
prejudice of Kansas City. The whole region was on treacherous
ground in the middle 1850's; one false step or one sudden, unfair
thrust by an aspiring rival might end the game in calamity.

Finally—signal of a new stage in city growth—the resolutions
evinced a clear concern for the rise of an agricultural hinterland
immediately west of the city. The resolution quoted above is
representative: it invites Southerners to come and help make
Kansas a slave state. There is no way to prove that the invitation
was disingenuous; the signers may actually have intended it in
its explicit sense. To ask for "peaceful competition" in the settling
of Kansas, however, to insist on it as the only legitimate way, was
to concede the game to the Free State interests. It is not possible
to show that Kansas City businessmen did, or did not, realize this
result at the time. On the assumption that some did and some did
not, the resolutions as framed suited both parties equally well.

That the influential businessmen of the community recognized what the development of Kansas could mean to Kansas City
was revealed in another way in the testimony of Kansas City men
before the Howard Committee. William S. Chick, Charles Spalding, Jesse Riddlesbarger, Charles Kearney, Alexander Gilham,
E. C. McCarty, Dr. Isaac Ridge, and Mayor Milton J. Payne were
all called as witnesses. Their testimony, gently phrased and confined to generalities, at times came close to a "plague on both your
houses" attitude. Nevertheless, their sentiments were revealed to
be unmistakably pro-Southern; in their evidence they explained
the proslavery violence so as to seem to extenuate it. The grava-

men of their complaint against the Northeasterners was that those migrants allegedly came to Kansas not to farm but only to vote—after which they returned to the East! The implication is obvious: Had the Free State migrants carried plows, yokes, and other such equipment with them they would have been welcome, irrespective of their politics.[41]

Of the Kansas City witnesses just named, at least two, Chick and Riddlesbarger, operated a commission business for the New England Emigrant Aid Company. Charles Robinson, Free State governor in Kansas, described his experience in Kansas City in 1854 when he was looking for channels through which company goods and people could be directed. "Here were found," Robinson wrote, "besides the noisy proslavery advocates, several quiet, civil and accommodating business men. . . . All these gentlemen welcomed Free State men with as much cordiality as proslavery [men], and some of them with more." When Robinson was later arrested and was awaiting trial for "treason," for resisting proslavery authorities in Kansas, Dr. Ridge, himself a slaveowner, did his best to have the prisoner released.[42]

The kind of growth which the Kansas Citians wanted, the possibilities for which were becoming larger every day in the middle 1850's, was incompatible with a staunchly "Missourian" position during the border troubles. It was a circumstance in which the chosen future was incompatible with the past. An important newcomer to Kansas City at this time must be noticed here, and the notice may serve to make this point clearer. Kersey Coates came from a wealthy Philadelphia family, and by the 1850's he was associated with Thaddeus Stevens in the practice of law. During the winter of 1854-55, he left Philadelphia for a western trip, partly on his own account and partly as agent for an emigrant aid company which had been formed in that city. Coates was thirty-one at the time. In Kansas, he became prominent in the Free State movement. Robinson suggested his name for territorial delegate to Congress, and Samuel Pomeroy acknowl-

---

[41] This paragraph generalizes the testimony of the men named in the *Howard Report*, pp. 835-36, 856-57, 844-46, 852-53, 848-51, 837-38, 861-62, 855-56.

[42] Charles Robinson, *op. cit.*, pp. 69-70, 272.

edged Coates's effective fund-raising activities in Pennsylvania. One Howard Committee witness mentioned a violent altercation during the November, 1854, election at which "Mr. Coates, now of Kansas City," had been present. Coates had made no secret of his opinion of the proslavery men on this occasion, and was driven from the scene by an angry mob.[43]

During the same period, however, Coates had decided that Kansas City land would be a good investment for the group he was representing. He could not persuade them of this, and consequently borrowed enough money to buy a tract on his own account. Returning east to be married and to bring his young bride to their new home, he was back in Kansas City by the spring of 1856. In view of his acknowledged prominence among the Free State leaders, it might be surprising that Coates's name was never mentioned in the *Enterprise* in any connection with the border troubles. Robinson, John Brown, and James H. Lane frequently were targets for Van Horn's editorial venom, but Coates escaped it entirely. In November, 1856, his name appeared in the paper in a list of directors of the newly organized Kansas City, Hannibal & St. Joseph Railroad Company. From early in 1857 advertisements regularly appeared in the paper for "Coates & Company," real estate brokers, and Van Horn solicited the favorable attention of his readers to these advertisements. Regardless of its background and its sympathies, the Kansas City elite must have seen that Coates possessed the abilities and qualities they needed. The first of Kansas City's historians says so, and one of the city officials during the border troubles claimed, retrospectively, that he, too, had seen the value of such men as Coates: "I saw," former Marshal J. P. Howe told a reporter many years later, "that it would not do to drive such men as Kersey Coates, Dave Hood, and the Eldridges away from town."[44]

---

[43] *Coates Memorial,* pp. 40-41, 175-80; *Howard Report,* p. 37. Kersey Coates was Robinson's attorney during the latter's brief incarceration mentioned above.

[44] Miller, in *History of Jackson County, Missouri,* pp. 429-30; *Coates Memorial,* pp. 113-14 n.

Kansas City's position, while clear, was a difficult one to maintain, and Robert Van Horn demonstrated his considerable journalistic talent by rationalizing the position extremely well. Essentially, his technique was to drown out political controversy by stressing economic issues. This method enabled him to protect Kansas City's reputation: "Frankly and decidedly pro-slavery," he wrote, "we desire to be effectively and intelligently so."[45] The implied contrast was posited against the wild and irresponsible elements centering in Westport and Independence.

Whenever possible, Van Horn duly excoriated Free State leaders (except Coates), and in doing so he frequently tied their crimes to the worst possible: that of injuring Kansas City's prospects. Thus James Redpath, one of the most important Eastern newspaper correspondents during the border troubles, was labeled a British abolitionist, "his hireling pen devoted to the abuse of Kansas City and Westport, decrying their business advantages and the character of their citizens." But the editor liked it best when he could find evidence that the troubles were subsiding and constructive activities about to resume. He felt fairly sure in November, 1855, that "the reign of lawlessness in Kansas has seen its culmination." A year later he was still optimistic: "We feel safe in saying that the troubles are ended."[46]

Van Horn's natural reluctance to publicize news of violent outbreaks irritated some of his readers. Criticizing other journals which printed sensational stories, he revealed that he was often asked "Why does not the *Enterprise* give . . . more news?" The reason was obvious:

> It is well known that the press and demagogues in the Eastern States, and even nearer home, seize on everything looking like difficulty in the Territory to feed the morbid feelings of an excited public, and it is the duty of those who control the primary channels of Kansas news to be well-advised . . . before they unwittingly minister to this pestilent disposition to detract from our good name.

[45] *Enterprise*, February 16, 1856.

[46] *Enterprise*, November 24, 1855, September 20, 1856.

The harassed editor did his best to counteract the effect of disturbing rumors and garbled accounts of disasters; he frequently assured everyone that the roads around Kansas City were perfectly safe, contrary to the widespread impression.[47]

Everything that came to Van Horn's notice which could be stretched to include considerations of business advantage was duly reported in that light, even the presence of the Howard Committee in Kansas City to investigate the border troubles. This investigation, Van Horn said, would give the legislators "a fair opportunity of judging the rapid advancement of this western empire."[48] He never stopped reminding his readers of the business treasures that were waiting for them as soon as the disturbances should come to an end. Kansas trade would "pour down upon us like an avalanche." According to one correspondent whose letter Van Horn printed, "Let peace and quiet reign and your city will receive a large accession next Spring if all signs fail not." Another writer, in almost identical language, admonished readers of the *Enterprise*, "Your city and State will receive large accessions to the population in the Spring if wise counsels prevail." Best of all, Van Horn was to report happily on one occasion, Robinson and Pomeroy had sat down with Jeff Buford and Colonel Titus, another proslavery leader, around a table at the American Hotel where the four "pledged each others' healths in the choicest Heidsieck."[49]

Another facet of Van Horn's elaborate editorial policy during the troubled period suggests a sort of "cultural self-defense" necessary to the increasingly self-conscious city. After all, most of the Kansas Citians were from Missouri and other Southern states. The charge of "border ruffianism" leveled against the proslavery party by Eastern journalists could cut deeply. The "border ruffian" was a man of violence who had no respect for law, order, and the security of property; he was a barbarian and almost by definition unfit for respectable urban living; he was certainly no

[47] *Enterprise*, September 13, October 25, 1856.

[48] *Enterprise*, April 19, 1856.

[49] Both correspondences and the "Heidsieck" item are in *Enterprise*, December 20, 1856.

promising material for economic development. A "border ruffian" might have nothing to do with pro- or anti-slavery principles. The significance of the label threatened Kansas Citians in a way transcending those principles.

Considerable local effort went into creating a more appealing image of the western Missourian in general. As a matter of fact, so said Van Horn, the border people were *not* like the caricature drawn by the Eastern press. According to one of his essays on the "border ruffian," the stigmatized men were most attractive: "Daring, athletic, fearless . . . of grenadier height, with the shoulders of an Atlas and a Yankee Sullivan fist, a mild, peaceful, harmless, rollicking, good-humored kind of fellow when not provoked. . . ." Always ready to defend his country when at war, the so-called ruffian quickly reverted to peaceable civilian status: He "dresses like a gentleman, takes his drink, and . . . becomes as social and good-natured as ever." These genial giants would, of course, never dream of forcibly interfering with a decent man's politics or of molesting his legitimately owned property. On another occasion Van Horn related the story of a Free Stater in need who had been, to his own surprise, befriended by men whom he would have considered to be "border ruffians." These men did not let political differences interfere with their benevolence. "That's right, Mr. King," they had said to the Free Stater, "vote just as you think—we wish every man to enjoy his opinion." The result was that Mr. King was eager to convince people back east that the border Missourians were fine people, even though honestly mistaken on the slavery question.[50]

Van Horn took up the same theme at the Democratic National Convention in Cincinnati in 1856. Here was an excellent platform from which to state his case, and a Cincinnati paper printed an article about its former townsman. He had introduced himself as a "border ruffian," adding that he had never killed an abolitionist, burned down a house, or even voted in a Kansas election. He defended the Missourians who had crossed into Kansas, and tried to reduce the whole conflict to a simple question of land claims. When the Yankees got to Kansas, according

[50] *Enterprise*, September 20, August 9, 1856.

to Van Horn, they had found the best claims taken up and quickly invented the term "border ruffian" in their effort to drive the Missouri claimants off the land.[51]

Associated with this cultural argument was the question of where Kansas City stood on the conflict of principles which had touched off the border war: Which side did the city take? Free State publicists frequently gave out stories about leading Kansas Citians who had cooperated with the proslavery element. William Phillips, for example, claimed that Mayor Payne had raised two hundred men and a thousand dollars to assist the Missourians. John Doy, another ardent Free State man, noted that while he and his party were coming up the river on a steamboat, they were warned of a "hot" reception awaiting them in Kansas City.[52] Van Horn engaged in some controversy with a Westport editor who apparently felt that public meetings in Kansas City did not pass proslavery resolutions that were strong enough to be effective. More explicitly, Van Horn replied bitterly to an attack in the Lawrence (Kansas) *Herald of Freedom*. Because Kansas City had always been ready to protect all law-abiding people, he wrote that after the troubles had quieted "our city was stigmatized by over-zealous proslavery men as an 'Abolition hole.' "[53] A policy of neutralism, whatever may have been its success in urban strategy, clearly satisfied none of the partisans.

The border troubles surely taught a lesson about partisan politics in general. The lesson, at least in Kansas City, was that politics was bad, and best avoided if at all possible. A wise man would not even attempt to analyze the history of the conflict: "It requires," wrote Van Horn, "a calmer state of feeling than exists on either side to investigate . . . with that calmness requisite for so important a matter. Indeed, we are not sure but that the least said, the better for all." When he was in a more partisan mood he could always blame the troubles on "*political* influences in the Eastern portion of the Republic. . . ."[54]

---

[51] Clipped in *Enterprise*, June 7, 1856.

[52] Phillips, *op. cit.*, p. 167; his story cannot be checked, but seems unlikely to this writer. Doy, *op. cit.*, p. 7; he adds that the "reception" did not materialize.

[53] *Enterprise*, January 12, 1856; January 17, 1857.

[54] *Enterprise*, December 15 and 22, 1855.

These matters were by no means confined to newspaper discussion. On July 8, 1855, John Johnson, for a brief time one of Kansas City's early mayors, wrote to his son William that the family had just been to church and then to a good Sunday meal, evidence that "both physical and spiritual food" was available "even in this land of, so-called, Missouri ruffians. . . ." Just at present, continued Johnson,

> there is no excitement in politics . . . and all will remain quiet probably until some other irritating causes rise out of the present chaotic mass of politics in the U.S. [If you should come to Kansas City:] it would be judicious to have little to say on the slavery question. . . . There are many who are very sore on that subject and who soon get excited.

Johnson did not feel this kind of excitement was good for the enterprise at the junction of the Kaw and the Missouri, where things were so hopeful otherwise.

> Our incipient city does not grow as yet, though there is some prospect of its taking a start this season. It is geographically one of the best positions in the whole country. . . . I do believe that when the political troubles of the nation become settled this city will not be [a city] only in name but in reality.[55]

If only the political troubles could be solved. . . . "What the end will be," Johnson concluded in the letter quoted, "no man can tell."

And, indeed, no man could tell. In spite of the avidity with which Van Horn noted every hopeful sign that the disturbances were subsiding, in spite of their actual subsidence in Kansas City's immediate vicinity after 1856, the end was still far off. So far, Kansas City had found a tortuous path through the dangers of the period, and had followed it safely. Her early historians understood well enough. The city builders, wrote Miller of this period, "wanted the trade of the new population and were averse to methods that disturbed society and deprived them of it."

[55] MS in possession of Miss Frances Berenice Ford, Kansas City, Missouri.

Theodore Case, who had arrived in the city in 1857, told substantially the same story in his history of the city; the population was largely Southern in sympathy, he said, but wanted mostly "to make a little money from both sides."[56]

The border troubles coincided with a new and crucial stage in Kansas City's development: the settlement of its immediate hinterland. It is likely that each of these processes obscured the other. Intertwined with both were difficult questions of culture and politics. It is possible that these trying years helped prepare Kansas Citians for the ordeal of the Civil War, as Case suggests. At any rate, Kansas City shaped itself politically so as to follow the main chance in the 1850's; it was to do so again in the 1860's, under infinitely more difficult circumstances.

[56] Miller, in *History of Jackson County, Missouri*, p. 429; Case, *History*, p. 70.

CHAPTER 4

The Railroad Matrix

IN THE fall of 1854 two men came west, scouting for one of the many emigrant aid companies which were then forming. Looking over Kansas City, the two agents noted its fine rock landing and estimated its population at between six hundred and a thousand persons. "City," they thought, "is a somewhat ambitious title for the little village of Kansas, but it may be presumed to have a prospective import, referring rather to the possible than the actual." Already beginning to attract Eastern capital, the place vied with other border towns for the lion's share of emigrant, Santa Fe, and California trade. From the wharf, these observers saw the freighted wagon trains girding for the trip to New Mexico, "an American caravan, preparing to cross the American desert." All in all, they speculated, Kansas City's prospects were bright; only a shortsighted and doctrinaire attachment to the proslavery cause seemed likely to mar them. But this was by no means sure to be the case. "Prejudices which imbitter different sections against each other," the two men went on, ". . . are often modified, or entirely removed, by mutual contact, business intercourse, and social relations, and it would not be surprising if slaveholders and abolitionists should yet unite their interests and efforts, in building a city where, as yet, there is little but the name."[1]

A shrewd comment. Conflicting party politics were irrelevant to the project of establishing Kansas City, and that is why the border troubles came as a rude interruption to more interesting activities: the urban enterprise itself, and all the individual activities within and around it. Many things were necessary—city government and street improvements, hotel space, large warehouses, wholesaling establishments, the attention of wealthy men,

[1] C. B. Boynton and T. B. Mason, *A Journey Through Kansas* (Cincinnati: Moore, Wilstach & Keys, 1855), pp. 20-21. These men represented the Cincinnati "Kansas League."

immigration, and so on—and on the rim of the Great Plains, the key to them all was the railroad. In December, 1853, the wife of a prominent local man wrote her children suggesting that they buy a farm in the rich countryside around the town. "The next thing is," she continued, "the railroad is located to this County and the inhabitants of this place are sure the terminus will be at this point. Then, of course, we shall soon have a large City." Her husband, in another letter written a year and a half later, compared Kansas City's natural position with that of St. Louis and Chicago and insisted "this *must* eventually become a great railroad center, but not until the territory beyond becomes settled with a considerable population. . . ."[2]

Only by developing a productive hinterland could you build a city and gather in the rewards of city building in the western Middle West. By 1860 pack trains and wagons were almost obsolete; even river steamboats could no longer serve the growing plains population. A local publicist whose work was partly financed and officially approved by the Kansas City Council in 1858, had only an ill-concealed scorn for entrepreneurs who relied on outworn modes of transport. "Years ago," he wrote, "steamboat commerce would build up a city in perhaps half a century. But in these days, when there is but little old fogy notion about the rise and progress of western cities, it is useless to think or talk about building up a city in the west, no matter how many steamboats we have . . . unless we have railroads we shall never have a city."[3]

Railroads would bring people and goods from the east, not only to Kansas City but also to the plains beyond, from which in turn the city would draw the increasing agricultural harvest to send back east. It was this pleasing prospect into which the slavery struggle broke, and again it was this prospect which determined the neutralist position taken by the Kansas Citians

---

2 Diana Johnson to William and Sara Vliet, Kansas City, December 4, 1853; John Johnson to William Vliet, July 8, 1855. MSS in possession of Miss Frances Berenice Ford, Kansas City, Missouri.

3 Charles C. Spalding, *Annals of the City of Kansas and the Great Western Plains* (Kansas City: Van Horn & Abeel, 1858), p. 57.

during the struggle. But even without the border troubles, the transport situation would have been difficult. When the letters just quoted were written, there were no railroads near Kansas City; when Spalding wrote, there were none; when the Civil War broke out, there were none. Not until late in 1865 did the first locomotive arrive from the east. During the whole twelve-year period, there was always a possibility—sometimes a strong possibility—that the main lines might go to some other Missouri River city. St. Joseph was always a competitor, as was Atchison, Kansas, after 1854. More important because more powerful was the interest in a railroad stemming from Leavenworth. In the circumstances, Kansas City's railroad program became a community enterprise around which gathered all of the individual resources which could be mustered in a new western city. Other developments continued, of course; new businesses and residents arrived in the city. But much of this growth must have been based on hopes that the railroad program would be carried to fruition, and the new arrivals as they came were quickly drawn into a community organized more and more forcefully around the need for rail transportation.

Kansas Citians could not build the railroads themselves, because they had not the money. Even St. Louis, with federal and state aid, had completed only 37 miles of the Pacific Railroad of Missouri by 1853 and only 181 miles by 1861, when the war broke out. The Hannibal and St. Joseph Railroad Company, on the other hand, with no more public help but with the backing of Boston capitalists, had crossed the state and was in full operation by February, 1859. The kind of investment which railroad building needed was to be found not in the West but rather back in the East, in Boston, Philadelphia, and New York. The steamboat industry had never fallen entirely into Eastern hands, because the necessary outlay was not so great. With the passing of the riverboat era, however, one kind of local independence was lost. About all a western town could do in the new conditions was to advertise itself, line up its legislators behind chartered paper roads, mobilize its electorate behind tempting city bond issues, and hope to attract a favorable nod from one of the older cities. Since all the neighboring towns had the same ambitions, the story in each case is a story of town rivalry.

In Kansas City, as in other places similarly situated, the railroad program involved two main tasks. To accomplish the first, the community at large had to stand as one man behind offers which the city might make in trying to secure the necessary Eastern backing. To some extent, this called for an educational campaign; even if local residents did not need to be told that railroads were desirable, they did need to know which projects were to be supported at what times. It would not do for half the people to be pulling strongly for one particular connection at the time arrangements for another connection were at a delicate stage of negotiation. Again, it would be helpful for everyone to know the arguments. There were good reasons to be offered in favor of Kansas City as a railroad center. Its merchants trading twice a year in eastern cities or its newcomers writing to friends back home in eastern states could do good propaganda work if they were well supplied with ammunition.

The second task was to advertise the city in influential circles. A community consisting of active and wide-awake businessmen united in favor of railroad enterprise and enjoying unparalleled natural advantages—what a tempting picture this was to show to investors! The picture had to be well drawn and frequently presented; as long as a Bostonian might reasonably ask, "Where in the world is Kansas City?" little could be hoped for in the way of railroad building at the juncture of the Missouri and the Kansas.

Just as Robert Van Horn had proved himself an unusually competent editor in his handling of the touchy issues raised by the border troubles, he showed outstanding ability again in the matter of agitation for a railroad. Almost immediately after taking over the *Enterprise* he began printing a series of letters signed "L"; identified only as an early pioneer who had seen the country around him grow, "L" was, as most of his local readers probably knew, Johnston Lykins.[4] The articles set forth a theory of economic history which could have been taken almost verbatim from Gilpin's speeches and writings. The theory, which was simply an elaborate prophecy, seemed to guarantee the future existence of a great metropolis near the point at which the Missouri River turned north. "Commerce," wrote Lykins, "like the star of empire wends its way to the West; and commerce creates at given distances commercial centres." A staggered line connecting the major cities between New York and St. Louis showed (or could be made to show) that these centers lay between three hundred and four hundred miles apart. Continental development was now, in the 1850's, at a stage where a new commercial center must appear; the logic of river courses and distances pointed clearly to Kansas City.

With this informing confidence, Lykins projected a number of lines radiating from the town, on which rails should be laid. First would come the Kansas Valley road along the Kansas River into the West; it would serve as a westward extension of Missouri's Pacific Railroad, already creeping toward Kansas City. Next would come a southern connection with Galveston, Texas, tapping a mineral-rich countryside as well as the fertile, tropical staple crop region around the Gulf of Mexico. Finally, a road must run north to the Great Lakes, through an area rapidly growing in population, and connecting with the natural water highway eastward.

Having thus neatly boxed the compass around Kansas City, Lykins suggested the awe-inspiring consequences of completing these projects. The tropical South and the temperate North, the agricultural fertility of the West, and the industrial power of the East—all would meet in this great central emporium. Nature had made it potentially the hub of direct trade with an area which stretched away over a thousand miles in every direction: "No

---

4 The letters ran serially in issues of the *Kansas City Enterprise* from November 3, 1855, to February 2, 1856. The issue containing the first letter apparently does not survive, but all the letters were reprinted by Van Horn as a pamphlet, *Railroads Chartered and Projected Centering in Kansas City* (n.p., n.d.), of which there is a copy in the Library of the State Historical Society of Missouri, Columbia, Missouri.

other city has such a background—no other such promise of magnificent greatness." The restless energy of Europe and the incalculable wealth of Asia would meet here, with Kansas City astride the link.

Van Horn not only ran these articles in his paper, along with appropriate editorial applause, but also published them together as a pamphlet. It was entitled *Railroads Chartered and Projected Centering at Kansas City,* and made an impressive boosting piece for distribution. The theory Lykins expounded could give local men that sense of coherence, of harmony in some general pattern which satisfies a deep human need. But there was more than theory in this pamphlet; its title indicated how city growth was to be promoted. The theory, or prophecy, was encouraging, of course; but as usual in such cases one had also to cooperate with destiny. Railroads must be chartered and "projected," even if the actual construction was a far-distant hope; the city must offer to exchange its bonds for railroad stock. In short, local residents must prepare to mortgage their future to a vision of progress.

The accretions from successive waves of business on the western border—fur trade, Indian trade, westward migration, and the dawning possibility of land speculation—had built the nucleus of a business community at Kansas City. Municipal incorporation and the newspaper project gave evidence not only of its cohesion but also of its aims. Subjected to a fiery test during the years 1854 to 1856, the cohesion grew stronger and the aims clearer. The secretary of the New England Emigrant Aid Company assured Easterners in 1857 that no further dangers were to be anticipated during the passage through Kansas City, "the inhabitants of that region having become fully convinced by dearbought experience, of the serious injury . . . to their business prospects, by diverting both trade and travel into other channels." One of the company's best-known backers had already described, for the same clientele, Kansas City's rock landing and the Missouri railroad, "which gives its inhabitants great hopes that it will become a great commercial city."[5]

These "inhabitants" made up the group for which local publicists wrote and spoke. Originally an almost random association of western opportunists, this group was in the process of becoming a kind of elite. Not that there was anything very exclusive about it; anyone could join for as long as he wanted to commit himself to the location's prospect and could show talent (or merely energy) with which to help develop that prospect. But this group did shape the community's polity. During the whole period through the immediate postwar years, the group remained small; expressed as a fraction of the city's rapidly growing population it became, in fact, smaller. Between ten and twenty men held the local situation in hand from 1838 to 1868 and made the decisions by which "Kansas City" sought the rewards Gilpin had outlined for it.

The stake came from two sources, which were not always really separate: investment in trade and investment in land.[6] While these two interests were quite compatible and frequently existed together in the same person, the evidence shows that land and attitudes toward it were fundamental. Real estate first provided a base for trading operations; later on, trade became a means of driving up the value of real estate. None of the early mercantile enterprises survived the Civil War intact, but most of the men who had important landholdings in the 1850's either continued to watch over them during the war or else returned to the city after a wartime sojourn elsewhere and picked up where they had left off.

Some of the early traders have already been mentioned in Chapter Three. Chick, Gilliss, Northrup, and McGee had been

[5] Thomas H. Webb, *Information for Kanzas Emigrants* (Boston: Mudge, 1857), p. 6; Edward Everett Hale, *Kanzas and Nebraska* (Boston: Phelps, Sampson & Company, 1854), pp. 123-24.

[6] Pioneer research for this section was done by Dr. Charles N. Glaab, and for more detail and full documentation the reader is referred to his article, "Business Patterns in the Growth of a Midwestern City: The Kansas City Business Community before the Civil War," *Business History Review*, XXXII (Summer, 1959), 156-74.

carrying on their mercantile activities near the landing since the 1840's. They bought land almost by second nature, perhaps just because it was "there"—cheap; nearly everyone who came west with a dollar to his name bought some land. But at first these landholdings, beyond what could be farmed, were not the most important concerns of the owners. James H. McGee died in 1840 and William Miles Chick in 1847; each left several sons who apparently in each case divided up the different lines of trade among them. Thus, Allen B. H. McGee took over some of the Indian trade his father had developed and later went into the outfitting business on a large scale; John C. Frémont twice called on him to serve expedition trains. Milton McGee, after a tempestuous youth which included Army service in the Seminole War and a trip to California in 1843, held some Indian trade interests and also built a large hotel.[7] Similarly, three sons of William M. Chick carried on various enterprises in which the father had built at least a nascent interest. With all these mercantile activities between them, it seems significant that of James McGee's many sons only two, and of Chick's only one continued to figure in the Kansas City power elite.

In one or two instances a properly ramifying mercantile business, unattached to landholdings, was enough to keep a man in Kansas City at least until the Civil War and to maintain him for a period in this decision-making group. The most prominent examples are Hiram Northrup and the third son of William Miles Chick, whose name was Joseph. Northrup, as already noted, was the first man to build a wholesaling business at the landing by supplying individual Indian traders in the territory. Joseph Chick, after an apprenticeship as clerk in Northrup's firm, became a full partner and developed a wholesale grocery trade with the Santa Fe trains. Doubtless because of the character of their own wholesaling operations, Northrup and Chick added banking to their extensive interests around 1856, becoming the first bankers in Kansas City. Apart from Van Horn, however, they are the only

---

[7] See R. Richard Wohl, "Three Generations of Business Enterprise in a Midwestern City: The McGees of Kansas City," *Journal of Economic History* (December, 1956), pp. 514-28.

two city builders in those early years who did not have important real-estate interests on the site.

A group of professional men also bought land, but these investments were at first secondary to other matters. Three doctors (Francis A. Rice, Isaac M. Ridge, and Johnston Lykins) and two ministers (Nathan Scarritt and Edward T. Peery), all of whose names appeared high on the city's tax lists for many years, show the composition of this group. To it should be added John Calvin McCoy, whose increasing concern for his lands began, as he grew older, to supplant his interest in surveying.

Following hard upon the opening of Kansas and Nebraska, numbers of Eastern men came west bringing considerable cash and, in some instances, good business connections back home, with the single purpose of finding promising real estate speculations. Many of these men went into the new territory, but some stopped at Kansas City. Perhaps most important among them was Kersey Coates, who bought a string of town lots and almost immediately joined the local power elite in trying to make the city grow. Another newcomer, in 1856, was Thomas H. Swope. Kentucky-born, with a Yale degree and with money to invest, Swope looked over the newly opened land and bought thirty acres of town property from Thomas Smart. He continued to add to his holdings, buying and selling with a keen instinct for profit, and acquired one of the biggest fortunes in the city. During the 1850's such men were arriving, buying land, and laying out additions.

They were joined in their real estate speculations by men who were already in the area and who now began to shift their interest from other activities into land development. Charles Kearney, who had operated a Santa Fe business in Westport since 1852, moved north to Kansas City four years later and bought a tract of land to develop. Joseph C. Ranson, an Irish immigrant who had been an important commission and grocery merchant in the town, disposed of these enterprises entirely in 1858 in favor of promoting a city addition. John W. Reid, a well-known Jackson County farmer and leading proslavery organizer during the border troubles, bought his plot of Kansas City ground in 1856.

The little trading community, in other words, was fast becoming a real estate center. A "landed interest" of a very special kind was developing. There could be nothing conservative about it; this land was not designed for country-seat estates but for quick urban growth. Only so could it serve the purpose of the owners, who had unquestionably in many cases gone deeply into debt in order to buy it. As Kansas City took shape, its power elite came to consist almost entirely of real estate owners working together in order to make their site a railroad hub for what Gilpin had called "the pastoral garden of the world."

From the beginning, the uncertain progress of the Pacific Railroad of Missouri commanded attention on the state's western border. It may have been that while the tracks came west, even if they came very slowly, the Kansas Citians felt that the golden prophecies of Gilpin and Lykins would be fulfilled with hardly the lifting of a local hand. As the state legislature continued to grant the railroad favor after favor, the *Enterprise* duly celebrated each instance. But the Pacific consistently refused to designate its western border terminal. On one occasion, when asked to do so by a delegation from Kansas City, the management was decidedly cool and suggested that it would be more profitable for the railroad to stay well away from competition with river transportation.[8] This may have been no more than an effort to lever substantial contributions for the railroad out of Kansas City pockets, but it made a point which was none the less valid: the prophecy of Kansas City's greatness was not self-fulfilling.

There were two ways in which the local business group could supplement the theory which Lykins had worked out for them— two ways in which they could help fulfill the prophecy. First of all, companies could be organized with charter rights to build

[8] M. J. Payne, "City of Kansas . . . ," in H. L. Conard (ed.), *Encyclopedia of the History of Missouri* (New York: Southern History Company, 1901), I, 623-24. Payne was a member of the delegation.

certain lines. The next step would then be to ask help from Eastern financiers for what would appear to be going concerns. In reality, none of these chartered companies ever got far past the "paper railroad" stage. But there was a second card to play: public assistance. If a paper railroad was organized by Kansas City men, the local electorate might then vote to exchange municipal bonds for shares of stock; in that way, the assets of the paper railroad would include a lien on the taxing power of the city itself. This device would help to interest outsiders in the proposition, and might give Kansas City a degree of independence from the Pacific Railroad's directorate. Public assistance need not be limited to locally organized companies, but the pattern just sketched was followed most often; in fact, the local elite became so adept at manipulating public and private claims on future income that it is impossible now to follow all of their tracks.

So many railroad companies were chartered, reorganized, and chartered again that it would not repay the effort to list them all.[9] Railroad planning became, in effect, the organizing principle around which Kansas City was built. The early emphasis on several specific kinds of trade with several hinterlands which had brought together the town company nucleus now was concentrated upon securing the transportation agencies with which to carry the goods back and forth. Hence the flurry of charters and projects, most of which came to precisely nothing. They were sparks, or eccentric fragments, thrown off by the friction which the enduring effort generated.

The Kansas Valley Railroad, for example, which had been mentioned by Lykins in his over-all plan, was one of the first local companies for which a charter was obtained. The territorial legislature of Kansas granted the charter, which allowed the company to build west toward Fort Riley. Not a foot of rail or roadbed was ever laid by the Kansas Valley Railroad company. Two years passed before it was even organized, in 1857, at which

[9] Charles N. Glaab reached the same conclusion while preparing a 300-page history of local raidroad promotion in Kansas City from 1850 to 1875. See his *Kansas City and the Railroads* (Madison, Wisconsin: State Historical Society of Wisconsin, 1962.)

time Lykins became president and Coates, treasurer. The directors included several of the city addition promoters, and large quantities of stock were soon subscribed. Not paid, however. It is important to remember that, just as this was a paper railroad, the stock subscriptions remained nothing more than columns of the names of Kansas Citians with figures written after them. This charter might, of course, have been taken over by some Eastern group, in which case the city would have agreed to exchange its bonds for the stock, and the trains would ultimately have rolled. As it happened, the route later chosen for the Union Pacific's Eastern Division tapped the same area (although the route was not identical with that proposed for the Kansas Valley road), and nothing more was heard of the local project which Van Horn in 1859 had called "the grand enterprise of the present time."[10]

In large part the railroad boom which lasted in Kansas City up to the outbreak of the Civil War stemmed from efforts to threaten or otherwise influence the Pacific Railroad of Missouri. As the directors of that company continued to be coy, the Westerners tried to show either that it would be worth the Pacific's while to take over the paper railroads immediately and build them into extensions for itself, or that Kansas City had alternative Eastern connections which would, if completed, damage the St. Louis line's earning power. So the Kansas City, Hannibal & St. Joseph, the New Orleans, Shreveport & Kansas City, and an incorporated fantasia called the Kansas City, Galveston & Lake Superior came into being, along with a host of others. One curious result of all this activity was that after the war the city found itself linked with both St. Louis and Chicago; it also was by that time the terminus of the eastern division of the transcontinental Union Pacific, and plans called for another line projected toward the Gulf. None of these were sure, however, in the prewar years. The best bet was unquestionably the Pacific Railroad of Missouri, and around it the whole complex of activity and rhetoric turned.

---

[10] See *Statutes of the Territory of Kansas* (1855), pp. 926-30, for the charter; representative discussions of the Kansas Valley Railroad are in *Enterprise*, February 7 and April 11, 1857, and *Western Journal of Commerce*, August 18, 1859. Hereafter cited as *Journal*.

A brief examination of the Kansas City, Hannibal & St. Joseph project shows the reasons for the pre-eminence of the Pacific Railroad. Chartered in 1855, the ostensible purpose of this company was to connect with Missouri's northern land-grant railroad. The real intention was probably to threaten the Pacific. The fact that no moneyed men were even faintly interested in this charter never deterred its directors from acting as though they represented a going concern, nor Van Horn from propagandizing the Kansas City, Hannibal & St. Joseph as loudly and as frequently as he could through the columns of his newspaper. In fact, the failure of outside capital to seize this latest opportunity offered it by Kansas City led Van Horn along a path of argument which, outside of its context, would have to be called absurd. Local people, he wrote, would build the northern connections themselves. The K. C., H. & St. J. would avoid the trammels of corrupt legislators and speculators and would likewise escape control by outsiders ignorant of or inimical to Kansas City's interests; it would be "the people's road."

During a period when the Pacific directors seemed to be holding out on the western town, Van Horn attacked the very idea of state aid for railroads; in his view, it was "only another name for swindling." Companies which sought public largess would quickly disappear from sight "when no more money can be ground out of the burdened taxpayers. . . ." These fulminations were always associated with praise for the northern connection, which was to be financed entirely by honest Kansas City businessmen and operated solely in their interest. Dependence on the Pacific Railroad of Missouri, with its "interested contractors and . . . huckstering Directory," would be a thing of the past.[11]

If state aid was bad, however, the taxpayer could still contribute. At least $1,500,000 was foreseen in county subscriptions, and more in city bond issues. A new organization entered the lists in October, 1856, when the Kansas City Chamber of Commerce was organized. To judge from the surviving minutes, its purpose was simply to organize and direct the local railroad cam-

11 For the K.C., H. & St.J., see *Laws of Missouri, 1855*, pp. 138-39; *Enterprise*, December 27, 1855; January 5, July 12, August 16, and September 20, 1856.

paign. This body, in which all the leading promoters participated, unofficially superintended a rearrangement of the route of "the people's road," so that more towns and counties might be approached for money. In Kansas City steps followed a pattern which became representative in the years that followed: A public meeting called upon the city council to hold a special election on aid for the railroad; the council did so; on October 14, 1856, Kansas City voters overwhelmingly ratified the exchange of $150,000 worth of city bonds for stock in the company.[12]

Little more was heard of this project, in spite of the time and effort which had been lavished upon it. This was partly due to the panic of 1857, but even more to the condition of affairs respecting the Pacific Railroad. During this year and the next, negotiations were in progress which ended in the final selection of Kansas City as this railroad's western terminus. The negotiations involved bond-for-stock exchanges by Kansas City, Independence, and Jackson County, which were ultimately worked out satisfactorily (and of which more will be said below), and further state aid for the Pacific which Van Horn now supported with all his journalistic resources. The story in detail is long and complicated, with aid bills passed and aid bills rejected in the state legislature, each drawing the proper editorial comment in Kansas City. Finally, at a special session of the legislature in the spring of 1860, a generous package of grants and favors passed and seemed to clear away all obstacles to a quick completion of the line between Kansas City and St. Louis. The western city celebrated wildly. Affairs were apparently well lubricated with alcohol; cannon, bands, bonfires, and a monster parade along Main Street with a model railroad car in tow, all symbolized what Van Horn called "the inauguration of a new and glorious era. . . ."[13] Unfortunately, the Governor then vetoed this bill.

"Recreant to his vows, false to his pretensions, treacherous

12 *Enterprise,* October 4 and 18, 1856; Ordinance Record Book A (Office of the City Clerk, Kansas City, Missouri), p. 156; typescript "Minutes of Chamber of Commerce of Kansas City, Missouri, 1856-1879," Archives of the Native Sons of Kansas City, City Hall, Kansas City, Missouri.

13 See *Journal,* March 19, 1859, and March 15, 1860. The above paragraph can be documented almost at random from the paper's files during this period.

to his friends, and a traitor to Missouri," cried the *Western Journal of Commerce*, ". . . no man can defend him without taint and no man desires to extend a hand to raise him from the deep into which he has precipitated an honorable and distinguished name." Immediately, the campaign shifted its sights again to the northern connection, and now a use was found for the old Kansas City, Galveston & Lake Superior charter. The Chamber of Commerce had already tried, with some success, to interest the management of the Hannibal & St. Joseph (the land-grant road across northern Missouri, controlled by the Boston directors of the powerful Chicago, Burlington & Quincy system and not to be confused with the local paper railroad) in a Kansas City connection. Now, with the Pacific seemingly stalled by the infamous veto, another public meeting urged the council to call another election. Again the voters authorized an exchange of bonds for stock—this time to the amount of $200,000. Clay County, across the river, subscribed an additional $150,000. A serious effort by local residents to build at least a roadbed fifty-four miles to the town of Cameron, where it would join the H. & St. J., now got under way.[14]

The rest of this story belongs to a later chapter, but the extent to which this small project was actually completed makes a point worthy of notice here. "Mark the prediction," the *Journal* assured everyone in January, 1861, "that in less time than has been taken to talk about the Pacific Railroad, the K. C., G. & L. S. Railroad will be running from the sunny bay of Galveston to frigid Lake Superior and exchanging the commodities of the Antipodes at our wharf. . . ."[15] But it was not to be. With bonds, stock, and now and then even a little cash changing hands, with a contractor at work on the ground from October, 1860, to the outbreak of war, the roadbed alone was only two-thirds done. The city's bonds were practically worthless in New York. Clay

14 *ORB*, Book B, pp. 119, 132; Hannibal & St. Joseph Railroad Company, Red Label volume, in the Chicago, Burlington & Quincy Archives (Chicago, Illinois), especially letter from J. T. K. Hayward to John Brooks, October 19, 1859; Minute Books of the Kansas City, Galveston & Lake Superior Railroad Company, also the Kansas City & Cameron Railroad, Burlington Archives; *Journal*, October 11, 1860.

15 *Journal*, January 24, 1861.

County's bonds were a little better (because they were, in effect, state obligations), but not enough to pay the contractor anything approaching what was due him. Aid from the Eastern-backed Hannibal & St. Joseph company was contingent upon completion of this short roadbed, and during the war even the existing segment of it deteriorated so rapidly as to be almost useless when hostilities ceased. Judged by any criterion, the Kansas City railroad campaign up to April, 1861, appears almost to have been ludicrous, to have produced nothing but a battered thirty-five miles of grading and a substantial debt for a town of five thousand inhabitants—and to contrast strangely with the visions limned six years earlier in the Lykins railroad plan.

To see events in this light alone—the light of their concrete issue by the time of the Civil War—is to miss most of the story, however. The importance of the railroad campaign in Kansas City between 1855 and 1861 did not lie in the approach of rolling stock close to the city. Wagon trains and steamboats carried its trade quite adequately; there was no overflow of goods lying in warehouses or on docks. There was no question here of a flourishing urban center having outgrown existing agencies. By the 1860 census, the leading Missouri River towns lined up as follows:

St. Joseph	8,932
Leavenworth	7,429
Kansas City	4,418
Independence	3,164
Atchison	2,616
Wyandotte	1,920
Weston	1,816
Westport	1,195

Kansas City was neither the largest nor the fastest-growing settlement in the area; it was older than both Leavenworth and Atchison (as well as Wyandotte, which later became the nucleus of Kansas City, Kansas).

Taken alone, these figures are of little value. What must be seen is not simple economic growth but something more complicated: the creation of community—a group of people performing the same actions for the same reasons. In the present instance, the group was made up at first largely of city addition promoters; what they did (over and above their individual business concerns) was to make a series of gestures toward connecting themselves with the sources of economic growth. Their reasons lay somewhere in the contrast between existing conditions and an optimistic calculation of future prospects. The way to realization lay along iron rails, and therefore the community formed around the railroad campaign.

As has been said already, most of the movers in this campaign were owners of substantial amounts of real estate in or adjoining the town. Correlation between these names and the boards of directors of the various chartered companies ran very high. During and after the border troubles, the men who were trying to work out a politically noncommital platform for Kansas City were also busy surveying their land parcels into additions, offering single lots for sale, and devising ways to attract buyers.

There was McGee's Addition, for example, south of the city and centering along Grand Avenue, over which rumbled the thousands of wagons engaged in the Southwestern trade; by 1858, McGee claimed thirty-eight brick buildings and a population of seven hundred in his addition. Many incoming Germans settled there, which perhaps had something to do with the rapid moderation which McGee's political opinions underwent. There was Joseph C. Ranson's Addition, on which the owner had constructed a large brickyard. The buyer of a lot could get credit from Ranson on a sliding scale: If he erected a building costing $1,000, he paid Ranson 10 per cent, and if the building's cost ran to $5,000 no interest at all was charged. Coates's Addition, Lykins' Addition, Guinotte's Addition, and several others ringed and dotted the city, and in each case represented sharp interest in a long-term rise in real estate values. All of the owners claimed that they would not sell for speculative purposes, and while this may be doubted the claim itself is worth noting; some developers were said to sell lots only on condition that the buyer erect some kind of building (Coates was said to insist on brick structures).[16]

Several of the addition owners formed the heart of Kansas City's decision-making inner circle until after the Civil War. Their names appear in every important grouping which events made necessary or desirable. A rough view of this inner circle, or clique, or elite, can be derived from these groupings: the men who backed the *Enterprise* newspaper venture, the members of the first Chamber of Commerce, the directorates of six railroad companies and two local branches of St. Louis banks, and the delegates to a regional internal improvements convention—all between 1855 and 1863. The total number of names is fifty-two, which is not large, but yet is much larger than the group of decision-makers. Many of these names appear in only one group, but some again and again. Kersey Coates figures seven times on the list; Johnston Lykins, Joseph C. Ranson, and S. W. Bouton (at one time Coates's partner in real estate dealings), participated in six groups each; Northrup, Swope, Gilliss, and the Chick family appear in three.[17]

The make-up of these groups gives us a good start for filling in the elite list and makes the importance of real estate clear. Chick and Northrup represent the mercantile element. E. M. McGee's name appears only twice in the groups listed above, which somewhat underrepresents his importance; he was frequently in Jefferson City, in the state legislature, watching over the political interests of the Kansas City group. Again, while Van Horn was not a landowner and did not figure significantly as a director of business enterprises, he was obviously an important member of the elite; he was its intellectual, so to speak, providing it with verbal platforms and rationales. Milton J. Payne is another whose importance among the promoters does not emerge in real estate or in the business directories; three times elected mayor of

---

[16] The additions are described as of 1858, and as attractively as possible, by Spalding in his *Annals*, pp. 38-55; he had written a series of articles on the additions for the *Journal* in 1857 and now condensed these articles slightly.

[17] William H. Miller, *Early History of Kansas City* (Kansas City: Birdsall & Williams, 1881), lists the members of these groups on pp. 50, 67, 69, 75, 76, 77, 78, 107.

Kansas City in the 1850's, serving at least one term in the state legislature, often named on delegations to various conventions and conferences, Payne may have been the first political organizer in the city.

At any rate, the inner circle was small, and it diversified its functions. Southerners and Northerners got along amicably in this group, with the former predominating; more of the later members tended to be from the North, but this was not entirely the case. One section conspicuous by its absence from the inner circle was New England.

This was the group which made the most important decisions in Kansas City. The city charter, the financing of a newspaper, and the appearance of a chamber of commerce, which have been mentioned already, all bespoke response to the need for teamwork and specialization in an urban enterprise. Much of the work had to do with publicizing the city and its goals. Thus, in 1858 the Chamber of Commerce directed Van Horn to prepare a memorial to Congress on the advantages of Kansas City as an eastern terminus for the transcontinental railroad. Van Horn drew up a forceful paper, expanding on the Gilpin-Lykins geographical thesis in order to show that the route west from Kansas City was ideal, and the document was accordingly laid before Congress.[18] Again, in the same year, Charles Spalding was encouraged by Van Horn, the chamber, and the city council to write his *Annals*, which we have cited several times. Under Chamber of Commerce auspices, several hundred copies of a lithographed map were distributed in the eastern cities, showing in great detail the geographical conveniences which any railroads built from Kansas City would enjoy. In 1859 the same organization asked T. S. Case to write a full description of the city as he first

[18] In pamphlet form, this memorial is very rare: *Central Pacific Railway Route. Memorial to the Congress of the U.S. on the Subject of a Railway to the Pacific Ocean by the Valley of the Kansas River, or the Route of the 39th Parallel. From the Chamber of Commerce of the City of Kansas. Reported to the Chamber by R. T. Van Horn, Chairman of the R.R. Committee, April 27, 1858* (Kansas City: Western Journal of Commerce, 1858), 16 pp. Miller reproduces it verbatim, pp. 81-91. I have consulted the copy of the pamphlet in the Snyder Collection at the University of Kansas City. No railroad was built near the route Van Horn suggested.

saw it on his arrival two years earlier; it is probable that some kind of publication was in view for the manuscript Case composed, but nothing came of this project. Instead, the first regular business directory appeared in the following year. In 1860 the city printed its first official map, an attractively colored affair, five feet square and carefully laid out on high-grade map cloth.[19]

At the end of 1857 members of this city-building group sponsored a festive dinner at Col. Titus' Exchange Hotel. Western game made up the fare, and it was accompanied by plenty of good drinks. These continued long into the night as a series of toasts were consumed, with appropriate responses from one or another local figure: Northrup, Ranson, E. C. McCarty, Spalding, Van Horn, and others. Van Horn responded to the toast, "Railroads and the Press: Twin Brothers in Progress and Development," with a long discussion of the advantages which Kansas City offered to railroad builders and of the many good things which railroads would mean for the city. He had to admit that no railroads were there, as yet; years would pass before the first locomotive could enter the city. Their absence, however, was a relatively minor point; twelve years earlier, Chicago had no railroads, but now that metropolis had flung a ten-thousand-mile network about her in every direction. "Let the world know of us," Van Horn concluded, ". . . that here is the commercial center fixed by the laws of nature herself, and the capital of the world will stretch out its iron arms . . . the roads will be built." We need not doubt the report which assures us this speech drew wild applause.[20]

Even if it had not come relatively late in the line of toasts—assuming, that is, that Van Horn and his hearers had been entirely sober—the speech would have been enthusiastically received. It

[19] Case's manuscript and the city map are both preserved in the Archives of the Native Sons of Kansas City; another copy of this map is in the Snyder Collection at the University of Kansas City. For the railroad map, no copies of which are known to have survived, see Chamber of Commerce Minutes, March 3, April 14, 1857, p. 11. This map was apparently very similar to one printed in the *Journal*, November 29, 1862.

[20] This and other speeches at the banquet were reported in the *Journal*, January 2, 1858.

outlined exactly the inner circle's position toward events, and showed what they had to do to promote the city's growth: knit the citizens together around a plan for the future, and attract the attention of the outsiders who alone could supply the wherewithal to gain it. "Make it a *business rule*," wrote Spalding, "to never let a farmer go out of your store until you have said more or less to him about railroads." Later on, arguing for a project to aid the Pacific Railroad, Van Horn explained how "the masses of the people—the poor men," were the ones to benefit most from railroads. Laborers could expect good wages and a growing demand for their services if the city could secure the roads and the expansion which would be consequent upon their coming.[21]

But all efforts had frequently to pass the test of wider support within the city. Taking only the accepted pattern of railroad agitation for example, the progress from Chamber of Commerce discussion to public mass meeting to city council to electorate clearly depended for its success upon broad agreement by several hundred or more local voters with the expressed program of the city builders. The business community had to rally a larger community around its aims.

The impressive results which were achieved in winning popular support show that for such fundamental purposes as railroads the city electorate functioned as a well-oiled machine. Propositions to commit future tax revenue to the support of the companies steam-rollered through to legal form every time they were offered. The city's population was probably not much less than 1,000 in October, 1856, when the election to support the Kansas City, Hannibal & St. Joseph was held; only 5 negative votes were recorded. In April, 1860, when the population was around 4,000, only 9 votes opposed aid for the Kansas City, Galveston & Lake Superior Railroad. In September, 1859, when the question concerned county aid for the Pacific Railroad of Missouri, Kansas City's tally showed 1,667 votes in favor as against 8 opposed![22]

This kind of medicine was rather strong for the rest of the

---

21 *Enterprise*, August 15, 1857; *Journal*, September 8, 1859.

22 *Enterprise*, October 18, 1856; *Journal*, April 19, 1860; September 8, 1859.

county to take, and in the last-mentioned example (where county money was at stake) the cry of fraud was raised at once. This election had been county-wide, and elsewhere in the county the vote had run 862 to 465 against it. The Kansas City machine converted this rejection into a more than 2-to-1 approval. Since there were certainly fewer people in the city at the time of this 1859 election than the census takers counted for the following year, and since the weather had been unseasonably cold on the day of balloting, the charge of fraud seems well justified. Furthermore, there is no reason to imagine that the local promoters committed fraud for the first time on that particular occasion.[23] Fraudulent or not, the figures stood, as other startling figures stood before and after these.

The point to be emphasized here is that railroad propositions even in completely honest balloting would undoubtedly have gained heavy majorities in Kansas City. Whatever opposition there may have been has left absolutely no record, and while this does not mean that we must assume a population unanimously behind the city builders, it does mean that the machine managed to organize the kind of support they needed.

Certainly the leaders in Kansas City's railroad campaign were operating in favorable circumstances. Their community was younger than St. Joseph; no important interests that were bound inseparably with river-boating or in any other way threatened by railroads had arisen, as such interests apparently did arise in the older city upstream. Kansas City was older than Leavenworth, where not one but many railroad projects, often mutually conflicting, competed for popular support when bond issues were proposed. We may guess that Kansas City in the 1850's was new enough to retain an opportunistic flexibility, but old enough to have worked out and to support consistently one main line of attack.[24] Whatever the reasons, the main fact is clear: To the

---

[23] *Independence Messenger*, clipped in *Journal*, September 8, 1859; *Journal*, September 15, 1859; Westport *Border Star*, September 16, 1859.

[24] For St. Joseph, see Frank Popplewell, "St. Joseph as a Center of the Cattle Trade," *Missouri Historical Review*, XXXII (July, 1938). Data on Leavenworth are presented in Chapter 7.

extent that it made up a community at all, Kansas City's population gathered around the promise offered by rail transportation.

Even at this early period the Kansas City settlement was separating itself from its close neighbors. As in the border troubles, so too in the field of economic development this community failed to behave as most western Missourians thought Missouri towns ought to behave. Railroads and all the new forces they represented were regarded with at least some suspicion elsewhere in Jackson County and nearby. The proposal to aid the Kansas City, Galveston & Lake Superior in 1860 had rolled over all opposition in Kansas City, whereas in Clay County a complementary proposal passed only by a 3-to-2 margin. "Corporations," wrote a critic in the *Liberty Tribune,* "have no souls, and Railroad corporations least of any." According to another writer in the same paper, the bond proposal would only place local inhabitants in "the greedy grip of Boston capitalists . . . who will ultimately abolitionize the northern half of the state." During the controversy over the Jackson County subscription to Pacific Railroad stock, an Independence editor anxiously noted that if the Kansas City vote was to stand, it would mean the entire county's political dependence upon the smoothly functioning Kansas City clique.[25] Almost surrounded by settlers who regarded them in this jaundiced fashion, the Kansas Citians had all the more need to organize their urban enterprise tightly and efficiently.

Theodore Spencer Case, of an Ohio family, had enough money to attend a medical college at Columbus, whence he graduated in 1856. Rather than seek practice at home, however, he did as many others of his generation were doing: putting as much cash as possible in his pocket, he moved west. After having been fleeced of fifteen dollars in a Kansas town promotion, he found

[25] *History of Clay and Platte Counties* (St. Louis: National Historical Company, 1885), pp. 184-85; *Liberty Tribune,* May 18, June 8, 1860; *Independence Messenger,* clipped in *Journal,* September 8, 1859.

himself in Kansas City in May, 1857. Kansas City was then a town of no more than fifteen hundred inhabitants.[26]

It was raining when Case stepped onto the landing from the steamboat which had brought him to the town at the bend of the Missouri, and the scene was dismal in the extreme. Nearby, in front of the bluff, was the American Hotel (the one formerly used by the Emigrant Aid Company). It was a miserable place, but Case mistakenly thought it was the only hotel in town. Rather than follow many of his fellow travelers all the way to Westport, where accommodations were better, he made the American his base while looking over the raw settlement. The hotel and several warehouses dominated the levee, with a few small retail shops sandwiched in between the larger buildings. Only one street— Market, which later became Grand Avenue—was cut through to the levee from the south and could be used for business locations; on the rest the grades were still too steep, and the streets oppressively narrow. Smithies, saloons, and a few stores straggled along Market Street, ending in what seems to have been a little slum inhabited by some Irish settlers. South of the crest of the bluffs, more shops and saloons were joined by residences, in several of which room-and-board was offered. Farther south along Main Street the quality of the houses improved as one approached the neighborhood where lived the Northrups, the Ridges, the Campbells, and finally the McGees in their addition. A deep ravine meandered diagonally across the whole townsite, debouching in the river near the foot of Market Street. It was bridged only where it crossed Main and Market, and at the latter place the crossing was ramshackle and dangerous. Most people, it seemed, carried arms; the memory of the border troubles was

---

[26] See biographical sketch in Theodore S. Case, *History of Kansas City, Missouri* (Syracuse: D. Mason, 1888), pp. 460-63; also Alexander Majors, *Seventy Years on the Frontier* (Chicago and New York: Rand McNally & Company, 1893), p. 255. In his 1859 manuscript, which is the basis for this paragraph, Case dates his own arrival as 1857; records of the Starling Medical College, in the Library of the University of Chicago, Chicago, Illinois, date his graduation there as 1856. The sketch in Case's *History* gives 1853 for his arrival at Kansas City, and this error has been copied elsewhere. In addition to the manuscript, I have included some notes from a reminiscence by Case which appeared in the *Kansas City World*, July 12, 1897.

still fresh. Everywhere, land and shares were being bought and sold in feverish excitement.

Unable to find an office in Kansas City, Case gave up and went to Westport. He was back again by September, however, and this time to stay. He found an office now, on the third floor of a new dry-goods building which had been finished since May; with two men who served as city engineers, he paid fifteen dollars a month for this little headquarters. In spite of its unprepossessing aspect, Kansas City attracted Case. The quantities of hard money which circulated, the unsightly piles of Santa Fe merchandise, the mule teams, and the land speculation caught his interest with "the prospect of having made a good location" in his quest for a western home.

The community which Case now decided to join (and in the councils of which he quickly rose) had, of course, more enterprises in hand than the development of real estate and the agitation for railroads. Opportunities were expanding with each passing month. The Far Southwest had developed since 1848, under American control; although men still referred to "the Santa Fe trade," this business had expanded to regional proportions. Manufactured goods such as hardware, mining machinery, and groceries were replacing dry goods on the westward trip, and the trains now brought back wool instead of precious metals. J. S. Chick alone was freighting about half a million pounds of groceries annually in this way by 1860. Several miles from the city, on the Kansas prairies, were the corrals where the teams of the Southwestern traders rested, upon their arrival in the spring, while the merchants in charge went to Westport, Kansas City, or to St. Louis to complete their transactions. Bilingual advertising in the *Western Journal of Commerce*, English-Spanish, gave a surprisingly cosmopolitan impression and testified to the importance of the Southwestern outfitting business.[27]

A new trade area opened out, and the commerce of the

[27] In addition to the material cited in Chapter 3, see the article on Kansas City freighting contributed by J. S. Chick to the *Encyclopedia of the History of Missouri*, ed. H. L. Conard, II, 515-17; see also W. P. Tomlinson, *Kansas in 1858* (New York: H. Dayton; Indianapolis, Dayton & Asher, 1859), pp. 18-19.

prairies broadened accordingly when in 1858 a gold rush to Colorado set in. Rumors of rich mines in that region had been current since the time of Coronado. These rumors occurred in waves, at different times, and during the 1850's a number of expeditions prospected in the Rocky Mountains.[28] The *Daily Kansas City Western Journal of Commerce* had discussed the likelihood of Colorado gold as early as March, 1858, but the real furore broke at the end of August in that year, when John Cantrell of Westport returned home with pouches full of the precious dust from the Cherry Creek-South Platte district (where Denver grew up almost overnight the following year). "THE NEW ELDORADO!!!" trumpeted Van Horn, while the fever gripped his city. Within the next few days parties were "preparing for the diggings."[29]

In two weeks one Kansas City house alone outfitted thirty Colorado parties; the outfit necessary to four men prospecting for six months was usually put at something over five hundred dollars.[30] Not only did the provisioning of migrants mean business at Kansas City, but also the growth of the Cherry Creek settlement led some of the local grocery houses to set up branch stores there. Again the rivalry of the border towns asserted itself. Two guidebooks for hopeful Colorado prospectors appeared before the end of 1858; at least fifteen more followed in the next year. Many of them were designed to steer the migrants to one or another of these towns: Leavenworth, Lawrence, St. Joseph, Atchison, and Platte City all had their advocates, along with those for Kansas City. The guidebook stressing the advantages of Kansas City was put together by no less a publicist than William Gilpin. He addressed a mass meeting called by the Chamber of Commerce in November, 1858, to alert local citizens to the great opportunity which was before them. The *Journal* reported another mass meet-

---

[28] See L. R. Hafen (ed.), *Colorado Gold Rush: Contemporary Letters and Reports, 1858-1859* (Glendale, Calif.: A. H. Clark, 1941), and *Pike's Peak Gold Rush Guidebooks of 1859* (1941); Hafen cites Kansas City references among many others.

[29] *Journal*, August 26, 1858.

[30] *Missouri Democrat*, September 21, 1858, cited in Hafen, *Colorado Gold Rush*, p. 57.

ing in February, 1859, to devise means for keeping Leavenworth and St. Joseph from profiting unduly in the gold rush.

A fair amount of government contracting was done in the neighborhood. Most of this was connected with supplying the western forts, and it was a business over which Kansas City and Leavenworth struggled interminably. In 1858, when the great freighting firm of Russell, Majors & Waddell was in difficulties, a number of Kansas City businessmen deeded $60,000 worth of real estate to Alexander Majors, a Westport resident, contingent upon transfer of his government freighting business from Leavenworth. Majors had enough influence in the national capital to get the transfer approved, and a new increment to local trade thereby appeared. By 1860 commission charges on government freight in Kansas City amounted to $50,000, a tidy supplement to the $114,000 which private freighting business supplied.[31]

These lines of commerce which described Kansas City's economic base in the late 1850's supported an increasing superstructure. A new mercantile interest arose to join the earlier enterprises. In 1856 an Irish immigrant named Patrick Shannon induced his two brothers to come to Kansas City, one from St. Louis and the other from New Orleans. Both had been storekeepers, and in Kansas City the dry-goods firm of J. & P. Shannon soon occupied three floors of a downtown building and operated a branch store in St. Joseph.[32] Local meat packing was begun by a grocer, Michael Diveley, and a man named Mitchener who had been a packer in Cincinnati. A large chinaware house, D. M. Boland & Company, was established, importing directly from England to Kansas City through New Orleans.[33] The rapidly growing number of locally owned stores was augmented by branches which Eastern firms began to set up in the city: men's

---

31 *Journal*, May 24, 1860; the *Journal's* Annual Review for 1859 is quoted by James C. Malin in *Grassland Historical Studies: Natural Resources Utilization in a Background of Science and Technology*, Vol. I: *Geology and Geography* (Lawrence, Kansas: By the author, 1950), p. 218.

32 On the Shannons, see several clippings in "Kansas City Scrapbook," Native Sons of Kansas City, and *Journal*, June 4, 1859; January 19, July 12, 1860.

33 *Journal*, July 16, 1859; November 29, 1860.

clothing, dry goods, and hardware were the major lines that interested outsiders.

Van Horn noted all these new arrivals in the *Journal*, in which he devoted far more space to local and regional business than to party politics, thus reversing the proportions usually devoted to these topics in Western newspapers. He called signals, or tried to, for the business elite, stressing the importance of more wholesaling, insisting that additional hotels be erected, pointing out lines of enterprise in which it was clear to him that killings were waiting to be made in Kansas City. Van Horn frequently urged his townsmen to establish manufactures and not to rest content with a commercial base. He quoted with hearty approval some remarks made by Mayor G. M. B. Maughs in 1860, according to which "commerce *may* enrich a people—productive industry, manufactories, *will* do so. . . . We should supply Southwest Missouri, the greater portion of Kansas Territory, New Mexico and the Pike's Peak gold region with many of the wants of civilized society, machinery, farming implements, etc., manufactured here." Little came of these urgings, however; by the time the war broke out less than $200,000 worth of goods, at a most generous estimate, were made annually in Kansas City, while $4,250,000 worth had changed hands there in 1859.[34]

A considerable amount of Indian trade, based on the annuities which the federal government paid the tribes, was still carried on near the Missouri-Kansas border in the late 1850's. Van Horn put the figure at a million dollars, and E. M. McGee proudly advertised in the first printed city directory, in 1859, that he and his agents knew all the Indian languages and could contract efficiently for all clients. The possibilities of the Indian trade had been suggested to potential migrants by Secretary Thomas Webb of the New England Emigrant Aid Company. This business, however, was beginning to yield to another, which was to be far more important and which required in the end that the Indian give up the fertile Kansas lands guaranteed him forever in favor of American farmers who were now attacking "the desert."

In 1860 there were (officially) 107,000 Kansans, and many

[34] *Journal*, April 12, 1860.

of them—especially those in the southeastern region of settlement —traded at or through Kansas City. Their trade made up one of the factors which shaped that city's neutralism in 1855 and 1856, and Van Horn's *Journal* encouraged merchants in the river town to take all possible steps to build business connections in the territory. Although he had frequently aspersed the puritanical New Englanders during the border conflict, he now found them potentially valuable and even compatible neighbors.[35] Nevertheless, this local trade remained proportionately small before the war, and its greatest importance during these years was like that of the railroad campaign. It offered unlimited possibilities for the future, having "a prospective import, referring to the possible, rather than the actual."

The factor involved here was the passing of "the Great American Desert." In the 1850's, partly because of such Eastern interest in Western land as the emigrant aid companies represented, more and more commentators disputed the notion that the territory west of the Missouri border could not support a farming population. The two Cincinnati agents who were quoted at the beginning of this chapter announced themselves fully convinced that Kansas land was good, "and that future investigation will very much reduce the dimensions of what has been called the American desert." Edward Everett Hale took pains to describe the territory's excellent possibilities, "because the frequent statement and general impression is that those plains are wholly desert and worthless." And Thomas Webb cited a letter from an early Kansas settler to the effect that the whole desert idea was a myth which "Missouri people and superficial explorers have labored to create. . . ."[36]

For Kansas City the currency of the "desert" notion was a serious matter, as has been indicated already. Johnston Lykins, in his railroad letters to the *Enterprise*, had stressed the superb "background" of Kansas City. The character imputed to its hinterland defines a city's chances for growth, and the accepted view

---

[35] See an interesting account of his first trip into Kansas in *Journal*, May 29, 1858.

[36] Boynton and Mason, *A Journey Through Kansas*, p. 34; Hale, *Kanzas and Nebraska*, p. 112; Webb, *Information for Kanzas Emigrants*, p. 64 n.

of Kansas City's hinterland was changing basically during this early period. Nothing indicates that the city builders any more than generally sensed the process. The outpourings of Gilpin, Spalding, Lykins, and Van Horn can on no account be made to yield an accurate and detailed prediction of the future development of Kansas, even though local historians have credited them (and others) with this kind of prescience. Van Horn was highly inconsistent, actually holding on one occasion as late as 1857 that Kansas would be mostly a hemp- and tobacco-growing area. Even in 1860 he was just as convinced as most Americans were that the country west of Topeka was such as could support only one transcontinental railroad.[37] More often, of course, he followed the other publicists in pitching his optimism so broadly that it would embrace any kind of future development at all.

His assistant for a time on the *Journal,* Charles Spalding, devoted the first four pages of his *Annals of the City of Kansas,* in 1858, to a direct quotation from Gilpin on the fertility of the Great Plains, "the pastoral garden of the world." Gilpin, in his 1858 speech on the Colorado gold rush, used the occasion to express his favorite continental prophecy, complete with isothermal lines and what had become by this time a monotonous succession of great cities arising along them, naturally culminating in Kansas City. In 1859 Van Horn scornfully entitled an editorial on recent geographical publications, "The Desert: It Has Moved Again."

While they refused to accept any specific limit for their own venture, the Kansas City elite had inevitably to support the most optimistic estimate of the potentialities of their surrounding area. All the weapons of eloquence were turned against the unattractive desert-image. Word pictures were drawn of fertile soil, plentiful water, wealth of all kinds from the earth. Van Horn generalized the attack into something like a theory of city growth. If the notion of a desert typified a stingy and unkind Nature, the editor simply reversed this proposition. Natural forces had conspired, he

---

[37] See Albert D. Richardson, *Beyond the Mississippi* (Hartford: American Publishing Company, 1867), p. 29. Van Horn was justifying his proslavery position to Richardson and may not have taken his own forecast seriously. See *Journal,* August 16, 1860.

said, to bless Kansas City with such advantages as to assure its growth.

The theory was built on propositions already advanced by Gilpin and Lykins. The old *Public Ledger* had argued similarly in 1851, and indeed, most midwestern boosters have had recourse over the years to one or another variant. In the course of his Christmas Dinner speech, in 1857, Van Horn had expressed it ably. "God has marked out by topography the lines of commerce," he said,

> . . . and it is by studying these great tracings of the Almighty's finger that the pioneer of trade and the herald of civilization has selected the site of those gigantic cities of the Republic, and which has fixed upon the rock-bound bay of the Missouri and Kansas as the last great seat of wealth. . . . If men will only study topography, the problem is solved.

Happily for them, the Kansas Citians stood on the highway of progress. "Since the days of Columbus," the editor went on,

> commerce and enterprise have been seeking the *west*—west, west, has ever been the watchword—over the Atlantic, up the Potomac, across the Alleghenies, down the Ohio, over the Mississippi, up the Missouri. It is found at last. Kansas City stands on the extreme point of western navigation . . . beyond *us*, the west must come to us overland. I say again—the west at last is found.

After being interrupted at this point by the applause of his audience, Van Horn continued with discussion of the isothermal lines, those great belts of fertility which were thought to girdle the earth, marking out civilizations and trade areas:

> We are in the central parallel of population and production, and as sure as the sun in his course imparts to our valleys and plains the richest of his fructifying rays, just so sure will our fortune be great and certain.

Charles Spalding, in his own remarks at the banquet, gave an even simpler exposition of natural advantages. "Geography," he said, "tells us *all*, when correctly studied. . . ." The junction of the Missouri and the Kansas rivers lay squarely athwart the path of the future, which "will fix the grand proportions of Kansas City. The patent of the Deity is stamped upon each and all of these charters of our prosperity." Spalding managed to work the theory into most of the 116 pages of his *Annals of the City of Kansas*, published the following year. Kansas City's destiny was never very far from Van Horn's mind; in a private letter in 1858 he wrote that he could not understand why Providence had introduced mankind to the American continent first at its relatively uninteresting eastern gateways. The interior, the West, "is the masterpiece of creation and the perfection of topography."[38] Even Thomas Swope, discussing the real estate boom, attributed it to the presence of speculators who had originally gone to Leavenworth but had discerned superior natural advantages in Kansas City.

The theory served well enough for outside consumption or perhaps to invigorate a dispirited booster at home, but what would happen if Van Horn's readers and hearers in Kansas City took him seriously? "Where a town has commanding geographical advantages . . . ," he wrote, "then eastern cities *must* and will build railroads for us, and for themselves—railroads to connect with our superior commercial advantages." If that were so, the local residents need not bestir themselves. Apparently, some people believed inaction to be their role, and Van Horn had to add a corollary to his theory. The Westport newspaper suggested that Kansas Citians "plume themselves too much upon the advantages of their location," and Van Horn once remarked editorially that "the man who first used the expression 'natural advantages' ought to have been hung."[39] Enterprise must at least cooperate intelligently with Nature, and so the editor continued to adjure his fellows in this strange, two-fold way: First, they had a compelling geographical superiority which practically assured their future, but second, they must never stop doing all they could

[38] To I. Cartwright, Kansas City, February 27, 1858, Archives of the Native Sons of Kansas City.

[39] Westport *Border Star*, May 27, 1859; *Journal*, January 26, 1860.

to influence destiny. Streets must be graded, merchants must lay in adequate stocks of goods, voters must approve internal improvement programs, and so forth. Above all, partisan politics must be avoided or else relegated to the secondary position they deserved; city building was not a party matter.

It was unfortunately necessary for Kansas Citians to guard certain vital interests in the political arena, but the importance of politics was mostly that of its negative threat. "Congress may wrangle . . . this man or that man may succeed," Van Horn told his readers, "and neither the success of the one nor the failure of the other will build our railroads, regulate our banks, maintain our public institutions, or protect our growing internal interests." Spalding agreed; ideally, he wrote in the *Annals*, most Americans should pay attention to business and let politics be the concern only of the politicians.[40] If local men could see the bounties offered them by Nature, if they would deliberately work to improve these bounties, and if they would stay clear of the bog of politics, who could set a limit to the possible expansion of Kansas City?

In their search for an imagery adequate to this vision, the enthusiastic Westerners turned, curiously enough, to Oriental comparisons. Benton had already described Kansas as "rich like Egypt," and now in his railroad articles Johnston Lykins called it "the modern Egypt." Somewhat later he remarked that the West would soon support "cities . . . greater than Babylon, Nineveh, or Thebes," and still later Van Horn in the course of his first visit to Kansas Territory declared that the region "at once awakens in the imagination the romance of Oriental lands, palm trees, groves of orange, pomegranate and fig, and the aroma of spices becomes palpable to the sense." The editor was reminded of "the pastoral lands of Palestine and the plains of Arabia."[41] One final comparison could be predicted from those just quoted, and Lykins had in fact already drawn it in one of his original articles: "The passage from Galveston to Lake Superior will be through an enchanted Eden." The Great American Desert had outlived the pe-

---

[40] *Journal*, July 25, 1860; Spalding, *Annals*, p. 10.

[41] The last two quotations from Lykins and Van Horn are in *Enterprise*, February 14, 1857, and *Journal*, May 29, 1858.

riod of its romantic attractions, and it was swiftly being replaced with something better, namely, the Garden of the World.

Nature may or may not have given the town at the river junction special advantages over its rivals, but certain advantages were indisputable. The place grew steadily between 1854 and 1861, and the period was one of sustained prosperity. The panic of 1857 and the ensuing depression seem not to have affected the business of Kansas City directly, although their adverse effect on railroad building must be considered. In fact, Kansas City had some built-in guarantees against outright depression during these years, guarantees which her editor summed up under the rubric "border money." There was $1,000,000 in annuity payments to the Indians, $2,000,000 spent annually by the Army in this region, plus $200,000 in mail contracts; to this substantial extent the federal government was underwriting prosperity on the western border. In addition, there was $1,500,000 from Southwestern freighting and $300,000 from emigrants in search of any of half-a-dozen western Eldorados, and neither of these sources diminished noticeably in or after 1857. The total of $5,000,000 was calculated for the area between Independence and Atchison; Kansas City was forced to share this money with the competing towns, but the city's share was enough to give a solid underpinning to the expansive visions of the local businessmen.[42]

Real estate reflected these visions for a time, and up to 1859 the city experienced a typical Western land boom. "Property has advanced very much here since last winter," wrote Thomas Swope from Kansas City in 1856. Late in the same year he had bought land for $250 an acre for which he was offered $300 an acre the very next day and $600 three weeks later. He could have received $300 per lot for downtown property which had cost him that much per acre. In 1857 levee lots which had originally been sold from the Prudhomme estate for $200 to $300 were bringing

---

[42] *Journal,* November 14, 1857; the article is reproduced in Miller, *History,* pp. 69-70.

$10,000. Thirty-six acres of land on the fringe of the town, bought in 1848 by Dr. F. A. Rice, were assessed at $47,000 in 1857, at $53,500 in 1858, and $61,600 in 1859. During the same three years, Thomas Smart's tract appreciated from $20,000 to $39,000.[43] These tax assessment figures do not, of course, represent the real value of the land any more than they represent cash in someone's pocket. They do give a conservative picture of the kind of transactions which served as a background accompaniment to the exalted eloquence of the local boosters.

It is also worth remembering that real-estate values stood mostly for future expectations, not real wealth. Many western towns before and after the 1850's went through similar booms with similar figures—Leavenworth at that very time presented a comparable, perhaps even a more impressive, scene. Realization on this property, at least realization on a scale with its owners' ambitions, still lay in the town's increasingly clouded future.

These ambitions were in marked contrast to the appearance of Kansas City in the prewar period. Its site, thought one visitor in 1856, was the least likely on which to build a city:

> Perpendicular hills, hills oval, hills ragged, long slopes, abrupt ascents, with ravines and gorges deep or yawning wide in wild confusion—all seemed to forbid house-building thereabout. . . . The houses fronting the river are reared against the bluff, with its summit far above the roofs; and in the rear end, even in the third story, you have the earthy odor peculiar to a newly dug cellar.

Another observer concluded that "in this western world" it took very little indeed to make a city, if this were to be called one: houses plastered against the bluff, narrow streets jammed with wagons, cattle wandering about in large numbers to be sold to

---

[43] Swope's letter is reproduced photographically in *Kansas City Star*, June 19, 1921; manuscript Tax Assessment Book for 1857 and 1858, in possession of Miss Frances Berenice Ford; *Journal*, August 4, 1859. On Smart, see file of biographical cards, Archives of the Native Sons of Kansas City, for material gleaned from many sources.

emigrants. Contrasted with the beautiful Missouri countryside, the scene by the landing was depressing.[44]

Young Henry Villard, going west in 1859, found Leavenworth to be twice as big as Kansas City and regarded the latter's pretensions as absurd. It could show no more than "a few dozen buildings, including some brick warehouses" on the least wholesome site for possible city growth that Villard had ever seen. The amenities of decent living were almost entirely lacking, according to a British traveler who found the food and drink terrible and his hotel room full of bedbugs. "I had not been long in Kansas City," he wrote, "before I began to find out that I had indeed left all the delicacies or luxuries of life behind me."[45]

In these respects, all the commentators agreed; the city "does not impress the beholder very favorably." But the more perceptive—or the more sympathetic—among them sensed the essential element which did not meet the eye. It was, after all, a new town, and if it was still rough and uncomfortable to live in, its inhabitants had nevertheless engrossed a third of the Missouri River steamboat trade and nearly all of the trade with the Southwest. The projectors had some basis for their projections. Alexander Majors recalled the appearance of Kansas City in the 1850's very clearly: the line of shabby-looking warehouses along the levee, the assorted saloons, dry-goods, and grocery stores strung out between Wyandotte and Walnut streets, the bluff behind them covered with weeds, brush, and dead trees. He agreed with everyone else who knew, that neither of the two hotels (around 1856) was any good. "To a young man, however," Majors went on,

> the levee with its three or four steamers, large piles of Mexican freight, prairie schooners, mules, greasers, Indians, negroes, mudclerks, Frenchmen, consignees, emigrants, old set-

[44] George C. Smith, *Life and Times of George Foster Pierce* (Sparta, Georgia: Hancock, 1886), pp. 281-82, quoting a letter Pierce wrote from Kansas City late in 1856; Miriam D. Colt, *Went to Kansas* (Watertown, N. Y.: L. Ingalls, 1862), pp. 34-36, quoting her own diary.

[45] Henry Villard, *Memoirs* (New York: Houghton Mifflin Company, 1904), I, 101-2; Grantley F. Berkeley, *The English Sportsman in the Western Prairies* (London: Hurst & Blackett, 1861), pp. 151-54.

tlers, tenderfeet, hotel drummers, brass bands, omnibuses, etc., presented attractions not easily resisted.

There were, perhaps, fortunes to be made in a town of about 2,000, in a year when 27,000 emigrants stopped at one hotel alone.[46]

First of all in the list of obstacles to the city's growth, there stood the frowning bluffs just back from the river. The city government was put to work carving streets through the bluffs—the most important of all the jobs undertaken by government in the early history of the city. The assessor was kept busy with regular and special tax levies, while the council steadily raised the tax rate on real property. The earliest ordinance on the subject set the rate at one-third of 1 per cent, which was raised to two-fifths of 1 per cent early in 1855, and to the constitutional limit of half of 1 per cent in November of that same year. Almost as soon as the state acted to allow a higher rate, the city took advantage of the ruling, and by April, 1860, landowners were paying 1 per cent of their assessed valuation.

The job of road-making explains the importance of the city engineer in this period and why his salary was the highest of any official; in 1860 he was given an assistant, who drew $60 a month. The engineer surveyed the hills and the street lines to be cut through them, and turned in a formidable report in 1855 outlining the project of grading four north-south streets back from the levee: Main, Delaware, Wyandotte, and Market. A cut forty-seven feet deep at the top of the hill was necessary to provide a grade of eight feet in a hundred for Main Street. At one point along Walnut, fifty-four feet of rocky soil had to be excavated below the surface of the bluff. Nevertheless, work began in 1856 and continued thereafter until the war interrupted it; in 1865 it was resumed. This work was under way when T. S. Case arrived in Kansas City in May of 1857; by September, Main Street was

---

[46] Tomlinson, *Kansas in 1858*, pp. 17-18; Tomlinson apparently saw what he wrote about, but the reader should be warned that he was not above plagiarism. On pp. 19-20, he makes his own the passage from a Van Horn editorial on "the plains of Arabia" which I have already quoted, note 40. Alexander Majors, *Seventy Years*, pp. 255-57.

twelve feet lower than it had been in May, and the owners of buildings along it had already been forced to add stories beneath the original foundations.

Along with the grading, culverts and sewers had to be built for the new streets, and this task, too, was well begun by 1860. It would be very difficult, and perhaps impossible, to determine how much this work cost, but Payne estimated many years later that between 1855 and 1860 all public improvements except those on the wharf came to over $150,000;[47] grading, culverts, and sewers certainly made up most of that amount.

Social materials might have seemed as intractable as the hills to observers in the 1850's who tried to gauge Kansas City's chances for growth. Poverty probably did not constitute much of a problem, due to the fairly chronic shortage of labor. What charity was felt to be necessary was supplied by private subscriptions, benefit balls, and the like.[48] But the *Journal*, which always tried to represent the city in the best possible light, reported street fights frequently and complained of the presence of gamblers and professional swindlers in town. The fights often arose in connection with drinking; in 1857 (when Case put the population at not over fifteen hundred), $135,000 worth of whiskey was sold in Kansas City. Van Horn, of course, seized on this figure to recommend the establishment of locally owned distilleries! Prostitution seems to have flourished, no doubt due to the transient character of much of the city's population. Van Horn warned local authorities to act before citizens arranged a lynching party for some of the criminals: "Save our city from the scenes which must follow an uprising of the people."[49]

The "local authorities" might or might not have sufficed in the specific instance; they consisted of a chief of police with a regular force of two men and empowered to hire up to ten more to serve on a night patrol. Social peace could not depend on official sanctions in Kansas City any more than it could later in

[47] In addition to the Ordinance Record Book already cited, see Payne's article in Conard, *Encyclopedia*, I, 619. See also the Case manuscript cited above.

[48] *Journal*, December 4, 1858; January 8, 1859.

[49] *Journal*, April 12, 1860.

cow towns such as Dodge City or Wichita. Time alone could bring about the kind of order which Van Horn asked for; the character of the community had to change. Railroads and trade figures might indicate city growth, but city growth meant far more than those tangibles. Customs and institutions must develop in which a more or less stable social intercourse could maintain itself. The original French fur-trading community did have its characteristic and well-organized forms of recreation and entertainment, but that community no longer existed. Even though many of the French-Canadians survived, living on low-lying, marshy ground near the river, except for a few like the Chouteaus, they had and could have no influence on the new city. One social structure had gone, and the community needed to substitute another for it. Already, well before the Civil War, movement in this important direction had set in; efforts were being made to supply the amenities which visitors had invariably found lacking, and it is a mistake to regard these efforts as in any way nonessential.

The increasing frequency with which balls, parties, and celebrations were held testifies to the emergence of a social order out of a chaos of individuals. Christmas, Easter, the anniversary of the Battle of New Orleans, the birthday of Thomas Paine—any event could and did serve as an excuse for some kind of an affair. Several hundred people, including some from neighboring towns, paid five dollars per ticket to attend a fancy-dress ball in Kansas City on Christmas Eve, 1858. Earlier in that same year the city officially celebrated Independence Day for the first time (E. M. McGee providing roast buffalo for the assembled throng), and still earlier the *Journal* had actually referred to one grand ball as a fitting finale to a brilliant social "season"! Expectations such as this word would excite might well have been disappointed at that time, but their appearance was an important milestone in the city's development.[50]

Regular entertainment facilities was another need which the would-be city felt, and the presence of chess clubs, photographic galleries, and lectures such as one before the Young Men's Mer-

[50] *Journal*, December 11, 1858; January 1, 1859; June 12, March 6, 1858.

cantile Library Association entitled "Life at Sea," gave evidence
that Kansas Citians would pay for a wide range of offerings.[51]
More important to most people were the traveling circuses which
passed through town. Over two thousand people attended one of
these—which unfortunately broke up in a fight.[52] More important
still, at least as far as city growth was concerned, was the theater.
Several transient companies gave performances in Kansas City
in the late 1850's and also gave Van Horn another topic on which
to admonish his clientele. The city, he wrote, could support a
permanent theater. Why? Because a theater is something that
real cities always support, a feature of civilization, so to speak;
hence, "our young metropolis" should have one.[53] In similar vein,
the newspaper urged support for the efforts of local men to
establish a library: "One of the most prominent indications of an
elevated intellect and superior moral culture of a community. . . .
The want of a good library containing judicious selections from
authors on all prominent subjects has long been felt in this
place."[54]

Efforts to found theaters and libraries in Kansas City came to
very little in the prewar years, just as efforts to build railroads
produced no tracks during the same period. In both cases, what
was done had "a prospective import." More could be said for a
few private schools which were established. The most successful
seems to have been a young ladies' seminary conducted by one
John H. Luther. Beginning with primary subjects such as spelling,
reading, and writing, the course worked through geography and
arithmetic and on into high-school Latin, Greek, and algebra. A
high-school semester cost fifteen dollars in tuition; if piano lessons
were desired, they cost an additional twenty-five dollars. This
school began its operations in September, 1857, and by 1859 almost one hundred girls were attending. Luther's school, along
with private Catholic and German schools, was exempted from
city taxation.[55]

51 *Journal*, January 29, February 26, 1859; February 27, 1858.
52 *Journal*, May 22, 1858.
53 *Journal*, April 30, May 14, and July 9, 1859.
54 *Journal*, February 13, 1858; May 7, July 21, 1859.
55 *Journal*, February 20, 1858; May 7, 1859; *ORB*, Book B, p. 66.

But private institutions became less and less adequate. They were relatively expensive, and they were not within easy distance of the most heavily populated neighborhoods in the city. The one public school was a district school and was entirely inaccessible for Kansas City children. A school census at the end of 1858 showed two hundred and seventy children in the age group seven to sixteen, of whom nine-tenths were not attending school. This fraction seems very high; a *Journal* correspondent two months later put the total figure at four hundred, of whom only half were in school and only one-fourth in school full time. He drew the best moral for time and place: "If our city would employ the most effectual means for a steady growth . . . let her do for education what other cities have done. . . ." Still, the local authorities were only debating how a schoolhouse might be put up when the Civil War burst upon all the city's shining prospects.[56]

Voluntary organizations, of course, played an important role in cementing a viable social structure in Kansas City. Mention of Protestant and Catholic churches, Masonic lodges, the Odd Fellows, and other associations began to appear more and more frequently in the paper's columns, especially with notices of meetings or social occasions. In this area of the city's life the two leading immigrant groups were both prominent. A Shamrock Benevolent Society was in existence by 1858; it seems to have met regularly, organizing St. Valentine's parties and balls celebrating Washington's birthday, as well as carrying out some charitable activities. The Germans were, if anything, more active than the Irish. They sponsored singing-society festivals, Schiller festivals, dancing parties, a sax-horn band which on one occasion even the Irish borrowed, and finally, a German-language newspaper. Groups like these, in the highly unsettled scene which the city presented in the 1850's, must have provided significant social ballast for the young community.

In all of these activities the local residents can be seen trying to tame themselves and their neighbors into some kind of cohesive group. If they had to agitate together for railroads, they had also to live together day by day. Such cooperation made

[56] *Journal*, February 2, 26, May 14, 1859.

necessary a great deal in the way of predictable behavior and mutually understood relationships. In their efforts to ornament, to provide a few "frills" for daily life, they were moving with sure instinct against those elements of their enterprise which struck visitors so unfavorably. In 1855 some kind of a tally revealed that there were 478 Kansas Citians; on the basis of the very conservative 1860 census figure, 4,418, it appears that almost a hundred newcomers arrived every month in the interim. In spite of the enormous difficulty which those figures make clear, the beginnings of community were equally clear by 1860.

Both the Irish and the Germans were toasted at the great 1857 Christmas banquet at which the sax-horn band supplied the music. An older foreign group was also to have received a toast and to have supplied a response. But—unconsciously pointing a symbolism as accurate as it was sad—the chairman was forced to explain that whoever was to have represented the old *voyageurs* had been unable to attend the feast.

William Miles Chick

Dr. Johnston Lykins

John Calvin McCoy

Kersey Coates

Robert Thompson Van Horn

Charles Kearney

Milton J. Payne

Dr. Theodore S. Case

City of Kansas
From Charles C. Spalding's *Annals of the
City of Kansas,* 1858

Camp Union, Tenth and Central Streets, 1861-1865

Westport Landing in 1848

North along Main from Tenth Street,
about 1868

The Levee in 1867
From Nathan H. Parker's *Gazetteer of Missouri,* 1867

North along Delaware Street from Third, 1869

East along Second Street from Wyandotte, 1869

East along Second Street to Main, 1869
Watkins Bank on right, Mechanics Bank (Stage Terminus)
on left; Shannon Home, top left

Charles C. Spalding   John W. Reid

Southwest Corner of Second and Main Streets, 1868
Watkins Bank, successor to Northrup & Chick, on corner

North along Main Street from Missouri Avenue, 1871

The Opening of the Hannibal Bridge, July, 1869

CHAPTER 5

"We Have Held On as a Community"

KANSAS CITY's early historians almost completely ignored the
Civil War epoch except for a highly exciting battle which
happened in and around Westport late in 1864. Even though this
dearth of contemporary records means that many first-hand
sources have been lost, it is both understandable and pardonable,
for the real history of the war in Kansas City does not fit at all
into the urban tableau which these writers strove to present. It is
instead a history of hopes dashed and former friends at gun-point
against each other. The early agreement to subordinate differences in order to build a city and to prosper with its growth was
not entirely destroyed during the war, but it could be supported
only by arms. The vision of wealth in "the Pastoral Garden of the
World" was seen suddenly to rest behind Union bayonets.

Kansas City had grown so rapidly that no one knew better
than roughly how many people lived there at the end of the
1850's. The federal census for 1860 listed 4,414 persons. The city
assessor for the previous year, S. W. Bouton, said he had counted
7,180 citizens in midsummer, 1859. Bouton may have included a
good many transients in order to pad his total, but it is reasonable to suppose that by the end of the winter of 1860-61, well over
5,000 people were calling the place their home. Fast as it was,
this growth was felt to be solid—not purely speculative, as was
alleged to be the case in the larger border towns, Leavenworth
and St. Joseph. The expansion was not "beyond the agricultural
population behind us—and we trust never to see it exceed its
proper ratio in this respect; for a solid substantial growth . . . is
much better than a feverish or forced increase based upon three
percent a month as is now the case with most western towns."
Railroad connections east and west and the occupation of Kansas
and Nebraska would make it possible to show even better figures
soon, or so it was hoped. "Tell them we are building a great city

157

here," wrote the editor of the *Western Journal of Commerce,* "and that the locomotive must drink from the Missouri at Kansas City in January, 1861, at which time [and in which case] Kansas City will contain a population of 18,000 inhabitants. . . ." It seemed clear to the writer that by 1864 there would be 28,000 Kansas Citians.[1]

This was not to be the case; instead of continued growth, the year 1864 was to see a Kansas City of shrunken population, dilapidated aspect, no railroads, and under military control and the imminent threat of having its streets and squares and warehouses turned into a battlefield for contending armies. The Missouri-Kansas troubles had given a brief glimpse of what could happen to the place when sectional rivalries flared into violence. Kansas City was situated on the border of a border state; Southern and Northern migrants met on its levee. To the extent that they became "Kansas Citians"—to the extent that they identified themselves with the exploitation of the Great West and invested their fortunes in it—they could submerge their differences in the pursuit of a common ambition. Real and enduring warfare, however, would strain this business compromise within the city; outside of it, in the encircling area, suspicion of the big town with its Easterners, Northerners, foreigners, and its everlasting pursuit of the almighty dollar would congeal into bitter hatred. On three sides the city would be surrounded by "bushwackers," and on the fourth, the westward side, their Kansan counterparts, the "jayhawkers," would roam at will. Guerrillas would lie in wait along the roads to the city, ravaging the countryside, burning farms, and making legitimate commerce all but impossible. The city would be strangled.

It is likely that most Kansas Citians tried not to think about the increasing probability of civil war. Certainly in 1859 and through most of 1860, the prospect of war was given little space in the local newspaper. Editor Van Horn made a point of playing

1 *Western Journal of Commerce,* July 21, August 25, 1859.

down political struggles as much as he could, and he gave more space to railroad projects, new stores and businesses, and general advice on the ways to win wealth in a Western city than he gave to conventions, platforms, elections, and threats of secession. In order to became a Missourian he had naturally become a Democrat, and he dutifully excoriated the sectional bias of the Republican party. In order to further the designs of his city, however, he was a Union Democrat. If abolitionists and Black Republicans took a position in politics which could be described only as perverse, the same was true of the Southern "fire-eaters." Both groups were unaccountably (and culpably) willing to sacrifice everyone else's interest to their own romantic notions.

In the election of 1860, Stephen A. Douglas was the only candidate for any practical man holding these views; impractical men with the same views might support John Bell and his Constitutional Union party. These two candidates stood for moderation and peace, and together they almost monopolized Kansas City's vote. Still, the extent of the Breckinridge Democrats' strength elsewhere in the county, with its implications of a more vigorous pro-Southern point of view, was noticeable. Lincoln's showing was the smallest of all for the whole county, although he ran ahead of Breckinridge in the city; the fact that there was any Lincoln showing at all was evidence of the disturbing influence which the rise of a city brought to the Missouri frontier. On election day, capitalist Kersey Coates mustered the Lincoln men, some of them fearful for their personal safety, and marched them in semimilitary order to the polling place. Of Lincoln's 191 Jackson County votes, Kansas City accounted for all but 6:

PRESIDENTIAL ELECTION OF 1860 IN KANSAS CITY[2]

Douglas	487
Bell	368
Lincoln	185
Breckinridge	131

At all events the national impact of this election hung like a

[2] *Journal,* November 8, 1860; see also the issue of November 15, for the county returns. In Jackson County, Bell got about 1,400 votes, Douglas slightly over 1,000, and Breckinridge slightly under 1,000.

pall over the local scene. "Nothing but the interposition of an over-ruling Providence," sighed the *Journal*'s editor when the count was in, could now fend off civil war.[3] This paper had consistently expressed a pro-Southern attitude in all respects save those which the near future would now show really to have counted. The choice between the ideals and rhetoric of South Carolina and Black Republicanism was not a welcome one to make, but the choice between secession and union was absolutely clear. Romantic politics and interesting constitutional theories, after all, built no railroads, supplied no immigrants, invested no capital, and developed no wests. The *Journal*, accustomed by now to hanging on to the essential core of the city-building consensus in the midst of dangerous political crosscurrents, blamed the nation's troubles on New England and then set out another and more important proposition which all Southerners could understand equally well: Only an overt violation of the Constitution by the newly elected administration would justify the South in forcible resistance. The implication was that nothing else would.[4] If any issues of the *Journal* were printed between March and May, 1861, they seem unfortunately not to have survived. Nevertheless, the firing on Fort Sumter clearly gave the Kansas City editor what he needed: an excuse for casting his lot with the much-maligned North.

Everyone in Kansas City did not agree with him, however, and therein lay seeds of disaster. Missouri remained a divided state throughout the war, and nowhere was division more bitter than on its western edge. Immediately across the line was Kansas, and between the two states a blood feud had begun years earlier. From Kansas came the raids of John Brown, James Montgomery, and Charles Jennison, with the political influence of James Lane in the background. Into Kansas went Charles Hambleton from southwest Missouri on his retaliatory mission in which he shot down a dozen helpless and unarmed Kansans. When the Civil War broke out, Montgomery, Jennison, and Lane were suddenly clothed in one or another degree with the authority of the Union,

[3] *Journal*, November 8, 1860.
[4] *Ibid.*

or of the State of Kansas. Western Missourians had to protect themselves somehow, and in so doing they were likely to find themselves opposing Federal or partly Federal forces—this regardless of their views on secession or slavery, assuming they had any views on those subjects. There followed inevitably the development of guerrilla warfare, in which men were shot from ambush and regular forces tried one after another measure of harsh and thorough repression in the effort to beat down the guerrillas. In the entire border region, the balance of forces was most delicate and the impact of the struggle most devastating in Jackson County.[5]

Whatever the effects of the war period were for other Western cities, in Kansas City it meant four years of uncertainty and almost unbearable tension. Throughout these years, most of the state of Missouri was a no man's land. Influential men in both Union and Confederate councils rated its strategic importance highly; as one Confederate sympathizer urged, Missouri leaned toward the South, but was surrounded on three sides by free states. "Missouri cannot be secured to the South," he told Jefferson Davis, "unless the country west of it is taken possession of and held by the Confederate States." Prompt action might gain not only Missouri but also Kansas and Colorado for the Confederacy.[6] But both sides employed their major forces elsewhere, and neither was ever able to consider Missouri securely in its pocket. The chief interest of the war in this state centered upon the relationship between military power and civilian authority and upon the long contest between regular troops and guerrilla fighters.

The state administration in 1860 had been elected on a Douglas platform, but Governor Claiborne Jackson and many of his friends entertained the idea of secession—or at the very least "neutrality"—from an early date. A convention was called in March, 1861, to consider the subject of Missouri's federal rela-

[5] Richard Brownlee, *Gray Ghosts of the Confederacy* (Baton Rouge: Louisiana State University Press, 1958), is excellent on the general subject of guerrilla warfare in the border region.

[6] F. J. Marshall, Marysville, Kansas, to Jefferson Davis, May 20, 1861, *Official Records, Union and Confederate Armies* . . . , Series I, Vol. XIII, 578-79. Hereafter cited as *ORR*.

tions; the western border elected pro-Union delegates, as did most
of the rest of the state, and the convention adjourned pro tempore,
having rejected all radical propositions. Jackson and his associates now needed to find other tactics, and these seemed to be
most readily available in the military field. With control of a
sizable armed force of their own, these men might keep Missouri
closed to Federal troops, even if they did not officially take the
state out of the Union.

The firing on Sumter, Lincoln's call for 75,000 Union volunteers, and probably the decision of Virginia to join the Confederacy simplified matters somewhat, at least by forcing the ines-
capable alternatives further into the open. Secession strength in
Missouri began to organize and move. On the western border a
band of Confederate sympathizers dashed into Liberty, in Clay
County, and seized the federal arsenal there. At about the same
time—late in April—Jackson called the legislature into special session and ordered the militia into summer encampment. At the
head of eight hundred men, with cannon supplied by the Confederate Government, the Governor was not far away from a
much larger federal arsenal in St. Louis. With the Regular Army
in the area under hesitant, almost somnolent, leadership, it
seemed inevitable that the arsenal would fall; with it would go
control of St. Louis, and most of the rest of Missouri as well.[7]

A good many Kansas Citians watched these events with
dread; the whole area around them was sure to become a sham-
bles if the passions of five years earlier were unleashed again. On
the border there were no mistaken notions of "the erring sisters"
departing in peace; secession meant war. What a war would
mean was set out graphically by Dr. Johnston Lykins in an open
"letter to the people" which the *Journal* printed on January 31,
1861. Lykins was Southern by birth and sympathy; his wife was
later forced to leave the city because she favored the Confederacy
so vocally. Still, the land-developing, railroad-planning, city-
building Lykins, for twenty years identified with the growth of

[7] The opening of the Civil War in Missouri can best be studied in the first
few chapters of Brownlee, *op. cit.*, and in Wiley Britton, *The Civil War on the
Border* (New York: G. P. Putnam, 1899), I.

Kansas City, could see nothing attractive in the prospect before him as of early 1861. War meant not only the destruction of the beautiful American idea, as Lykins painted it, of a land "where under his own vine and fig tree, the citizen may enjoy the fruits of his labor, with none to molest him or make him afraid. . . ." War would also bring anarchy and pillage "and subject us to the rule of the tyrant, the robber, the pirate—and our wives, daughters and mothers to the brutality and lust of fiends in human shape. *Do not say this cannot be*—that this is far off—that we shall not see it. . . ." Lykins spared his readers nothing: towns would be sacked, cities destroyed, farms burned, banks robbed. Already, he computed conservatively, the very threat of secession had cost Missourians about $100,000,000 in the decline of property values. Calling attention to his status as an old citizen, Lykins concluded with a strong pro-Union appeal.

So, too, during the election of the "federal relations" convention already mentioned, the *Journal* insisted that only the most positive pro-Union candidates be supported. Its editor backed up Lykins' adjurations with figures of his own, showing the collapse of values which readers could expect close upon the heels of secession.

Deploring secession, however, was one thing; taking action against it when it stood on the threshold was quite another. While Kansas City's Union element agonized over decisions, feeling for the most part no love for either side in the North-South conflict, the secessionists went vigorously ahead with their plans. Across the state, in St. Louis, the Civil War had already arrived. A quick reorganization of federal forces put them under decisive Union control; Governor Jackson's men had been surrounded and disarmed, and the St. Louis arsenal saved. Jackson immediately cried out that Missouri was being invaded by a hostile army and asked for fifty thousand volunteers to repulse the invader. Command of state forces was given General Sterling Price, a popular figure with something of a military reputation dating from the Mexican War. The legislature now gave Jackson generous appropriations to support his "defensive" preparations.

In the area around Kansas City, events were taking an ominous direction. A former Westport editor had moved his plant to Kansas City, and was issuing enthusiastically pro-Southern news and comment in a paper called the *Star*.[8] In neighboring Independence, three companies of volunteers had answered Governor Jackson's call. One company invaded Kansas City and seized from the Chouteau warehouse a large consignment of arms destined for New Mexico. The city was about to be invaded and secured for the Confederacy; about a thousand men gathered for this purpose at a farm on the road between Independence and Westport. "It is well known," wrote the correspondent for an Atchison newspaper, "that Union men are leaving St. Joseph and Kansas City on account of the ascendancy in those places of fanatical pro-slavery men." According to a letter in the *Leavenworth Times*, Kansas City was fairly churning:

> Secession stalks abroad unrebuked and Unionism, with its majority of three to one, succumbs in terror. . . . Republicans are scarce and scary, and many are leaving the city. Business enjoys a sweet repose, and the classic and sublime spectacle of a city in ruins seems about to present itself in unwholesome shape to our view.

One man who tried to publish a Republican paper in Kansas City was driven out; several large mercantile firms had moved or were about to move their offices.[9]

But some of the men, at least, who had sunk every hope into Kansas City's future had not done so in order to see the prize snatched from their nerveless fingers. Backed into a corner, they fought to save their investment, and whether they liked it or not this meant that they fought for the Union. They rallied around

---

8 No surviving issues of the *Star* have been found; its items were frequently clipped in the *Journal* during these days. Some time in 1861 the editor, whose name was H. M. McCarty, moved his enterprise to Independence, where it was later destroyed by Union soldiers.

9 *ORR*, Ser. I, Vol. I, 652; Atchison *Weekly Champion*, May 4, 1861; *Leavenworth Times*, May 2, 3, 1861. See also *ORR*, Ser. I, Vol. I, 661: "Union men are leaving Missouri in swarms, and unless matters change within a week a reign of terror will exist about St. Joseph." General Harney, in St. Louis, received appeals from Unionists who were being threatened "more especially at and in the vicinity of Springfield, Hannibal, Saint Joseph, and Kansas City." *ORR*, Ser. I, Vol. III, 379-80.

R. T. Van Horn, who was elected mayor in April, 1861, in a close contest against the incumbent, Dr. G. M. B. Maughs. Governor Jackson's friends in the legislature now took a hand in the city's affairs by divesting its new mayor and council of all police powers.[10] Van Horn quietly left the city and crossed the state to St. Louis, where he explained his difficult situation to F. P. Blair and General Nathaniel Lyon. The upshot was a major's commission for Van Horn in an improvised organization called the Enlisted Missouri Militia, with authorization to enroll a Union battalion in Kansas City.

At the same time, Captain W. E. Prince, of the Regular Army at Fort Leavenworth, was introduced to Van Horn, and the two men concerted plans to stem the tide of Confederate success which threatened to engulf Kansas City. By the end of May, Van Horn was back home; what he could not do as mayor he could now do as major. Meanwhile, men and guns had been loaded onto a steamboat at the big fort up river. On June 9 it dropped down to Kansas City. Secession flags were waving everywhere, and as the boat pulled up to the levee a motley crowd rushed to board it. They backed up quickly, however, as Union troops with fixed bayonets, led by Captain Prince, marched down the gangplank and formed quietly on the wharf. Horse-drawn cannon followed them off the boat, and the whole force moved off along Main Street and about the city.

Prince stayed long enough to disperse the secession force and to protect Van Horn while the Enrolled Missouri Militia signed up, and then returned to Fort Leavenworth.[11] Having organized his force, Van Horn almost immediately had to use some of it; he marched south and joined some Kansas troops who were trying to break up a large band of guerrilla fighters near Harrisonville. On his return he learned that secessionists were looting banks in some towns in the vicinity, so he confiscated

10 *Laws of the State of Missouri*, 21st General Assembly (Jefferson City: W. G. Cheeney, 1861), pp. 64-67.

11 These events are described in the typescript of a speech by Van Horn before the Loyal Legion, June, 1907; Van Horn Papers, Archives of the Native Sons of Kansas City, City Hall, Kansas City, Missouri.

all the cash in Kansas City's two branch banks (the Union and the Mechanics), amounting to $143,000, and sent it to Leavenworth for safekeeping.[12]

During most of the war Kansas City was practically a beleaguered and usually an occupied town. Its trade was crippled, and those of its earlier residents who remained in town began to accuse each other of treachery and rebellion; much property changed hands as owners moved from the city or sold land to raise money to satisfy taxes. All the while, differences between the city and the country grew sharper, until by the end of the war Kansas City was something of a cultural island, isolated as to opinions and motives from the farms and smaller towns around it.

Part of this isolation was due to military uncertainties. In the best of circumstances, the Federal army could secure only the cities—Kansas City and usually Independence—but it never controlled the rolling, farm-dotted lands which surrounded them. Even this control of the cities, however, was far from sure, and on more than one occasion the Federal authorities were ready to give up Kansas City and retire to Fort Leavenworth. Thus in August, 1861, as General Price pushed north toward the Missouri River, it was thought that when he reached it he might turn west. It might then be necessary, Prince wrote to Van Horn,

> to withdraw your force from Kansas City; you will therefore hold it in readiness to move immediately . . . and inasmuch as the means of communication with your place is daily, so regulate the amount of supplies in your camp as would be most economical to the Government should it become necessary to abandon the place.

Again, the worried Van Horn heard from Leavenworth that no reinforcements could be sent him: "You must retreat on Wyandotte, thence to this place, if you cannot hold your own."[13]

12 Van Horn to Prince, August 24, 1861, Van Horn Papers, State Historical Society of Missouri, Columbia, Missouri; see Joseph Klassen, "Kansas City's Van Horn" (unpublished M.A. thesis, University of Kansas City, 1958), pp. 88-89.

13 Van Horn Papers; cited by Klassen, op. cit., pp. 87-88.

As it happened, General Price did not strike at Kansas City, but rather at Lexington, about fifty miles downstream. Van Horn's Kansas City force, along with another from St. Joseph, was sent to help the defenders; nevertheless, Lexington fell on September 20, after siege and a sharp attack. (Van Horn and the other survivors got back to Kansas City about a month later by virtue of an exchange of prisoners.) Shortly after he had taken Lexington, the Confederate general retired from the area and retreated into Arkansas.

The Price campaign serves to illustrate the situation of Missouri in the war period. Each side could thrust deeply into the other's territory, but neither had the requisite numbers and equipment to hold the ground taken. Missourians came to talk of the year's five seasons: spring, summer, Price's raid, fall, and winter. Federal authorities did their utmost to secure railroad and river communications between the larger places in the state and devoted the rest of their forces to futile efforts at stamping out the guerrilla warfare which settled in as the normal condition, especially on the western border.

The engagements between the contending armies were far from the worst threat in Kansas City's Civil War trial. Much worse was the guerrilla action, and this, of course, is tied in directly with the state of opinion and emotion in the border area. For four years bands of irregulars roamed the country around Kansas City, robbing wagon trains, destroying bridges, firing on railroad trains and steamboats, harrying Federal troops and Union sympathizers. These bands were, in general, supported by the rural and small-town populace, which quartered and fed them and misled the pursuing troops. Kansas City's safety lay in quelling the guerrillas, and the guerrillas could be reached only through the civilians who helped them; thus an economic problem became a military problem and then, immediately, a political problem.

No one will ever know to what extent the popular state of mind which sustained the guerrilla bands in the border counties was prosecession and to what extent it was simply anti-Kansas. Charles Jennison, for example, had now become a colonel; under his command, in the summer of 1861, was the newly organized Seventh Kansas Cavalry. Ordered to Kansas City in September, it marched down from Leavenworth, raiding as it came. The Kansans were apparently convinced that all Missourians were avidly pro-Confederate and that the highest ideal any of them possessed was that of chattel slavery. Swinging into Independence, the Seventh paused. Commanding the regiment at the time was Major D. R. Anthony, a radical Republican editor who had settled in Leavenworth in the 1850's during the Kansas conflict. Anthony summoned the inhabitants of Independence to gather in the public square; here, he read them a lecture on their sins, promised dire retaliation in case any Unionists should be harmed, confiscated fifteen wagonloads of property owned by proslavery citizens, and led his detachment on to Kansas City.[14]

Anthony's action set a pleasant pattern for political warfare in and around Kansas City, and it was not an isolated event. James Lane was now a general, and while Price had moved north through Missouri in July and August, Lane had marched along the state line just west of the Confederate army, leading a column of Kansans. By the time Lane's force got to the river, according to a recent scholarly study, "a million dollars worth of property had been stolen or destroyed, and Osceola, one of the largest towns in western Missouri, had ceased to exist." In July, when Major Van Horn reached Harrisonville, he found that the Kansans, with whom his command was to cooperate, had already looted most of the stores in the place.[15]

Such raiding, continuing as it did throughout the war, shaped life in Kansas City. Kersey Coates's daughter recalled many instances at night when she and her mother retired to the basement of their house for safety, the men being out on patrol duty. "Every event of this stormy period," she wrote,

> was of gruesome coloring. The cannon was constantly repeating the signal of alarm given by the pickets stationed on the outskirts of the city. . . . Indiscriminate shooting continued

[14] S. N. Fox, "The Story of the Seventh Kansas," *Kansas Historical Collections*, VIII (1903-1904), pp. 13-49.

[15] Brownlee, *op. cit.*, pp. 38-39, 43.

among the guards, a bullet whizzing through our bedroom one morning at the break of day. Evidence of war was on every side.

According to a journalist visiting the city in the summer of 1863, there was not a safe road leading into Kansas City; everyone carried arms and slept with revolvers under pillows. City property values had depreciated by half. "One not acquainted, by practical experience, with the state of this society," he wrote, "cannot realize the constant insecurity for life and property felt by the citizens."[16]

It was a special kind of war, described by one resident during those years as "organized assassination modified by theft and arson. . . ." Ambush made the short ride from Kansas City to Independence extremely dangerous, even in convoy. Coates became a militia colonel, and on at least one occasion was ordered to picket all the roads leading out of the city. "I can see no other way," wrote his superior officer, "to arrange the efficient protection of the town at present." Within the city, the business community seemed to be either pro-Confederate or else almost paralyzed. Van Horn reported that he could get no help "on the part of the men of wealth here," and conceded that the only support the government could find was that induced by the power of its guns. High society in Kansas City was either secessionist or neutral, while the only real pro-Union strength was supplied by the Germans, the Irish, and those Americans who had come from Northern states. "I am totally surrounded," he wrote, "by a hostile sentiment, and by a hatred of the government, which no county in South Carolina can surpass."[17]

Meanwhile, he and his men were hastily fortifying an area about 200 feet square at the corner of Tenth and Central streets.

[16] Laura Coates Reed (ed.), *In Memoriam, Sarah Walter Chandler Coates* (Kansas City: Franklin-Hudson, n.d.), pp. 56-57; hereafter cited as *Coates Memorial;* Lela Barnes (ed.), "An Editor Looks at Early-Day Kansas: The Letters of Charles Monroe Chase," *Kansas Historical Quarterly,* XXVI (Summer, 1960), 118.

[17] *Coates Memorial,* pp. 56-57; Daniel Geary, "War Incidents in Kansas City," *Kansas Historical Collections,* XI (1909-10), 287-88; *Coates Memorial,* Col. J. H. Ford to Coates, May 2, 1864, pp. 181-84; Van Horn to Prince, August 24, 1861, *op. cit.,* also Van Horn's 1907 speech before the Loyal Legion, *op. cit.*

Built during the last ten days of June, 1861, the place came to be called "Camp Union"; it could house three companies, and across Tenth Street were forage yards and a stable. For four years Camp Union housed various volunteer and regular units, the normal complement being about 270 men. The whole neighborhood was given over to military drill.[18]

Union strength had begun to show, and over the long pull its staying power would tell. Without an important Federal fort within thirty miles of Kansas City, however, the subsequent history of the place would have been vastly different. As things were, the city remained more or less an armed camp in the center of a region which became more and more strongly anti-Union. Journalists quickly noted a difference between Kansas City, where Union forces dominated, and Independence, where (as one of them wrote) "I have yet to see a Union man in the place." The city-county tension, now and then explicit during the border troubles, came to be notorious. In 1862, to choose one example, the *Journal's* editor was arguing that Kansas City might be willing to bargain with other sections in the same electoral district for the nomination of candidates for the legislature; any man chosen, however, "must be free of all prejudice against this city. . . ." Later in the same year Van Horn ran against one M. Trefren for the state senate; in Jackson County he piled up a better than 2-to-1 majority, while in Cass County his majority was less than 10 votes out of more than 300 cast.[19]

There were, of course, Unionists in Independence, but they were apparently cowed into silence. Once the *Journal's* editor received a strange-looking package in the mail which he hesitated to open, fearing that it might be an infernal machine. It proved to be two bottles of wine, with this anonymous note: "Accept these . . . from the unconditional Union men of Independence. Please hit the traitors again."[20]

The city found itself in the middle of warring forces, as it

18 T. S. Case, in *Coates Memorial*, p. 186.

19 *Leavenworth Times*, July 21, 1861; *Daily Kansas City Journal of Commerce*, April 30, December 5 and 7, 1862. Hereafter cited as *DJC*.

20 *DJC*, July 3, 1862.

had five years before. There were the pro-Southerners at home who must be put down; at the same time, there were the Lanes and the Jennisons across the line in Kansas, whose radicalism would just as soon raze Kansas City as name it. Again there was the same platform-making job to be done, a reputation to be published. Since Van Horn was in the Army (and, in 1862, on his way to Shiloh and thence to the state legislature), his place at the *Journal* was now filled by his earlier partner, David K. Abeel. Although lacking Van Horn's talent, Abeel was nevertheless an effective writer, and he did his level best to keep the *Journal* what it had been, the verbal representative of Kansas City's general welfare. The task became more difficult as time passed and the war forced moderate men toward immoderate positions.

Abeel took up where Van Horn had left off, attacking with even-handed impartiality both the Missourians whose loyalty to the Union was dubious and the Kansas brigands who cloaked their jayhawking under Union authority.[21] At the same time he stressed the importance of maintaining a good reputation in Kansas where, after all, the future of Kansas City lay. "Observation has assured us," he wrote, "that a mistaken notion prevails widely throughout Kansas and southern Missouri, respecting the political orthodoxy of Kansas City." Anything which might correct this notion—such as forthright support for the Federal troops or a spectacular patriotic display on July 4—drew Abeel's hearty approval.[22]

But political orthodoxy during civil wars is a tricky proposition, and Abeel found himself less and less able to define it adequately. Starting from almost Lincolnesque defense of the Union pure and simple, he went on to emancipation, confiscation of rebel property, and increasingly exigent demands for decisive military policy which, to be effective, had to be radical. As he defined his position more closely, he lost friends and alienated sympathy. From the first, Abeel had attacked editorially "the

---

[21] See almost any issue of the *Journal* during the months of April and May, 1862.

[22] *DJC*, May 30, 1862.

prominent secesh of our city," although he did not mention names. Even this general censure got him into trouble, and although it is impossible to document local criticisms of him, it is clear that they were made, and that they grew louder. In the summer of 1862 he had to defend himself against the charge that, by washing dirty linen in public, he was in effect slandering Kansas City.

A new daily paper was started (of which we have no copies) which apparently tried to capitalize on the unpopularity of Abeel's references to "rebel sympathizers in our midst." Its prospectus (quoted in the *Journal*, June 18, 1862) announced the enterprise as firmly pro-Union but disclaimed the presence of even one "sympathizer with bushwhacking among our respectable citizens." This, according to Abeel, turned on the definition of "respectable," but he welcomed the appearance of the new paper, which was called *The Press*, apparently willing that it should make the first move. Nevertheless, from this point on—until he had to suspend publication in August—the *Journal* editor was almost constantly defending his policy against implicit criticism that it was bad for Kansas City to advertise the presence of anti-Union sentiment. "If there are no secession or bushwhacking sympathizers in our midst," he asked, "why are certain individuals grumbling and growling about the course of the *Journal*?" Abeel asked only that citizens should speak out clearly "for or against the measures they desire to have adopted to restore *security* to our business interests."

The Press obviously took some business away from the *Journal;* ten of its regular advertisers disappeared from *Journal* columns. Most of them were relatively small firms, but they included a fair-sized grocery establishment, an important lumber dealer, and one of the largest river-traffic agents in the area. As already mentioned, the *Journal* was forced to suspend publication in August, while *The Press* apparently continued for a few weeks thereafter, and then it disappeared.

Meanwhile, an event occurred which revealed starkly the dilemmas of a moderate position. On August 12 a Leavenworth paper carried a startling rumor that the guerrillas had rallied in force and had taken the town of Independence; an assault on Kansas City was expected momentarily. The part of the rumor which concerned Independence proved to be entirely true, despite the fact that the town was garrisoned by five hundred regular troops under Col. J. T. Buel. Partly due to Buel's lack of preparedness, he was completely surprised on the afternoon of August 11 by a force of about a thousand bushwhackers from the countryside. After a brief and one-sided skirmish, Buel surrendered. The guerrillas took what provisions they could carry and left. As soon as the news of this daring thrust reached Kansas City, all business was suspended, and the Union men formed hastily for defense. Reinforcements reached the city from Johnson County and from Fort Leavenworth the next day, and the danger of an attack subsided. But the rebels were not caught; they simply melted into the landscape; at any time they might descend again. "Reason tells us quite plainly," wrote a Leavenworth editor, "that the capture of Kansas City will be almost, if not quite, as easy. . . . After Kansas City comes Leavenworth."[23]

The effect of these events was to drive the Kansas City leadership toward an ever more radical position in order to retain its connection with the Union—and its hopes of benefiting from that connection. In the 1850's it had been possible to find some middle ground; that was no longer the case. Even as late as the summer of 1862, Abeel was trying to define a moderate pro-Union stance. The war was unfortunate, of course, but some good results might be expected: greater democracy, an increasing importance of the common man in politics, and an accelerated exploitation of the natural resources of the United States: "A new energy will be given to enterprise in all the territory comprising those [at present Confederate] States. . . . We have ample assurances that the present war will pay."[24] Abeel consistently commended the conservative Union utterances of the district's Congressional representative, Thomas L. Price.

But in order to win, one needed a forthright, decisive military

---

[23] See Britton, op. cit., pp. 314-25; Leavenworth Times, August 15, 1862; also Freedom's Champion (Atchison), August 16, 1862.

[24] DJC, June 12, 1862.

program. In order to get such a program, it appeared, one had to root out the men like Col. Buel in the Federal Army's hierarchy. To do this was necessarily to become "radical." Abeel moved steadily leftward, especially after the Independence raid. In doing so he failed to keep his footing on the slippery ground of city politics.

The parlous condition of the Missouri border had excited a good deal of attention by this time in the upper councils of the Union forces. General Benjamin Loan, in charge of what was called in 1862 "the District of Central Missouri," reported to his superior from Lexington, just east of Jackson County, that

> the condition of the Union citizens in this county could not well be worse than it is. They dare not remain on their farms. . . . It will require very prompt and severe measures to correct these wrongs, but I propose doing it at once, and you may prepare yourself for a vast amount of unnecessary complaining on the part of the erring brethren when the correction is applied.

Loan, as it happened, probably looked forward to the application he envisaged; he was a St. Joseph resident, and one of the few fire-breathing radicals on the border. Still, his notions were cogent as the situation deteriorated, and the much less vindictive General Samuel P. Curtis, in St. Louis, approved Loan's letter, remarking in answer to it, "I trust you may be able to create some terror in the rebel camps near Lexington."[25]

One idea for pacifying the countryside, which had already been tried in St. Louis County, was that of levying special penal assessments on Confederate sympathizers in districts where guerrillas were active. The proceeds were used to equip loyal militia and reimburse Unionists who had suffered from bushwhacking depredations. In June, 1862, it was decided to apply this system to the entire state. In each subdivision of the District of Missouri, the commanding officer was to appoint county boards, "selected from the most respectable and reliable citizens of the

25 ORR, Ser. I, Vol. XIII, 753-54; Loan to Maj. Gen. S. R. Curtis, October 20, 1862; Curtis to Loan, October 23, 1862, ibid., p. 758.

county," which were in their turn to list the names of all in the area whose loyalty was doubtful. A schedule of assessments was established, providing for payment of five thousand dollars for each Unionist killed, one thousand to five thousand dollars for each one wounded, and full value for all property destroyed in raids. These amounts were to be raised by levies on the wealth of the listed inhabitants, pro rata.[26]

Acting under the provisions of this scheme, various Missouri localities proceeded with assessment orders; the sum of five thousand dollars was levied on Boonville, fifteen thousand on Lexington, fifteen thousand dollars on Saline County, and so on. General Loan pushed the policy enthusiastically. On the eve of a trip to Independence, he explained to Curtis that one object of his actions was

> to break up the social relations here. Good society . . . as it is termed, is exclusively rebel. Another motive is that the traders, merchants, and bankers, who transact the business of the country, are all traitors . . . and are making large fortunes as the reward for their disloyalty. . . . In Jackson, Cass, Johnson and Saline, the same course will be pursued until none but loyal men will be allowed to remain at large in the country. . . .

On November 17, 1862, the blow fell on Jackson County: According to Special Order 37, District of Central Missouri, the sum of fifteen thousand dollars was levied "upon the disloyal inhabitants of Jackson County," of which half was to support the militia and half to relieve destitute families of Union soldiers. Colonel William R. Penick, commanding at Independence, was ordered to provide for the assessment in the regular way.[27]

The difficulty of enforcing the measure was increased by the circumstance that clear polarities, such as radical-conservative, Republican-Democrat, unionist-secessionist, could not define the tangle of personal and political relationships that existed among the men who wanted to preserve their boom town on the Mis-

[26] *Ibid.*, pp. 11-12, 446-47.

[27] *Ibid.*, pp. 806-7, 800.

souri border. Coates and Van Horn both exerted themselves now as well as during the entire war period to protect associates who were—justly or unjustly—suspected of Confederate leanings. They did this at some risk to themselves, given the character of that period. Coates, for example, worked closely with George Caleb Bingham, a Union Democrat and already a well-known painter, who had moved to Kansas City shortly before the war and had since become state treasurer in the Gamble administration.[28] Coates and Bingham tried to get commercial restrictions on Kansas City lifted; they hoped that radical Army officers might be transferred out of Kansas City. Interestingly enough, just before the assessment order was issued, they were lobbying for the appointment of Frank Foster to a responsible military position.[29]

The assessment faced these men with a difficult problem. If enforced, it would have blasted the inner group of Kansas City's business and social leadership into fragments. William Gilliss, W. H. Chick, William Gregory, F. H. and W. J. Jarboe, E. C. McCarty, A. B. H. McGee, Mrs. Benoist Troost, J. C. Ranson, and John Calvin McCoy—these were only the most prominent of many well-known Kansas City names on the list. (McCoy's prorated share, $243, was the highest.)[30] Coates and Foster went into action to block enforcement. They reached Governor Gamble at the state capital; through Milton J. Payne, they reached General Curtis in St. Louis. Through one Abram Comingo, a Jackson County Union Democrat, they sent the case all the way to Washington, besieging the Missouri Congressional delegation, the President, and the Secretary of War.[31]

28 There are several book-length studies of Bingham. See, most conveniently, the sketch in H. L. Conard (ed.), *Encyclopedia of the History of Missouri* (New York: Southern History Company, 1901), I, 274-75, and Bingham's letters published in *Missouri Historical Review*, XXXII (1937-38), XXXIII (1938-39).

29 See the letters from Bingham to Coates on these matters in *Coates Memorial*, pp. 181 ff.

30 *DJC*, December 26, 1862; presumably Abeel published the list as a Christmas gift for the assessees.

31 The chronology is not at all clear in the antiassessment struggle; see *Coates Memorial*, p. 60; also six confiscated letters relating to Comingo's mission published in the *DJC*, March 26, 1863.

With this sort of agitation on their behalf, it is not surprising that many of the assessees did not pay their fines. Editor Abeel, who had by now become an enthusiastic radical, fumed against the obstructive action. He threatened the reluctant assessees with military coercion; he published their names in his paper; he applauded when several of them (including Gilliss, Ridge, Riddlesbarger, and McCarty) were thrown into jail one evening, and lamented when they were unaccountably released the next day.

But the opposition was too strong for Abeel, and too well organized. On January 13, 1863, orders came from St. Louis to suspend collection of the assessment, and a week later the Secretary of War instructed General Curtis to leave the suspension in effect until further orders—which never arrived. Some money had already been collected; no one knows what happened to it. Special Order 37 was never revoked; it simply lapsed.[32] The controversy and the bitterness which the surviving records of the assessment highlight, however, were neither born with it nor did they die with it.

The radicals must have smarted under their failure with the assessment. Their target from now on was Kersey Coates, who had marshaled the straggling Lincoln voters in Kansas City only three years earlier! Abeel claimed editorially that sinister influences had given Coates his colonelcy in the Enrolled Missouri Militia, "for the great majority of the men he commands utterly repudiate him. . . ." General Loan telegraphed St. Louis headquarters that he expected serious danger in Kansas City from widespread Unionist opposition to Coates.[33] But radicalism threatened a town-building brotherhood which had grown over the past years and by 1863 was much stronger than party politics. Abeel had gone too far; he had tangled with the wrong opponent. In his hands, the *Journal* had failed to find the consensus platform, and it no longer spoke for whatever Kansas City was being shaped to mean. During the first three months of 1863 the editor continued his attack on Coates, a man who protected rebels. He

[32] *DJC*, December 25 to January 21, 1862-63; *ORR*, Ser. I, Vol. XXII, Pt. 2, 17-18, 42-43, 47-48, 64.

[33] *DJC*, January 28, 1863; *ORR, op. cit.*, p. 111, February 14, 1863.

mentioned a rumor that Coates was about to start a local paper of his own. Then came a rather dramatic end to the story: Toward the close of March, Abeel announced that he had sold the *Journal* to one T. Dwight Thatcher of Lawrence, Kansas. In April the change-over was made; Thatcher took over the *Journal*, the attacks on Coates stopped abruptly, and David Abeel left Kansas City.

In this troubled situation the Kansas City businessmen who remained in the city through the war (and these included most of the important landowners) were straining themselves simply to hang on. While they fended off secessionist temptations on one hand and pro-Northern radicalism on the other, the blunt physical facts of warfare threatened to paralyze all their commercial activities. Population shrank; accurate figures are not available, but the estimate generally given is that Kansas City lost about half its people during the war years—the boom process had reversed.[34] Streets and buildings could not be maintained; a series of fires destroyed four of the largest warehouses, and for a time fire insurance could not be had on any terms. A Leavenworth correspondent described Kansas City as "completely dead, so far as business is concerned, and in this respect [the place] presents a marked contrast to its appearance in '56 when I first visited it. A perfect Sabbath reigns there. . . ." Property was for sale cheap, much of it for unpaid taxes. Normal municipal operations were barely sustained; the *Journal* once chided officials for allowing a corpse to remain unburied all day on the levee.[35]

All constructive action blocked for the time, the Kansas Citians could only try to keep possibilities open so that their urban enterprise might have a fighting chance against its rivals whenever the war ended. The Chamber of Commerce was reactivated in July, 1862; Coates was president, John C. Gage recording secretary, and T. S. Case corresponding secretary (all these men had

34 T. S. Case, in *Coates Memorial*, p. 169.

35 *Leavenworth Times*, June 16, 1861, April 6, 1862; *DJC*, May 2, 15, 31, 1862.

come to town after 1855). The chamber quickly arranged to print a map in the *Journal* which suitably demonstrated the city's geographical advantages for railroad building. It also lobbied among the military authorities to ensure adequate protection on the Santa Fe trail. The chamber also urged local merchants to advertise regularly in the newspapers of towns in southeastern Kansas.[36] These activities were clearly holding operations. Among the city's chances, railroads made up by far the most important, and something more on this subject will be said in the next chapter. Now, while the laying of track east of the city had to be deferred, the only thing to do was to keep reminding Easterners that Kansas City existed and could serve them well when the time came—and also to remind local people that, no matter how dark the present might be, they still held a counter for the future. "Certain parties," Abeel had written, obviously referring to rival town interests,

> may be surprised to find that the very occurrences of this war, and the contact of certain politicians with the despised "natural advantages" of this city, may have been the very thing that has operated to secure to us the splendid prize which otherwise we might have fought [for] in vain.[37]

The traditional Santa Fe trade (actually a regional, Southwestern trade) had also to be protected, as far as this was possible. The chaotic condition of Kansas, however, where the Confederacy enlisted Indian support as well as that of guerrillas like Quantrill, made it difficult. Kansas City unquestionably lost, at least temporarily, a substantial portion of its former commerce of the prairies. Much of it switched to Leavenworth, where an editor discovered agents of W. H. Chick in 1862 trying to lure some of the Southwesterners back to Kansas City. According to

36 Transcript. "Minutes of the Chamber of Commerce, 1862-63," pp. 26-30, Archives of the Native Sons of Kansas City. Kansas City's lobbying in 1864 is reflected in *ORR*, Ser. I, Vol. XXXIV, Pt. 2, 486-87, 500-501; Pt. 3, 51 (a personal letter from Gen. E. B. Brown to Van Horn); Pt. 3, 614; Pt. 4, 433.

37 *DJC*, June 26, 1862.

the best figures there was a sharp drop in the value of New Mexican goods received at Kansas City:

1860	$386,172
1861	284,007
1862	205,308
1863	346,641

The closest student of the subject has concluded that after a disastrous decline to 1862, the city recovered steadily in this field until by 1864 it was probably sharing the Southwestern trade half-and-half with Leavenworth.[38]

Ever since the middle 1850's the newer and nearer hinterland, that in Kansas, had become more and more obviously important to the city. During the war more newspaper space was given to this potential breadbasket than to the wagon trains on the Santa Fe road. Business and politics were hard to separate here. Kansas was settled largely by staunch pro-Unionists; they might prefer to trade at Leavenworth, with their "own" people, so to speak. Soon after the outbreak of war, a Topeka newspaper expressed hope that Kansans, "who have heretofore done business with the merchants of Kansas City, will transfer their favors to a city on their own soil, that heartily sympathizes with them in their love of the Flag. . . ."[39] This was one of the pressures which drove the *Journal's* editor toward the radical position which finally resulted in his leaving the city. Abeel's successor, Thatcher, probably knew better when to keep his mouth shut, but he was a Kansan himself, and did what he could in the paper to soften Kansas-Missouri jealousies which might operate to Leavenworth's advantage.

More tangibly at issue was whether or not the roads around Kansas City were safe for country traders. Frequently they were not safe because of the terrible guerrilla warfare. Kansas City merchants, therefore, had an interest in effective military protec-

---

[38] *Leavenworth Times*, July 22, 1863; William Miller, *Early History of Kansas City* (Kansas City: Birdsall & Williams, 1881), p. 473; Walker Wyman, "Kansas City: A Famous Freighter Capital," *Kansas Historical Quarterly*, VI (1937), 10-12.

[39] Topeka *Record*, clipped in *Leavenworth Times*, May 3, 1861.

tion for this regional business, and this was a reason why the city's leadership could not afford completely to alienate the radicals, even though it might collectively detest them. The *Journal* often announced to its readers in the hinterland that the roads were safe, but these announcements were not reliable. Safe roads would have meant the suppression of the guerrilla bands, and this was never accomplished.

How could it be accomplished? Regular bodies of troops were obviously unequal to the task, at least in the available numbers; they were rarely able to lay eyes on the irregular border warriors, and they spent as much time tracking down rumors as in any other activity. The next approach was through the families of members of the bands, or through any apparently peaceable resident who was believed to be in league with them. The assessment had been an effort in this direction, and its failure has just been described. A more comprehensive scheme began to take shape in responsible military quarters during the winter of 1862-63: If the suspected relatives and other aiders-and-abettors of guerrillas were rounded up and kept in prison or sent entirely out of the region, the base of operation for those fighters would be undermined. They lived off the countryside; they relied on civilian sympathizers for much of their intelligence service. Abeel described a system of Confederate spying, informally organized, which effectively blanketed the county in favor of the guerrillas, "rebels on top of hills signalling others, and so forth."[40] If this base could be destroyed or weakened, the whole guerrilla campaign would subside.

During the summer of 1863, in one of the many reorganizations which characterized the Union military hierarchy in the West, John M. Schofield replaced Curtis as commanding general in St. Louis. Schofield set up a new territory, the "District of the Border," including the Missouri and Kansas counties over which the guerrillas had been roaming almost at will; he named Brigadier General Thomas Ewing to command it. In effect, Ewing at his Kansas City headquarters had only one assignment: pacify the border. The spring and summer had seen guerrilla warfare

40 *DJC,* June 17, 1862.

reach an intensity unusual even for this tortured area.[41] Ewing soon concluded that his best course would be to strike at the families of the bushwhackers. This meant arresting their wives, sisters, and sweethearts, and confining them in whatever space was available. Wartime Kansas City afforded little space, however, and Ewing had his aides draft Order Number Ten, which provided for the forcible transfer to Arkansas of several hundred of these people. With Schofield's approval, the order was promulgated August 18, 1863.

Events had already outrun Order Number Ten; it was to be forgotten almost immediately in the shadow of the greatest crime in the records of American guerrilla history. William Clarke Quantrill, whose name had long terrorized the land around Kansas City, had gone south to Texas in the winter of 1862-63. After some complicated negotiations, in which the Confederate military leaders seemed anxious to be rid of him, he started back toward Jackson County with a regular commission as captain. In the confused and conflicting sources, it is impossible to say when the project of a raid on Lawrence took shape in his mind. During June and July he seems to have started planning it and spying out the ground; arrangements were already being made while Ewing and Schofield were considering the advisability of Order Number Ten. Quantrill's partisans, during the second week in August, quietly gathered at a farm south of Kansas City and east of the state line.

While they were completing their plans, they received news which drove some of them mad with grief and fury. Several of the bushwhackers' female relatives had been confined by Ewing's orders in a Kansas City building on Grand Avenue, between Fourteenth and Fifteenth streets. This building was part of the so-called Metropolitan Block which E. M. McGee had put up in his addition. The materials were good, and the structure was strong. Apparently, however, the foundation had never been completed, and certainly no careful maintenance work had been done in the

---

[41] Brownlee, *op. cit.*, p. 113; see also Albert Castell's political-military study, *A Frontier State at War: Kansas, 1861-65* (Ithaca: Cornell University Press, 1958), p. 121 *et passim*.

two and a half years since the war had begun. The Confederate girls (most of them under twenty) had been placed on the second floor and apparently were leniently treated by Ewing's men in such matters as leave and daily exercise walks. In the basement of the same part of the Metropolitan Block, several women of easy virtue had been confined, and in the immediately adjoining part of the Block (southward) was a temporary Army guardhouse. The wall between the basement and the guardhouse had been broken through, as might have been predicted in the circumstances. Unfortunately, in the process some supporting beams had been removed, and the part of the building just south of the section where the Confederate girls were housed began to sag dangerously. On the morning of August 14, General Ewing was warned that the building might collapse; the grocer who occupied the floor just below the girls began moving his stocks out into the street. For the moment Ewing did nothing about the warning, and that afternoon the crucial sections of the Metropolitan Block collapsed.

Soldiers and civilians rushed to the spot and began trying to extricate the women who had been trapped in the wreckage. Most were critically injured, and four were dead.[42] Almost immediately a rumor started that Ewing or his soldiers had deliberately plotted the catastrophe, even that the building had been deliberately undermined so that it would fall and kill the girls. Whether or not the rumor was true—and it is supported by no testimony earlier than six years after the event—the guerrillas believed it. William Anderson (henceforward to be known as "Bloody Bill"), the Younger brothers, John McCorkle, and others in Quantrill's band whose women relatives had been badly hurt

[42] See Brownlee, op. cit., pp. 118-20; also William Connelly, Quantrill and the Border Wars (Cedar Rapids, Iowa: Torch Press, 1910), pp. 299-302. Connelly's mistakes can be corrected by reference to a working paper on the subject of the building collapse by Mildred C. Cox, now in the Archives of the Native Sons of Kansas City. The paper includes several affidavits which were sworn to about two weeks after the event, as well as testimony of considerably less reliability taken in the 1870's in connection with a claim by George Caleb Bingham for damages from the Government due to the building collapse. Also in the archives are one or two interviews made in the 1940's with people who were present as children at the time.

or killed (sisters of Anderson and McCorkle were killed), believed it. In a very few days they were moving toward Lawrence, home of Jim Lane and symbol of everything these men hated, with an extra increment of revenge and murder in their hearts.[43]

The sack of Lawrence need not be detailed here. Surprise was complete on the morning of August 21, 1863, and the Kansans were too stunned to resist. Quantrill's band rode out of the ruined, smoking town leaving at least 150 dead men behind them. The news stirred a nationwide storm, with its center on the Missouri-Kansas border. A great fear spread throughout the settled part of Kansas, and many towns expected the same fate as Lawrence. Cries that "Quantrill is coming!" were enough to depopulate temporarily some of these towns. At the same time, Kansas radicals tried to rally forces for a retaliatory invasion of Missouri. General Schofield wrote Ewing that this must be prevented but added that "nothing short of total devastation" of the border countryside would suffice to put down the bushwhackers.

Even had the guerrilla problem not been a permanent one calling for desperate remedies, the tensions left in the wake of Quantrill's Lawrence raid would have forced General Ewing to act in some spectacular way. On August 25 he promulgated the famous Order Number Eleven. As a scholar has observed elsewhere, this "completed the ruin of western Missouri."[44] Inhabitants of Jackson, Bates, and Cass counties, unless they lived within a mile of Kansas City, Independence, or any of three other military posts, were required to leave their homes within two weeks. Those who could not establish their loyalty to the satisfaction of the district Army authorities had to leave the district entirely.

By the end of the month, two-thirds of the population of the

---

[43] See Elmer Pigg, "Bloody Bill Anderson: Noted Guerrilla," *Trail Guide* (Kansas City: The Westerners, 1958), for the guerrillas' reaction to the news. No one should accept a story such as this against General Ewing without much better evidence than has been supplied so far; the collapse of buildings was unquestionably a rather common occurrence in western boom towns even without the obstacles to safe maintenance which the war brought with it. One such collapse is noted with no special comment in the *Journal*, June 18, 1859.

[44] Brownlee, *op. cit.*, p. 126; also Castell's chap. xi.

border counties had gone elsewhere; sixty-four Kansas Citians had been banished, ostensibly for the duration of the war. Among them were many of the city's best-known figures: Riddlesbarger, Gilliss, Holmes, Mrs. Lykins, W. G. Barkley, and others. Perhaps the most poignant sign of the temper of the times was the exile of John Calvin McCoy, among the earliest of pioneers on the site and former secretary of the Town Company of Kansas. From outside the city McCoy wrote to P. S. Brown, a business associate with whom he had real estate matters to negotiate. He proposed that they meet across the river in Liberty, adding, "I suppose it might not be safe for me to come to Kansas City."[45]

Although Order Number Eleven bore thus heavily on Kansas City and its immediate hinterland, it did not pacify the border. With the return of foliage in the early spring of 1864, the old conditions reappeared. The *Journal* noted ruefully that the Pacific Railroad of Missouri had been robbed so often it would probably have to be temporarily abandoned. It was said that beyond the various military posts the life of an openly loyal man in the countryside was hardly worth insuring. During the early months of 1864, Union authorities issued a good many permits allowing deportees to return to their homes, and the local editor argued that this policy effectively sabotaged Order Number Eleven.[46] Whatever the reasons, the order did not work. Nothing worked, and that was just the point: There could be no adequate military and political program for Kansas City in a country torn by civil war. Until the war should end, the city which had sought every means to hypothecate its future prospects would possess no future prospects at all.

Even the approaching collapse of the Confederacy seemed not to alleviate matters. As the summer months of 1864 drew near,

45 Kansas Citians against whom Order No. Eleven was directed are listed in an unpublished article by Alan W. Farley, Kansas City, Kansas: "The Bushwhacker Massacre at Lawrence." McCoy to Brown, November 11, 1863, Archives of the Native Sons of Kansas City.

46 *Journal*, May 28, July 2, 1864.

western Missouri was alive with bandits, both Kansan and Missourian, disaffected Indians were carrying out devastating raids in Kansas, and Quantrill was on his way back.[47] All the while, the season for Sterling Price's annual raid came closer. To all appearances the fall of 1864 would bring with it no more encouragement than the three previous ones had brought. Kansas City was still beleaguered, and it was about to face the largest military assault of the entire war.

Nervous Kansas Citians were already being enrolled into militia formations in June. Robert Van Horn, elected once again to the mayor's office (after a term in the state senate), busied himself throughout the summer, mustering 60-day volunteers, while military men and journalists speculated anxiously about Price's plans. He had started northward again, but not until October 5 did Union authorities in the state of Kansas fully understand that the Confederate Army was headed toward them. Even as late as October 15, Thatcher of the *Journal* was still not convinced that Kansas City would be attacked. Nevertheless, Van Horn issued a proclamation closing all places of business at 4:00 P.M., so that citizens might assemble with arms at the eastern and southern extremities of the city.[48]

Uncertainties about Price's movements simply testified to the fact that the western Missouri countryside was a great blank so far as Union intelligence was concerned. The old Confederate had marched up out of Arkansas, past Pilot Knob, bypassing Jefferson City, and had arrived at Lexington—the scene of his triumph three years earlier—on October 19. He had perhaps nine thousand men with him, in somewhat tatterdemalion array. At Lexington his troops fought a brief and sharp encounter with General James Blunt's regulars and chased them back to the Little Blue River, just east of Independence. All doubts were now at

---

[47] *Ibid.*, June 18, 1864; James Monaghan, *Civil War on the Western Border, 1854-1865* (Boston: Little, Brown & Company, 1955), pp. 307-10; Brownlee, *op. cit.*, pp. 187-97.

[48] *Journal*, June 18, September 8, October 15, 1864; *DJC*, October 11, 1864; Castell, *op. cit.*, chap. xi, is an excellent and detailed study of the 1864 Price raid, based on a large political background.

an end; Kansas City was Price's target, and if it fell he would go on to attack Fort Leavenworth.[49]

The Battle of Westport has been refought many times since; the numbers engaged have been totalled to make it a "Gettysburg of the West." Actually, it was no such thing. If Price had any strategy for his campaign, his best hope must have been that a victory at Kansas City, perhaps followed by one at Leavenworth, would make necessary a serious diversion of Union troops from east of the Mississippi, where Lee and Johnston were hard pressed in the fall of 1864. But hindsight suggests strongly that these victories were never even remotely possible. An anticipated rising of thousands of hypothetical pro-Confederate Missourians had not taken place when Price invaded the state, and the gathering of the Union forces was such that even a victory at Kansas City would have left him closely followed by an army larger and better equipped than his own. Price faced about ten thousand troops under General Curtis, whose headquarters for some time had been at Fort Leavenworth. At the same time, General Alfred Pleasonton was bringing twelve thousand Union soldiers up the Missouri from St. Louis; by the time Price pushed Blunt out of Lexington, this second Union army was already close upon his rear. Curtis planned three main defensive lines: He would stand against Price on the Big Blue River, between Independence and Kansas City; driven back, he would stand again barely east of Kansas City; if driven back again, he would retreat across the state line to a position east and south of Wyandotte, Kansas. At one or the other of these positions Price would certainly be caught and annihilated between Curtis' anvil and Pleasonton's hammer. Only a miracle could alter this projected outcome, and none was forthcoming.

Blunt held out briefly along the Little Blue, but on October

---

[49] For the Battle of Westport, I have used the *Official Records of the Rebellion*, the *Daily Kansas City Journal of Commerce*, books already cited by Monaghan, Brownlee, and Castell, and a detailed study: Paul B. Jenkins, *The Battle of Westport* (Kansas City: F. Hudson, 1906). An unpublished eye-witness account of the events of October 23 in Westport is in a letter from the Reverend J. B. Fuller to his father, October 24, 1864, in the Robert M. Snyder Collection, University of Kansas City Library.

21 he had to yield and retreat through Independence to the Big Blue, where he joined the rest of Curtis' army. Price drove through Independence right after Blunt and attacked the Big Blue line on the 22nd, Pleasonton's army entering Independence as Price's left it! The fight on the Big Blue became a flanking operation, and late in the day General Joseph Shelby, at Price's extreme left, got across the river around Curtis' right. This forced the Federals back to their line around Kansas City, into which they moved during the night of October 22-23, while Price's army followed Shelby's brigade across the Big Blue, leaving a force to hold the line against Pleasonton. From a north-to-south line of battle, the armies had now shifted so that they faced one another along an east-to-west line across a small rivulet called Brush Creek, which here ran south of Kansas City and just north of Westport. During the morning of the 23rd, then, the Union Army under Curtis felt out Price's front along Brush Creek, while Pleasonton was attacking the Big Blue line now held by Price's rear guard (literally, his right-flank guard). Kansas City's volunteers waited tensely all morning, while the Confederate lines held firm. An old resident of the area, however (never identified), had meanwhile offered to guide Curtis along a good route across Brush Creek of which Price's men were unaware. This good fortune brought Curtis' forces across the creek at 11:00 A.M., and at the same time the sound of guns to the east told that Pleasonton had crossed the Blue. Price's drive was halted. Word soon reached Colonel Kersey Coates that the Kansas City militia would not be needed.

The Battle of Westport was substantially the end of the Civil War in the West. Price's retreat with his regulars, southward along the state line, turned into a rout; the guerrillas became merely bandits and bank robbers as the rapidly approaching end of the war destroyed their military role. Among them were the James brothers, the Dalton gang, Cole Younger, and others—derelicts of war, who continued to kill people and to supply the material for romantic legends long after the war was done. But Kansas City was never again under a military threat. Shrunken and battered, it could look at wealthy and booming Leavenworth, twenty miles up the river and about five times the size of Kansas City, and consider how to rebuild the projects and possibilities of earlier years.

To a community which existed solely because of its business possibilities, the war on the border had threatened extinction. Money has always been scarce for the speculative boomer throughout American history; there has never been quite enough to ballast his inflated predictions. The same was true in prewar Kansas City, even when business was pouring in from the plains and mountains.[50] During the war, however, money was short for another reason: There was not enough business in the city to circulate it. Going into debt in order to acquire city land and pushing trade so that city land values would continue to rise, the Kansas City businessmen now found themselves suddenly without the rise necessary to ransom their investments. Mrs. Coates remembered the painful state of affairs during the war when—as she told her daughter years later—"it took every cent of money we could get to protect our property." She was never able to forget the first time they had to sell some of Coates's carefully acquired real estate (presumably in order to protect the rest): "I actually kissed the money, which I made Kersey bring home to show me."[51]

Another important Kansas Citian, later to serve as mayor and also wealthy by local standards, was E. M. McGee, son of the early land promoter. McGee, too, must have been heavily in debt; at any rate, he vigorously defended the proposal, in 1862, that the regular term of the Court of Common Pleas not be held, since too many substantial men would lose their property if it were. The time of troubles brought with it all kinds of legal actions; some merchants left the city permanently, some temporarily, and others had no money. Suits for attachment of property

[50] Shortage of business cash is mentioned many times by George Chace in his manuscript diary for the year 1860, now in the Kansas City Public Library.

[51] *Coates Memorial,* p. 61.

and mortgage foreclosure mounted alarmingly on the docket. The *Journal* opposed closing the court, arguing that it would damage the city's business reputation. McGee had no use for such puritanism and maintained that when the community's life was at stake desperate remedies were needed. McGee's characterization of those who insisted on business as usual in the matter of debt payments was savage. "Pitifully small creatures," he called them, "ten thousand of whose souls might hold a review on the point of a cambric needle and still have a whole universe of room left, they want Court to be held." What had such people as these to do with ambition and growth? Their hands were "always clenched as though holding a five cent piece; their heads bent down, hoping to find one." If they had their way, McGee could see little future for Kansas City: "Farewell enterprise! Farewell business! Welcome three per cent a month! and rents in advance!"[52]

For the moment, McGee's side lost; court was held and much property was sold cheap. The following year, however, McGee joined Milton Payne in the state legislature where (with Van Horn's assistance in the upper house) they helped put through laws which effectively suspended lien foreclosure in Kansas City and also released inhabitants of the area covered by Order Number Eleven from the burden of state taxes.[53] Creditors are good servants but bad masters, and cities are not built on 3 per cent a month.

Things wore a brighter aspect as seen from Leavenworth. That place, by the outbreak of the war, had already left Kansas City behind and claimed almost eight thousand inhabitants. During the war its population more than doubled. Leavenworth's journalists happily noted the influx of cash whenever Union troops were paid. Leavenworth's merchants had frequent opportunities to fill large Army contracts at the nearby fort; ironically, Theodore Case, now in the Quartermaster Corps, had sometimes to advertise in Leavenworth papers for materials which his Kansas City colleagues were probably unable to supply. Satis-

---

[52] *DJC*, April, 1862.
[53] Klassen, *op. cit.*, p. 99.

factory figures on Leavenworth's wartime trade are not easy to find, but the fort seems to have accounted for about half of the city's business.[54]

The same war which was slowly destroying Kansas City had infused its rival with additional sustenance. "The throng of people march on, busy, busy, busy, all the time," wrote a Leavenworth editor early in 1864:

> Business is at its topmost best. Wines flow and lager is abundant. Luxuries are common, as the sparkle of champagne and the whiff of the Havana prove. All over social life, outside the regions desolated by war, there is spirit, activity, and an energy which is broad and bounding. . . .

All this was going on while the "cottonwood" city's erstwhile competitors, St. Joseph and Kansas City, were facing ruin. Kansas City especially "would seem to excite pity far rather than strife," its levee deserted, stores closed, and some of its greatest warehouses (including Chick's) charred ruins because of a fire which had swept them unchecked early in 1862.[55] Circumstances, it seemed, had canceled Kansas City's "natural" advantages in favor of "unnatural" ones at Leavenworth. That rival had, according to a Kansas Citian, "grown and fattened on the woes of the border," had "turned an honest penny (and many a dishonest one, too) out of the misfortunes" of Kansans and Missourians alike.[56]

About all Kansas City had left by this time was its railroad plan—and this, in the end, was to prove more than enough. The Pacific Railroad of Missouri, even though hampered and damaged by wartime misfortunes, was aimed straight at Kansas City, and by now it was too late for this route to be changed. The location of the Pacific's still potential western terminus unquestionably weighed heavily in the Congressional debates over the east-

[54] *Leavenworth City Directory* (Leavenworth, Kansas: Daily Commercial Press, 1871), p. 1; *Leavenworth Times*, August 18, 1863; January 21, 1864; February 7, 1865; see also *Times*, June 9, 1861, on business stemming from the presence of soldiers and an Army freighting depot.

[55] *Leavenworth Times*, February 8, 1864; April 11 and 23, and June 4, 1862.

[56] *Journal*, March 18, 1865.

ern end or ends of the country's first transcontinental railroad. In June, 1862, the first transcontinental railroad act was passed; along with several later amendments, it provided for a trunk route westward, beginning at a point in Nebraska on the 100th meridian, with branches connecting the trunk to the main Missouri River towns. The terms of the act were such as to leave open all questions about which of these towns would derive the greatest advantage from it, and both Kansas City and Leavenworth editors jubilantly scouted the chances of their respective competitors.[57] Events other than legislation were to determine the end of the struggle, but the Act of Congress did give Kansas Citians tangible basis for hope at a time when it was badly needed. Incidentally, the Pacific Railroad Act provided the best of rationales for the city's wartime political program: Kansas City people, according to David K. Abeel, "ought . . . to realize the obligations of patriotism which . . . this bill imposes upon us."[58]

Just as in prewar years every possible excuse was seized upon for a demonstration of social and cultural amenities in the rough boom town, so during the war no opportunity was missed for collective action symbolizing a viable community life. Fourth-of-July festivities, for example, were elaborately planned and advertised, and became occasions for propagandizing the city's pro-Union orthodoxy. The most impressive instance of this kind of community behavior was the Sanitary Fair, held in the spring of 1864. During the preceding months, fairs had been held in major American cities to raise money for the work of the United States Sanitary Commission, which at that time took care of sick and wounded soldiers. Citizens contributed money or goods, and the proceeds were turned over to the commission. The idea of contributing for the commission's work spread, and early in January, 1864, a Sanitary Fair was held in Leavenworth which raised $3,000 for the worthy purpose. A great Mississippi Valley Fair was planned for May, in St. Louis. Kansas Citians could easily have sent their contributions to St. Louis individually, as was done in a number of Missouri towns. This might have been the

57 *DJC*, June 28, 1862; *Leavenworth Times*, August 26, 1862.
58 *DJC*, June 24, 1862.

most practicable way of doing things, and it was urged at first by the *Journal*. Soon, however, the idea developed that Kansas City should have its own fair. A mass meeting provided for the proper committees; all the prominent names (among those families which were still in the city) appeared on the lists; the *Journal* supported the plan, and soon a big community effort took form. For two months (from late March into early May) the Sanitary Fair was the main item of local interest as reflected in the newspaper, almost displacing bushwhackers and railroads. Wives and daughters joined in; committees and subcommittees grew to be enormous (at least 125 different names appear in the *Journal* in connection with the fair), all with the object of producing an event "creditable to our city."[59]

The fair opened in Long's Hall on May 11. For three days the auctions went on, accompanied by entertainment: a band, the German singers, tableaux, and dancing in the evening. Every kind of pressure was used to encourage liberal contributions; the *Journal* published several lists from which rather interesting data can be drawn. Although the plains trade had revived somewhat by 1864, cash was still short; the highest individual cash gift was $50, and this came from Captain Case of the Quartermaster Corps. Van Horn, who probably scraped the bottom of the barrel, came up with $10, and most of the big names in the city gave less than that. Cyprien Chouteau, James H. McGee, Jr., John C. Gage, and Thomas Smart gave $5 each (in most cases in addition to other kinds of contributions). Half of this was all that such men as P. S. Brown and Johnston Lykins could manage. A number of laborers in the quartermaster's employ collectively gave $17.50. More than half the total proceeds of the fair came from the auctioning of other contributions, and these included a wide variety of goods: quilts, old pictures, a violin, a barrel of vinegar, cigars, a brand-new whisky barrel, and so on. Case, E. M. McGee, and Kersey Coates each contributed a city lot from their land holdings.

When the fair's executive committee (Kersey Coates, chairman) met to wind up accounts, it was able to send just over

[59] *Journal*, March 26, 1864.

$3,500 to St. Louis. The fair had incurred some expenses, which would probably bring the gross income close to $4,000. Five months earlier Leavenworth had gathered up almost as much from a fair which its press had scarcely noticed, and its citizens had sent sizable individual contributions to the St. Louis fair. The grand total received in St. Louis from all sources was $300,000. Kansas City's bit would hardly have been missed, and it was small indeed in comparison with the five- and six-digit figures recorded by the nation's larger cities. Still, the amount raised by the Kansas City fair averaged a dollar per person, which compares most favorably with the amounts contributed in Milwaukee, Cincinnati, Chicago, New York, and other places. Proportionately, it would compare favorably with any united charity campaign today. The effort, in other words, was a powerful one. Its main significance, however, was certainly not financial. The fair raised some money, but of more import for the city's future, it was a rallying point around which enthusiasm could be generated in a badly hurt and deeply depressed community.

Toward the end of the Civil War, Kansas City rebuilt its plans and hopes. For the first time in the city's history, destitution was a problem. Not only were Kansas Citians in hard circumstances, but Westport also appealed for help. Shortly after the Battle of Westport, a charity ball was held to benefit the neighboring community. At about the same time, Mayor Van Horn announced that the Kansas City government could not help all its destitute citizens: "There should be a community effort in this direction."[60] The needs of Unionist refugees from the countryside and of wives and children of Federal soldiers intensified the problem. Four hundred dollars had been raised by private contributions—sufficient only for the month of December.

Still, poverty was not the only concern of the day. A series of festive celebrations was joyously reported by the *Journal*: One, at the local quartermaster building, saluted the fall of Charleston;

[60] *Journal*, November 19, December 17, 1864.

the quartermaster captain gave a ball for his employees for which the building was beautifully illuminated; a few days later there was a masquerade ball which "will be remembered by the gay revellers as a season of unbridled pleasure and merriment."[61]

In March, 1865, the tax assessor was again at work, and familiar names appeared on his list with property holdings valued at more than twenty thousand dollars: the Campbells, McGee, Majors, Guinotte, Smart, Coates, and others.[62] Again, however, future prospects were more imposing than present wealth. As soon as the border was quieted, a tide of immigration could be expected. "For men of capital," wrote editor Thatcher, "now is the most favorable time possible for them to make a strike. . . . There is not a more promising town in the whole West than Kansas City, and we hold out open arms to every loyal immigrant from whatever quarter he may come." The Chamber of Commerce should immediately reorganize and go into action. Public schools must be readied: "The kind of immigration which we are now looking for to increase our city is a kind that sends its children to school. . . ." It was time to build a good library to keep the leisure of the city's young men properly occupied, "and how much such a thing would add to the comfort of living here."[63]

These themes were all expanded upon repeatedly and at length in the press. Thatcher made the cardinal point in an editorial on the surrender of the Confederacy. "The local history of Kansas City for the last two [sic] years," he wrote,

> has been exciting and varied. . . . We have lived much of the time like a fortified garrison. . . . Amid all difficulties, our people have preserved a good heart and hope, until now a better day seems to be dawning upon us. . . . Everything presages a bright future for Kansas City.

On another occasion he said succinctly, "We have held on as a

[61] *Journal,* February 4, 18, 25, 1865.

[62] *Journal,* March 4, 1865.

[63] *Journal,* March 4 and 11, January 28, February 18, 1865.

community."[64] Somewhat battered as well as reduced in wealth, the city's corps of leaders now turned to the job of regaining a competitive position among the towns of the middle Missouri Valley. The question of where the regional metropolis would develop had not yet been settled.

[64] *Journal,* April 15, April 8, 1865.

CHAPTER 6

The Metropolis

THE MIDDLE and lower Missouri Valley, locale of so much optimistic town-boosting in the 1850's, suffered grievously during the Civil War. Hopes were suspended, ambitions frustrated, and fortunes lost. Understandably, with the end of the war rival energies were immediately marshaled again and rival publicists once more sounded calls to drive ahead. The mayor of Atchison, Kansas, informed his constituents that their townsite gave them "unparalleled advantages as a shipping point." He added, "Let us improve them." St. Joseph, Missouri, the oldest competitor of all, was warned editorially that the time for action had come. That city, according to its newspaper, was "at the head of the list in the Missouri Valley. To preserve her superiority, vigilance and intelligence in the management of local interests are necessary." Leavenworth, Kansas, fortune's favorite among the river towns during the war and much larger than any of the others at its close, was in the fight; the *Leavenworth Times* campaigned "to stimulate all to prompt and united action *now*, to the exercise of that wise business energy which retains *what it has*, and builds upon it securely." Thirty miles downstream, Kansas City's *Journal of Commerce* announced that "it will be to our eternal shame if, with all the advantages over every other town to transact the business of this region, we fail to do it through the imbecility or indolence of our citizens."[1]

An unprejudiced observer, just after the war, might have hesitated to predict which town would ultimately dominate the middle stretches of the Missouri Valley, but he would probably have ruled out Kansas City. Albert Richardson, the New York journalist, found Leavenworth a much more impressive place in 1866; it had five newspapers, many brick buildings, well-lighted

[1] *Atchison Daily Champion*, May 9, 1865; St. Joseph *Gazette*, July 9, 1868; *Leavenworth Times*, September 5, 1865; *Western Journal of Commerce*, September 16, 1865.

streets, and other amenities which gave it what he called "the air of a metropolis." St. Joseph and Kansas City, on the other hand, were paying the price of earlier political uncertainties and would have to surrender any urban pretensions they might once have had. Another visitor from the East thought Leavenworth attractive and metropolitan; there was no poverty, no reminders of the recent war. More important because it might have influenced Kansas City's future more directly, was the comment of one R. C. Watson, treasurer of the Hannibal and St. Joseph Railroad and representative of powerful Eastern investment interests. "I was very much impressed with Leavenworth," he wrote to an associate, "which *pro rata* is as much a wonder as Chicago, and it seems to me it will not do to turn a cold shoulder on that place."[2]

Briefly, then, the years 1865 to 1870 witnessed renewed urban competition near the Missouri's "great bend," in which the Kansas City business community overcame the gravest disadvantages to emerge as the winner. The story is intertwined with that of the first permanent railroad bridge over the river, which was opened at Kansas City in 1869. The bridge has figured largely in all the later histories of the city and in various ways: Its location at Kansas City is used to explain the pre-eminence of the city over its rivals; in another way conversely, the decision to build the bridge at this point is used as evidence of the impressive natural advantages and managerial virtues of the city.

The period, however, is more complicated than this division of opinion suggests. Geography, the internal history of Kansas City, the pattern of agricultural expansion in neighboring Kansas, and the decisions of men as far away as Boston all worked together in the shaping of the city's postwar recovery. The story raises questions of determinism, enterprise, and chance—questions which it cannot answer. By 1870 certain paths had been taken,

---

2 A. D. Richardson, *Beyond the Mississippi* (Hartford, Connecticut: American Publishing Co., 1867), pp. 549-50; Josiah Copley, *Kansas City and the Country Beyond* (Philadelphia: J. B. Lippincott Company), pp. 45-46; R. C. Watson to James Joy, May 17, 1867, Joy Papers, Burton Historical Collections (Detroit, Michigan), cited in Charles N. Glaab, "Kansas City's Hannibal Bridge: Western Town Booming and Eastern Capital," *The Trail Guide*, IV, No. 1 (Kansas City: The Westerners, March, 1959), p. 14.

and certain alternatives had disappeared; a new piece had been added to the mosaic design of American metropolitan geography.

Probably there were three thousand to four thousand people living in Kansas City during the winter of 1864-65. Between hope for growth and fear of collapse, the place was so unsettled that the population figure must have changed significantly from month to month. By September, 1865, the *Journal* was claiming "nearly or quite 10,000"; two other local sources give between 15,000 and 16,000 for 1866,[3] and both were certainly exaggerating. The war had considerably rearranged Kansas City's business community. A city directory published for 1860-61 listed 1,400 names; the next directory was for the years 1865-66, and of its 1,100 names only 280 had appeared in the earlier one. The number of carpenters and builders declined from twenty-one to eleven, and only four of the eleven names appear in both directories. Boot-and-shoe establishments numbered twelve at the war's outbreak and seven at its close; only one name appears in both lists. The number of grocers increased from twenty-seven to thirty, and of the thirty grocers in 1865-66, twenty-seven were newcomers.[4]

Among the business elite there was both change and continuity. Franklin Conant left the city early in the war, and his property was sold for taxes. Jesse Riddlesbarger was a casualty of Order Number Eleven. Hiram Northrup and Joseph Chick both went to New York City during the war and did not return until the 1870's. W. G. Barkley left Kansas City for Montana and never came back. By 1867 W. H. Chick had removed his headquarters to St. Louis. These men had nearly all stressed mercantile activi-

---

[3] Theodore Case, "Kansas City in the War," *Kansas City World*, August 1, 1897; *Journal*, September 2, 1865; *Kansas City Directory and Reference Book for 1867-68* (Quincy, Illinois: Excelsior Book and Job Office, n.d.), p. 10; *A History of Kansas City, Missouri, Her Business, Population, etc.* (Kansas City: City Council and Board of Trade, 1873), p. 18.

[4] *Kansas City Directory and Business Mirror for 1860-61* (Indianapolis: James Sutherland, n.d.); *Kansas City Business Directory and Mirror for 1865-66* (Kansas City: Millett & Sloan, n.d.).

ties over whatever real estate business they had done. The owners of city additions apparently were more likely to remain through the town's time of troubles: Kersey Coates, E. M. McGee, Johnston Lykins, D. M. Jarboe, John W. Reid, Nathan Scarritt, John Campbell, and Thomas Swope were still watching over their Kansas City investments after the war, and John Calvin McCoy returned after a wartime exile to buy and sell land. A dividing line between real estate and merchandising cannot be too sharply drawn, however, as several prominent prewar merchants stayed in Kansas City and played important roles in its affairs. Louis Hammerslough and Patrick Shannon continued their dry-goods lines; Michael Diveley was active in business and politics during and after the war; Charles Kearney became more deeply involved in the city's postwar railroad campaigns and Nehemiah Holmes began promoting street transportation enterprises. Both of the two directories mentioned above list eighteen physicians, and on these two lists eight names are common to both. Five of Kansas City's thirty-four lawyers in 1865-66 had also been listed before the war, and all of them continued in public concerns: J. S. Boreman, H. B. Bouton, P. S. Brown, John C. Gage, and D. A. N. Grover.

All in all, the Kansas City power elite remained intact during the years 1860 to 1870 to a degree which seems remarkable for a border town at that time. Of the twenty men who led in organizing the Chamber of Commerce in 1857, at least one had died, and twelve others were still active publicly as well as privately in Kansas City by 1867. All of the five local men who figured directly in gaining the Hannibal Bridge (see below) were prewar residents: Coates, Reid, Kearney, Van Horn, and Case.

There were, of course, newcomers who joined the group of city leaders. Three important examples may be mentioned here because their interests reflected the increasing complication of the city's economic base. Thomas B. Bullene, born in New York State, had been taken when still a child to Wisconsin by his parents. Between 1849 and 1856 he carried on a mercantile business in Lyons, Wisconsin, with his brother. From there he went to Iowa where he continued in business of one or another kind until

1863, when he came to Kansas City. Franklin Conant's defunct general store had been bought by Coates and Gilliss not long before this time, and now Bullene bought Gilliss' share. The firm of Coates and Bullene operated for about a year, at which time Coates left the partnership; Bullene's brother joined him in Kansas City some time before 1867, and the name of the firm became Bullene Brothers and Emery. (The firm is still in existence as Emery, Bird, Thayer, one of the city's largest department stores.) T. B. Bullene did not wait long after his arrival in Kansas City to join the Chamber of Commerce; he was a member in July, 1863, and by November, 1865, he appeared on a chamber committee engaged in railroad lobbying. Bullene was one of sixty-seven men who organized the first Board of Trade, in February, 1869; he was already on the board of directors of the First National Bank, which, according to a local source, "included the cream of the business community."[5]

Whereas Bullene had bought an already large retail store and then supervised its further expansion as the city grew, Howard M. Holden illustrates a different kind of business continuity: He came to the city and gathered the pieces of a whole industry, rationalizing them into a more efficient structure. The young industry was livestock (and meat packing), and Holden's agency was financial. A New Englander by birth, Holden had engaged in banking in Iowa during the 1850's. He was successful, and in 1866 he brought his accumulated gains to Kansas City, sinking most of his money—$80,000—in the newly organized First National Bank which he proceeded to guide as it supported local meat packing, cattle raisers in the hinterland, and later, the grain trade. As a majority stockholder in what soon became (for a time) the city's leading financial institution, Holden influenced every important business development. He also, during the

5 The typescript of a diary kept by Bullene is in the Archives of the Native Sons of Kansas City; see also Laura Coates Reed (ed.), *In Memoriam, Sarah Walter Chandler Coates* (Kansas City: Franklin-Hudson, n.d.), p. 167; transcript of Minutes of the Chamber of Commerce, Archives of the Native Sons of Kansas City, pp. 29, 34; William Miller, *Early History of Kansas City* (Kansas City: Birdsall & Williams, 1881), p. 492, and the biographical sketch in the same book, p. 746; *Kansas City Times*, January 10, 1875.

1870's, interested himself in many civic matters and was prominently involved in the effort to construct a water system. His arrival in 1866 may be compared with that of Kersey Coates a
decade earlier, and his role in the city's affairs was to resemble
that which the older man had already assumed.[6]

A third newcomer to Kansas City's business community was
Henry J. Latshaw, who arrived late in 1865. Born in Canada, he
was reared in upstate New York and Toledo, Ohio; his father had
been engaged in flour milling. Latshaw served in the Quartermaster Corps of the Union Army, and after being mustered out he
spent a short time in Canadian oil speculation. Apparently in
search of wider fields, he turned to the "new West," and started
for Omaha. Instead of going there, however, he stayed in Kansas
City where, as it turned out, he found ample opportunities. Latshaw went into partnership with one R. W. Quade in an extensive
lumber business which prospered and sent its agents all over
Missouri, Nebraska, Kansas, and the Indian Territory. In 1871
Latshaw shifted from lumber to grain, just as Kansas City was
about to become a major grain market and milling center. Meanwhile, he had joined, or was co-opted by, the group of men, still
relatively small, which tried to guide the city in large policy matters. His name appears in connection with railroad enterprises,
banking, and the Board of Trade. In later years his fortunes continued to rise with the expansion of grain and milling, and his
biographer claimed that Latshaw's fame was "co-extensive with
the Missouri Valley."[7]

There were other important newcomers, of course, many of
them; but these three may be regarded as more or less representative for the higher circles of business at least. Rather than
sudden dramatic change, the picture is one of new men joining
already well-established local figures. The dates of arrival of
Bullene, Latshaw, and Holden suggest that the gaining of the
Missouri River bridge was not so much a cause as an effect of

6 H. L. Conard (ed.), *Encyclopedia of the History of Missouri* (New York:
Southern History Company, 1901), III, 265-67.

7 *U.S. Biographical Dictionary* (New York, Chicago, St. Louis, and Kansas
City: U.S. Biographical Publishing Company, 1878), Missouri Volume, p. 54.

enterprise and growth. The first two men came to Kansas City before the outcome of the bridge negotiations was at all certain, and Holden apparently moved in during their course. It is to the story of that bridge that we must now turn, picking up enough of the complicated background to see these events in their proper setting.

The border troubles, the Pacific Railroad Act, and the war had shown how vitally national party politics could affect local affairs; Kansas City's business leadership needed competent scouting in Washington. Their man was at hand in the person of Robert T. Van Horn. His journalistic work had shown that he could take a large view of the city's interests and, moreover, that he could represent these interests effectively. During the war years, he had been successively mayor, combat officer, state senator, and mayor once again. In each post he had shown decisive ability, and as time passed he showed (as he had shown once before) political adaptability as well. This former Whig and then Democrat was now on his way to becoming a Radical Republican—"and again," to quote a perceptive local biographer, "he was on the side where he could do the most good for the town."[8]

Near the end of August, 1864, the city council issued a circular urging the Mayor's nomination to Congress on the Union ticket. Although he had arrived in the city less than ten years earlier, he was now described as an "old resident . . . perhaps better than any other man acquainted with our interests and wants." According to one of the Missouri senators, Lincoln himself was strongly in favor of Van Horn's nomination. The nomination was unanimous, but the election revealed an old tension in the district. In Jackson County Van Horn received a comfortable majority of 600 votes over his strongest opponent; Platte and Clay counties, however, gave majorities to the opponent. Even in Jackson County outside of Kansas City the election was close,

8 Theodore S. Case, *History of Kansas City, Missouri* (Syracuse: D. Mason, 1888), pp. 434-35.

but the local machine was still reliable, and Van Horn took his seat in Washington. He was re-elected in 1866. In 1868 the Democrats were finally able to beat him, but by that time (as will be seen below) most of what was necessary to the Kansas City business group had already been accomplished.[9]

To understand what was accomplished, we must pick up once more the tangled threads of the railroad campaign. In 1861 Congress had not yet settled upon an eastern terminus for the proposed transcontinental line. The Pacific Railroad of Missouri's western end was still about ninety miles from Kansas City. The Hannibal and St. Joseph Railroad (controlled by the directorate of the Burlington and part of that company's developing system) was in operation between those two towns, and the Kansas Citians had tried and failed to build a fifty-mile northward connection with it. Kansas City had no railroads as the war began, and the fate of these three possible connections would determine the shape of urban growth in the entire area.[10]

When Lincoln signed the Pacific Railroad Act in June, 1862, one phase of the problem began to clarify. The Act provided for an eastern division point near the middle of Nebraska, from which branches should be built to four points; these, it was settled by executive order, were Sioux City, Omaha, Atchison, and the junction of the Kansas and Missouri rivers. At the same time, the Hannibal and St. Joseph was built west from St. Joseph, and a Leavenworth company was given a vaguely defined authority to build westward into Kansas. Both of these lines were to connect with the branch running from the junction of the rivers to the Nebraska division point. Conceivably, the Leavenworth company could have built from Wyandotte, Kansas, to Leavenworth, and then west. Nothing in the Pacific Railroad Act made it possible to predict which line would become the most important, or

9 Circular, August 30, 1864, Archives of the Native Sons of Kansas City; John B. Henderson to Van Horn, August 31, 1864, Van Horn Papers, Archives of the Native Sons of Kansas City; *Journal,* November 12 and 29, 1864.

10 The description of Kansas City's railroad negotiations is drawn from Charles N. Glaab, *Kansas City and the Railroads* (Madison, Wisconsin: State Historical Society of Wisconsin, 1962). The material was prepared by Dr. Glaab as a research working paper on the History of Kansas City Project.

in the case of the Kansas roads, specifically where they would run.

Construction began in both Leavenworth and Kansas City in October, 1862. Financial troubles and arguments, sometimes violent, among the directors, brought work to a halt more than once; uncertainty continued to hang over the western connection. In 1864 Congress amended the Pacific Railroad Act to provide that the Eastern Division of the Union Pacific (which Kansas Citians hoped would become "their" branch of the transcontinental railroad) should go through Lawrence, Kansas, and that the line from Leavenworth should make its connection there. This decision may have simplified the planners' problems in some respects, but it also brought Lawrence into the competition, with Kansas' Senator James Lane using his considerable influence in its behalf.

The transcontinental railroad was only one element, however, in some very complicated political geography. The great desideratum for each of these towns was not simply to be a way station on a railroad, but to be a connecting point, the center of a great regional interchange of goods and men. During the bleak summer of 1863, one visitor to both places wrote of Leavenworth and Kansas City that both

> are sanguine in their expectations, and about equally confi-
> dent in their ultimate success in the race for importance.
> They are now balancing, but a few more years will settle
> the question and do away with all rivalry. The world will
> soon speak of one of these places as one of the thriving cities
> of the country—and the other, the world won't speak of at
> all.[11]

Leavenworth, Kansas City, and now Lawrence, began projecting lines toward Galveston, Texas, at about the same time the events just described were taking place. Each was also vitally interested in what the war-battered Pacific Railroad of Missouri might do, and each (plus St. Joseph) sparred with the others to gain a Chicago connection.

[11] Lela Barnes (ed.), "An Editor Looks at Early-Day Kansas: The Letters of Charles Monroe Chase," *Kansas Historical Quarterly*, XXVI (Summer, 1960), 117.

The progress of the Pacific Railroad of Missouri had affected the decision to locate a branch of the proposed transcontinental railroad somewhere in the Kansas City area, but during the early years of the war the road west from St. Louis sank into even deeper difficulties than those which had plagued it in the 1850's. The legislature was asked periodically to help the Pacific, usually by assuming part of its debt. Kansas City's representatives in the state capital supported these requests, threatening that if their eastern Missouri colleagues did not vote with them on the aid measures they would throw all their city's support to the Cameron project, which benefited Chicago over St. Louis.

Some important financial relief was given the Pacific in 1864, and again its line crept toward Kansas City. After a brief skirmish between two groups of Kansas City landowners, the council passed an ordinance granting a right-of-way along the levee, for which the railroad agreed to pay the city $25,000, to be used for street improvements; the ordinance was ratified in a referendum election, 270 to 107. Although the final picture of the railroad routes was not yet clear, pieces were falling into place. Rail service between Kansas City and Lawrence had begun December 19, 1864, and the first locomotive on the Pacific Railroad of Missouri pulled into Kansas City amidst great public rejoicing, on September 21, 1865.

But Kansas City might yet have been bypassed in favor of another potential railroad center. Plans were afoot in 1865 and 1866 for the Pacific Railroad of Missouri to build a line straight from Pleasant Hill, Missouri, to Lawrence. The proposed line would have passed about twenty miles south of Kansas City. If Lawrence had then completed its railroad to Galveston the cutoff would have posed a very serious threat to the city's ambitions. There were also proposals to build the Pacific of Missouri around the bend in the river to Leavenworth; this possibility, along with Leavenworth's imminent connection with the transcontinental railroad, also menaced the Kansas Citians' plans for the future.

The result of the railroad campaign came to depend upon a connection with Chicago, which would be determined by the location of a permanent bridge across the Missouri River. The choice of a route to Chicago was primarily in the hands of the group of Boston capitalists who were building the great Chicago, Burlington, & Quincy system in the West. These men had more cash, more political influence, and more experience in rail development than the Pacific Railroad of Missouri directorate, to say nothing of the river-town campaigners. They had, after all, pushed the Hannibal road across Missouri much more efficiently than the men in St. Louis had managed the Pacific. Now their aim was to penetrate the new Southwest, and their choice of where to cross the Missouri River was to decide the long struggle between the rival towns. By the end of the war, it was clear that this choice would lie between Leavenworth and Kansas City.

The "Cameron road"—Kansas City's projected connection with the Hannibal and St. Joseph—had played a double part in the city's railroad planning since the late fifties. Obviously, substantial advantages would flow from such a link, if it was ever completed; at the same time the loudly advertised intentions to complete it threatened the Pacific Railroad of Missouri and compelled it to locate its western terminus in Kansas City. Events showed clearly, however, that local enterprise alone could not build even this short link, and well before the Civil War the Kansas Citians had tried to interest the Hannibal and St. Joseph directors in their proposed Cameron connection. Their success was minimal, but the Hannibal's general superintendent, J. T. K. Hayward, urged the value of the line on his employers, and a contract was negotiated in 1860: The Hannibal company would equip and operate trains between Kansas City and Cameron in return for certain financial arrangements by the Kansas City company, which were to be effected when that company had completed the roadbed.[12] War had brought to an end the halting efforts at construction which had been made; the partially graded roadbed

---

[12] This northern connection involved several corporate rubrics, and to note them here would only complicate the text. The earliest charter in this direction was for a "Kansas City, Hannibal, & St. Joseph" railroad company. In 1857 another charter denominated the "Kansas City, Galveston, & Lake Superior" company. In 1864 in the course of a reorganization, its name was changed to the "Kansas City and Cameron Railroad Company." In this chapter, I refer to the project simply as "the northern connection," or as "the Cameron road."

deteriorated, and the contract with the Hannibal and St. Joseph lapsed.

Late in 1864 the Chamber of Commerce appointed Johnston Lykins, Kersey Coates, and Theodore Case to set the dormant Cameron project in motion again. They made efforts in various directions—even tried to give the company away to anyone who could make a going concern of it. Meanwhile, a group of Kansas Citians headed by Van Horn and Payne had received from the legislature a charter for a company to bridge the river at Kansas City. No results developed from any of these efforts, and in 1865 Leavenworth promoters organized their own company to build a line to Cameron. In the autumn of 1865, agents of both "Cameron roads" met with the Hannibal directors. The Kansas Citians, who had already been rebuffed in other quarters, again came away empty-handed, while Leavenworth's representatives got an agreement that the Hannibal and St. Joseph would guarantee their company's first-mortgage bonds once its roadbed was finished. It was learned later that Hayward had changed his originally favorable opinion of the Kansas City connection and was doing his best to support Leavenworth's bid; although no longer general superintendent, he was retained in a somewhat vague advisory capacity with the Hannibal road.

Casting about for any expedient, the Kansas City and Cameron directors recalled that the Pacific of Missouri had recently paid the city the agreed $25,000 in return for the levee right-of-way. Although the voters had already ratified that agreement which specified that the money should be used for street improvements, Coates now asked the council to use the funds to pay a contractor for more work on the Cameron roadbed! It was done; the line between public and private responsibility was characteristically vague. Work was started again, but it could not go far; $225,000 more was needed to complete the job. Shortly thereafter, S. W. Bouton tried to sell some Kansas City bonds for the Cameron road, but found them unmarketable. He returned from the East with a very pessimistic view of the prospects.

Those prospects were, in fact, about as dim during the winter months of 1865-66 as they ever had been. The Pacific of Missouri might bypass Kansas City to the south, or it might run its line through to Leavenworth. Leavenworth now seemed to have the ear of the Hannibal directors, and was about to build toward Cameron. No group in Kansas City could command enough cash to carry through any project which might exert a decisive influence on the course of events.

At this point another figure entered the story, and the community leaders improvised another device to serve their campaign. The Bostonians at the head of the Burlington system had found in a man named James F. Joy an eminently satisfactory Western agent; they entrusted to him most of the decisions which had to be made in the interests of their vast and growing network. Joy was a Harvard man who had moved west in the 1830's. From his Detroit law office he had been active in building the Michigan Central, and by 1865 he had accumulated years of wide experience in the problems of railroading. It was with this man that representatives from Kansas City and Leavenworth had dealt when the Leavenworth men got the bond guarantee for their Cameron line.

Joy, however, was by no means committed to Leavenworth. The Kansas Citians, having failed to give him their paper railroad, now began—quite literally—to sell him part of their town in furtherance of their railroad plan. During the war several of them had come into control of a "West Kansas Land Company"; the name referred to the city, not the state, and the purpose of the company had been to pool land speculations in the northwestern corner of Kansas City. At some time during the 1865-66 winter, Joy had become interested in this company, and through the agency of Theodore Case, he began buying shares. Case was also a Cameron road director; in 1866 Charles Kearney was president of both railroad and land company, and within a year or so James F. Joy was the biggest shareholder in the West Kansas Land Company.

Now the affairs of the Cameron road began to straighten out; where all had been dark and unpromising during the winter, by the end of spring, 1866, things were moving forward. After a new financial settlement, the contractor agreed to resume work on the roadbed. Late in May, Case, Coates, and Reid traveled to Boston to negotiate for equipment. The Hannibal directors at that time were considering a firmer Leavenworth commitment, but the "three very respectable gentlemen from Kansas City," as the treasurer of the Hannibal described them in a letter to Joy, made a good impression. They presented a strong case for aid to the Kansas City and Cameron Railroad, and the Bostonians hesitated between the claims of the rival towns.[13] They placed the whole matter in the hands of their Western agent.

Joy went to Kansas City, where he encouraged the local men and made a few arrangements—probably including purchase of additional West Kansas Land Company stock. The Burlington company would need bridges over the Mississippi at Quincy, Illinois, and over the Missouri wherever their road crossed it. Railroad bridges over navigable waterways had in the past led to inconvenient litigation, and the company wanted specific Congressional authorization for these projects. It also wanted a federal land grant for a proposed extension south to the Gulf of Mexico. The Kansas Citians already had a bridge company charter, and they also had a paper railroad called the Missouri River, Fort Scott, & Gulf. Van Horn, now in Washington, was instructed to support the bridge authorization proposal and also a land grant for the Missouri River, Fort Scott, & Gulf; he was further informed that Joy would see to it that the Burlington lobby worked with him.

Van Horn's Kansas City bridge proposal went into an omnibus bridge authorization bill as an amendment. The bill passed late in July after a routine parliamentary course and over minor opposition. Leavenworth's guardians had apparently not been alerted to what was going on in the background; the *Leavenworth Times*'s Washington correspondent did not even mention the passage of the omnibus bill, and the *Congressional Record*

---

13 Existing accounts of these negotiations are inaccurate in several important respects. At this point, it may be well to stress that the Kansas Citians had no contractual claim whatsoever on the Hannibal directors; the 1860 contract had lapsed. Again, there is no certainty that Leavenworth representatives could have made a contract with the Hannibal company, since they, too, had been unable to complete their promised roadbed.

reveals no efforts of any kind in connection with it by Kansas representatives. During the same weeks Van Horn strenuously supported the land-grant proposal also; it was at least as important to Joy as the bridge authorizations, and it passed at about the same time after a bitter fight.

There were still some negotiations between Kansas City and the Hannibal company, and Leavenworth continued its efforts to secure the railroad. But the decision had been made. In 1867 the Cameron road was, in effect, given to the Burlington directors; construction of railroad and bridge was now in the hands of a group which could carry the job through, and work went rapidly forward. This was actually the end of premetropolitan competition among the river towns near the Missouri's great bend. As Senator Thomas Hart Benton allegedly had predicted in 1853, the future lay with Kansas City.

Why did the wealthy men in Boston build their link to Kansas City, and why did they decide to place their bridge there rather than at Leavenworth? Local tradition offers a compact (and eminently useful) explanation: Brilliant action by the city's enlightened business leaders drew Joy's attention—in the nick of time—to the compelling geographical advantages their site offered; along with Van Horn's quick political manipulation of the Congressional bridge authorization, these facts turned the trick. As it stands, the story is too simple and too obviously shaped to satisfy home-town pride. However, it does answer one of the key questions in Kansas City's history, and it does contain some truth.[14]

Geographical advantages there certainly were, in view of the Burlington's plans to push a line south to the Gulf of Mexico. In addition to reaching an ocean port, this line could tap what was in the 1860's the most rapidly growing section of the state of Kansas. The state's population rose from 107,000 to 365,000 (an

---

[14] See two articles by Charles N. Glaab, "The Hannibal Bridge and the Legend of Local Enterprise," Central Mississippi Valley American Studies Association *Bulletin*, II, No. 1 (Fall, 1958), 9-19; "Kansas City's Hannibal Bridge: Western Town-Booming and Eastern Capital," *op. cit.*, pp. 1-16. See also R. R. Wohl and A. T. Brown, "The Usable Past: A Study of Historical Traditions in Kansas City," *Huntington Library Quarterly*, XXIII (1960), 237-59.

increase of 240 per cent) between 1860 and 1870. By 1880 the figure was just under a million, the rate of increase being 170 per cent. In the same twenty years—most of the increase coming after the Civil War—the southeastern quarter of the state grew from 2,000 to over 220,000, with percentage increases from the 1860's and 1870's of 465 and 1,794, respectively.[15] To reach this territory from any point up the Missouri River from Kansas City would have required more bridges and hence additional expense.

With respect to the acuity of local leadership, it must be remembered that the Kansas Citians had worked out an agreed railroad plan ten years earlier and had kept to that plan ever since. They had organized the voting community dependably to support exchanges of city bonds for railroad stock or, for that matter, to support any other kind of aid to railroads which the Chamber of Commerce found desirable. And, while James Joy may have generated his own interest in town-land purchases, his way was made easy by the eager cooperation of the West Kansas Land Company. Matters had not been arranged so smoothly in Leavenworth; that community seemed to lack the kind of effective organization which the leading Kansas Citians had achieved. There were conflicting projects and rival bond issues, and the upriver city was unable to pursue a unified and consistent plan. "We have lost opportunities," lamented a Leavenworth editor, ". . . because, unlike Atchison or Lawrence . . . or Kansas City or St. Joseph in Missouri, we did not cling closely together for a home interest, a home success. . . . We permitted ourselves to be torn by party divisions and really to be governed by the tricksters and demagogues who led these divisions."[16]

Van Horn's Congressional negotiation for a bridge authorization was not so important by itself as legend would have it, but seen with his strenuous work for a land grant along the projected southern line, his political role must be given some weight. Perhaps it is best to say that the Kansas City leaders won their long

[15] Fred Durr, *Population and Labor Force,* which is Part IV in the series, *Economic Development of South Central Kansas* (Lawrence: University of Kansas Bureau of Business Research, 1957), p. 7.

[16] *Leavenworth Times,* August 16, 1865.

and often frustrating struggle for metropolitan status by tying themselves to the plans of the Burlington Railroad in the 1860's. Even this probably oversimplifies matters; Kansas City had already begun to recover from the war by 1866. Growth had resumed, and with growth there came change.

Arrangements between the Kansas Citians and the Hannibal-Burlington group were completed, in all essential matters, by the end of 1866. While the bridge was not opened until July, 1869, the certainty of its location and, as time passed, the visible progress on its construction were enough to guarantee the "prospects" which local publicists, then as always, described to anyone who would listen. "The bridge," said the 1867-68 Directory, "will be the making of the city."[17]

The intrinsic importance and the dramatic qualities of the Hannibal Bridge story have almost monopolized the attention of Kansas City historians when they have dealt with the years immediately following the Civil War. The texture of urban growth was actually thicker than the story of the bridge by itself can suggest. Many other events were occurring at the same time, and these, too, were intimately connected with the city's progress toward metropolitanism.

There is the matter of recognizing hinterlands, for example. In the earliest days, the Town of Kansas had looked far out across the "Great American Desert" to find its customers in Oregon, California, and New Mexico. During the dozen years or so preceding 1865, the market began gradually to change as the land immediately to the west increasingly attracted farmers. The fundamental change had come about by the later sixties; Kansas City's future no longer depended on the outfitting of emigrants or on the "commerce of the prairies." Still, there were curious holdovers from the past in the city's publicity. Shortly after the war, the *Journal* proclaimed that Far Western trade was coming

---

[17] *The Kansas City Directory & Reference Book for 1867-68* (Kansas City: Excelsior Book & Job Office), p. 11.

back to the city a thousandfold: "It is in that direction that we must look for our future market." The same article held up the tempting potential offered by the state of Kansas as a hemp-and-tobacco-growing region.[18]

Although the New Mexican trade was clearly of shrinking importance to the city, it commanded as much newspaper space in the postwar years as it ever had. According to the *Journal*, business was to be resumed as it had been before the great interruption. Fleets of wagons were described as they arrived; readers were assured that the commerce of the prairies was about to concentrate even more heavily in Kansas City than it had earlier. As late as May, 1866, the editor remarked that "the Santa Fe trade has fairly resumed its old status. . . ."[19]

Actually, while the city was approaching a turning point in its history, nothing in the record suggests any awareness of what lay in the near future. Growth, to be sure, was avidly sought and keenly anticipated. But it was pictured as a simple quantitative process; to that which had been, more would be added. The small town with its railroad plans, its Far Western trade, and its busy levee would become a large city with railroads, more active Far Western trade, and a busier levee. Awareness of qualitative changes that were in the offing made its way gradually and by indirection into the community's public consciousness as new interests joined old ones—then, after a period, the old interests were no longer mentioned.

As the railroad campaign in Kansas City approached its successful climax, railroad construction throughout the nation was rearranging regional trade patterns and making a good portion of the *Journal's* rhetoric obsolete long before it was abandoned. In April, 1866, for example, two published articles contrasted strangely. According to one of them, the westward extension of the Union Pacific would not affect the location of the New Mexican trade; according to the other, it had already affected it

18 *Journal*, May 5, 1865.

19 Walker Wyman, "Kansas City: A Famous Freighter Capital," *Kansas Historical Quarterly*, VI (1937), 13; *Journal*, April 21, May 26, 1866.

profoundly. "An occasional old and well-remembered sign," said the editor,

> is one of the few things which the Mexicans recognize as familiar and unchanged by the rapid improvements made here since their visits before the war. . . . The rush of the iron horse now scares them from their accustomed camp fires along the river bank, and but for such landmarks as the house of W. H. Chick & Co., they would hardly be certain of their locality.[20]

W. H. Chick and Company moved to St. Louis the following year.

Another indicator of change was the position of the Indians with respect to the city's wealth. Their trade had accounted for Westport's origin and had underpinned a good part of Kansas City's business in the 1850's, but by the end of the war the presence of Indians to the south and west had come to be regarded as nothing but an obstacle to future progress. Some of the tribes had sided with the Confederacy, and in September, 1865, a council was held at Fort Smith to write a peace treaty. The treaty was of great local importance because of the plan for a railroad line to the Gulf of Mexico, projected as early as 1856 in the incorporation of the Kansas City, Galveston & Lake Superior Railroad Company. From Kansas City to Fort Smith went a familiar lobby: Van Horn, E. M. McGee, and M. J. Payne, along with a Wyandot Indian named Matthew Mudeater.

There was no question but that the treaty would reduce the size of the Indians' landholdings, but provision for a railroad right-of-way was far from certain. Land taken from former pro-Confederate tribes was to be given to "friendly" tribes now being sent south for resettlement. Parties of men from other places as well as from Kansas City were on hand at the council and endeavored to convince the Government's commissioners "of the great good which . . . will result from a direct grant of land for railroad purposes through the country south of this."[21]

[20] *Journal*, April 28, 1866.

[21] *Journal*, September 16, 1865; see also the issues of September 23 and 30 for comments on the Fort Smith negotiations.

Ultimately, the treaty did provide for a right-of-way, but its disposition was a matter for Congress, and much work by Van Horn, along with the Burlington representatives, preceded the desired grant. The relationship between Indian lands and railroad politics was far too complicated to be taken up here, but it did involve urban rivalry. On one occasion, for example, the *Journal* called attention to disturbing rumors that Congress might extinguish Indian title to some Kansas lands in the interest of a line from Leavenworth to Fort Smith. This line could then connect with the one that had been planned between Pleasant Hill and Lawrence, bypassing Kansas City to the south. It was hoped, editorially, that congressmen would have enough sense not to yield to blandishments from Leavenworth. Kansas City, after all,

> is the point of all others which outside of local prejudices would be selected as the terminus of a national work intended to facilitate trade, to open up to the best advantage a region of country as yet almost unknown to commerce.[22]

Concern for the Indians certainly played no part in Kansas City deliberations. While railroads, cities, and land companies attacked the tribes' titles, lobbied against them in Congress, and tried to persuade them into hasty cessions of their land, the local paper looked askance on "eastern" sensitivities in these matters. It was not true, wrote the editor,

> that the people of the Great West are more blood-thirsty or less humane than the dwellers under the benignities of Eastern civilization. . . . It might straighten the vision of some of these cross-eyed editors to be scalped a few times.[23]

Just eight years earlier, Charles Spalding had pointed proudly to the Indians' annuities as one of the components of Kansas City's permanent prosperity.

Certain new emphases, therefore, did make their way into

---

22 *Journal*, August 19, 1865; see Paul W. Gates, *Fifty Million Acres* (Ithaca, New York: Cornell University Press, 1954), for the subject of Indian land cessions in Kansas.

23 *Journal*, October 21, 1865.

the local propaganda. More attention was given to the agricultural future of the immediate environment, and this required the revision of an old notion: "The idea that the Central and Western portion of [Kansas] is a Desert has been exploded." The *Journal* clipped this item from the Junction City, Kansas, *Union,* which went on to describe fields of wheat and corn, and "luxuriant grapes," amidst which tens of thousands of settlers could find "homes superior to any portion of the public domain." On another occasion the paper reprinted portions of a speech by William Gilpin in which that enthusiast portrayed the fertility of the plains in characteristic prose; the editor entitled the piece, "Great American Desert."[24] The desert had become a farming heartland, sending to Kansas City and other regional centers more and more livestock and grain, and receiving back increasing quantities of agricultural machinery and finished goods of all kinds. It was in enterprises associated with this exchange that the city's future lay—less romantic, perhaps, than the caravans to Santa Fe had been, but more profitable and more closely geared to urban growth.

Livestock trade and meat packing were the most important of the new enterprises which reshaped the city. Here, too, the story is one of rapidly increasing emphasis rather than of a completely new beginning. Cattle had been raised for the market in western Missouri years before the Civil War, and the supplying of emigrants to the Far West had stimulated a brisk livestock trade, especially at St. Joseph. After 1845, cattle from Texas were driven through Missouri on their way north, crossing the river on ferries at the Town of Kansas, Boonville, and other places.[25] By the later 1850's, cattle trading was significant in Kansas City, and one local promoter wrote that "it does not require the foresight of a prophet to foretell that at Kansas City will be located

[24] *Journal,* May 6, 1865; *DJC,* December 2, 1865.

[25] Clifford D. Carpenter, "The Early Cattle Trade in Missouri," *Missouri Historical Review,* XLVII (1953); Frank S. Popplewell, "St. Joseph, Missouri, as a Center of the Cattle Trade," *ibid.,* XXXII (1938), 443-57; Louis Pelzer, *The Cattlemen's Frontier* (Glendale, Calif.: A. H. Clark, 1936); Wayne Gard, *The Chisholm Trail* (Norman, Oklahoma: University of Oklahoma Press, 1954).

the great meat market for a large portion of the United States."[26]

As early as 1858 Michael Diveley and Henry Kelley each started pork-packing firms in Kansas City, and the following year J. S. Chick set up another. At about the same time, John L. Mitchener, a Philadelphian and first cousin of Kersey Coates, came to the city. He had already been a meat packer in Cincinnati, and he now opened the largest establishment in Kansas City. It included four buildings, the main one measuring 100 by 40 feet, and it turned out bedposts and soap as well as meat. When the war ruined this promising business, Mitchener went to Chicago, where he traded in livestock and played a part in the organizing of the Union Stockyards there.[27] The war apparently drove everyone but Diveley out of the business, but its last years saw a revival of the livestock trade at St. Joseph. That city had an eastward rail connection, and as millions of cattle were bought cheap in Texas and the long drives began again, St. Joseph was ready to profit from them.

But the cattle trade was about to be completely reorganized, and during the process of change Kansas City got its bridge and the resulting entry into Chicago. A complicating factor in the Texas cattle drives, almost from the beginning, had been a disease to which the longhorns were immune, but which they carried to other cattle. Among these other cattle the disease did great damage. Farmers in Missouri and elsewhere sometimes banded together to force the Texas drovers away, and the Missouri legislature passed laws against the entry of longhorns. The Texas cattle could come into western Kansas, however, and there they might be loaded onto cars along the Union Pacific (Eastern Division) line. There was business opportunity here, and while the Kansas Citians were pushing their railroad negotiations to a

---

[26] *Kansas City Enterprise*, November 24, 1855; see also James C. Malin, *Grassland Historical Studies* (Lawrence, Kansas: By the author, 1950), I, 249 ff; and Charles C. Spalding, *Annals of the City of Kansas and the Great Western Plains* (Kansas City: Van Horn & Abeel, 1858), pp. 78-80.

[27] Joseph McCoy, *Historic Sketches of the Cattle Trade of the South and Southwest* (Kansas City: Ramsey, Millett & Company, 1874), pp. 284-86; *Kansas City Daily Journal*, October 22, 1893.

successful close, another man discovered a future in the shipment of cattle by rail.[28]

Joseph G. McCoy, a native of Illinois (not related to the Kansas City McCoys mentioned earlier), had grown up in the cattle business. After the war he became interested in the possibility of a western marketing center for longhorns and began looking for a good place to start one. Experiences in Kansas City impressed him favorably; according to his memoirs, the strong local pride and boosting spirit of the businessmen were noteworthy. The Union Pacific (Eastern Division), now called the Kansas Pacific, ran to the city, and its directors agreed to ship his cattle when he should have any. When he negotiated for special shipping rates, McCoy found the Missouri Pacific uninterested, even scornful of his whole project, but the Hannibal and St. Joseph offered him good terms. On the basis of this agreement, he decided to go ahead, with Kansas City as his transfer point. He bought land in Abilene, Kansas, set up his yards, and established a hotel and a bank.[29]

Kansas City was now about to become a regional livestock center; having captured the choice railroad connection and the railroad bridge from Leavenworth, it now took most of the stock trade which St. Joseph had hoped to gain. This success brought with it the problem of establishing stockyards. In 1868 Mitchener had returned to Kansas City and tried to buy sixty acres of land from William Gilliss, but the arrangements had not been completed.[30] Two years later, however, the power of outside capital was again demonstrated as L. V. Morse, General Superintendent of the Hannibal and St. Joseph Railroad, along with James Joy, bought five acres on which they built eleven pens, fifteen unloading chutes, and a scale. Business almost immediately outgrew these facilities, and in the spring of 1871 the progenitor of the Kansas City Union Stockyards was organized. The original thir-

[28] Popplewell, op. cit., pp. 447-48; E. E. Dale, The Range Cattle Industry (Norman: University of Oklahoma Press, 1939), pp. 29-31; Gard, op. cit., pp. 55-56.

[29] McCoy, op. cit., pp. 40-66.

[30] H. M. Holden, "Stockyards of Kansas City," in Conard, Encyclopedia, VI, 90.

teen and a half acres of land was soon expanded.[31] An intriguing conjunction of dates at this point highlights the significance of the Hannibal Bridge in the growth of the city. The bridge was opened in 1869, and within a year and a half the stockyards were organized and were started on what was to be a career of accelerating expansion. St. Joseph had its own railroad bridge in 1873, and there, too, union stockyards were built the following year— but the packing business in St. Joseph was handicapped by Kansas City's head start of almost four years.

The livestock trade, like any other large operation, required money, and in greater and more reliable quantities than Kansas City was accustomed to handle. The business was seasonal, and those engaged in it needed capital to cover the time between purchase and sale. Until 1870 the buyers (and the packers as well) worked on a commission basis. It was a hazardous trade, and the picture is one of small firms operating on narrow margins and frequently disappearing. Edward W. Pattison, for example, born in Kentucky and raised on an Indiana farm, had carried on both livestock trade and meat packing in Indianapolis. In 1867 he moved to Junction City, Kansas, one of the Kansas Pacific's cow towns, and in 1868 he came to Kansas City, where he joined with J. W. L. Slavens to operate a packing plant. The partnership packed 4,000 cattle in that year. In 1869 Slavens sold his interest to one Dr. F. B. Nofsinger and joined with another man to form Ferguson, Slavens & Company. Shortly thereafter, Pattison sold his interest.[32]

As livestock and the associated meat-packing industry grew, they were in need of some rationalizing hand. By 1870, $3,000,000 a year in livestock trade money passed through Kansas City banks—commerce which would hardly have been possible had not Howard Holden and one or two others moved in during the later 1860's and arranged for adequate banking services to

---

31 See Cuthbert Powell, *Twenty Years of Kansas City's Livestock Trade and Traders* (Kansas City: Pearl Printing Company, 1893); also Arthur Charvat, "Growth and Development of the Kansas City Stock Yards" (unpublished M.A. thesis, University of Kansas City, 1948).

32 McCoy, *op. cit.*, pp. 319-32; *U.S. Biographical Dictionary*, Missouri volume, pp. 694-95.

handle the expansion.[33] Most significant, however, was the decision of the great Chicago firm of Plankinton and Armour, in 1870, to set up a packing plant at the head of the cattle trail. This brought a branch of the Armour family to Kansas City, along with the family's bank and—of course—the great and growing plant, symbol of the city's industrial future.

That growth generated problems was hardly evident in Kansas City before about 1870; how to achieve growth was the problem which its leadership had chosen to face. Difficulties of a different kind, however, were bound to arise as the town enterprise succeeded and as its unpaved streets, bedraggled buildings, and rough levee yielded to the thoroughfares, the warehouses and factories, and the steaming railroad yards of a nineteenth-century American city. Some of these difficulties had begun to manifest themselves before 1870, and in a small way they prefigured the kinds of trouble which were to confront Kansas Citians increasingly after that date.

In the first place, the organization of the business community was already less simple than it had been in the late 1850's. The Chamber of Commerce had suffered, along with everything else in the city, during the war; an early local chronicler who knew most of the principals characterized its wartime life as "ephemeral and spasmodic." After December, 1863, the chamber apparently did not meet at all until July, 1865, when it was reorganized under a charter from the state legislature. The names which appear in the minutes are almost all familiar; Coates's is the most prominent. Even so, meetings were infrequent. The chamber helped arrange a sale of city lots; it discussed such questions as street improvements, the desirability of a waterworks, the effort to get a United States customs house at Kansas City, and the distribution of city directories. More important were railroad matters connected with

---

[33] E. S. Osgood, *The Day of the Cattleman* (Minneapolis, Minnesota: University of Minnesota Press, 1929), pp. 38-44; Conard, *Encyclopedia*, III, 265-67.

the Hannibal Bridge negotiations; but after April, 1866, the organization went quietly out of existence.[34]

For a time—almost three years—no organization represented the business community as a whole. Then, in February, 1869, a Board of Trade appeared—"rendered necessary," our historian tells us, "by the old Chamber of Commerce having ceased to exist."[35] The new group began more auspiciously than the old one, and its roster included a fair sprinkling of names which were new to Kansas City in the postwar years. The board met weekly and dealt with the same variety of topics the chamber had considered. Soon, however, it began to lose its vitality. It did much in 1869, little in 1870, and in January of the following year a different group, called the Merchants Exchange, organized and became at least partly competitive with the board. An effort to consolidate the two failed; the Merchants Exchange lapsed, and the Board of Trade did almost nothing until 1872, when it was reorganized.[36]

Why had the organizing of Kansas City's business interests become so difficult? William Miller, secretary to the reorganized Board of Trade in the later 1870's, suggests that the problem stemmed from success. He points out in his *History of Kansas City* that the Chamber of Commerce, by 1866, had accomplished most of what it had originally set out to do. "Many of its leading members," accordingly,

> became connected with the enterprises which it had inaugurated, and were thus individually employed to such an extent that they could not attend to the affairs of the organization.

Still, this success had caused the city to grow, raising "a new class of interests," and leading to the establishment of the Board of Trade. The process, according to Miller, repeated itself with the board. Such success met its efforts in 1869 that "its members yielded to the same impulses . . . and devoted themselves to their

34 Miller, *History*, p. 480; *Journal*, October 21, 1865; Chamber of Commerce minutes, typescript in Archives of Native Sons of Kansas City, pp. 26-35.

35 Miller, *History*, p. 489.

36 *Ibid.*, pp. 493, 497-99, 501; *Kansas City Times*, December 20, 1872.

own affairs."[37] The true explanation may be slightly broader than this. During a period of such radical change, it must have been difficult—perhaps quite impossible—to set up and maintain a reliable and stable consensus of business interest. At any rate, the Kansas City business community was not again in the nineteenth century to be the close-knit, smoothly functioning machine which it had been, with the exception of the war years, through 1866.

There were other problems as the growing city manifested more and more needs. Fire protection was one of these. With reviving hopes and activities, more attention was given to this matter. From 1868 on, the editor of the *Journal* not only made news stories out of fires, but used them to point up the need for proper protective measures. These should include plenty of cisterns distributed throughout the city and a paid fire-fighting force. Early in 1868 the city council provided for a brick engine house (near the corner of Sixth and Main streets) and bought a steam fire engine in Seneca Falls, New York. Two hose carts and 2,000 feet of rubber hose were also provided, and the engine was fitted to be horse-drawn. The force consisted of a man to operate the engine at $75 a month, plus a stoker at $50, along with anyone who volunteered to help when a fire broke out. The arrangement was cumbersome in the extreme; sometimes the engine (called the "John Campbell") was rushed to the scene of a blaze only to stand idly because no one had brought the hose carts. Fortunately, no disastrous fires occurred during these years, but costly, localized fires were frequent. By the end of the 1860's some Kansas Citians were discussing the value of a city waterworks in relation to fire protection. A waterworks, however, would be expensive; constitutional limitations on the city's indebtedness forbade issuance of the necessary bonds. Not until 1875 would a waterworks be constructed—under private auspices—and until then the cisterns, the "John Campbell," two city employees, and the hope of timely downpours of rain constituted the city's protection against damage by fire.[38]

[37] Miller, *History,* pp. 492, 497.

[38] *Journal,* December 12, 1868; May 8 and 15, and July 3, 1869; January 29, 1870.

The schooling of children was another complex problem, although more of a beginning had been made by 1870 than was the case with fire protection. During 1867, consequent on state enabling legislation, the Kansas City School Board was organized, and it began the task of setting up a public school system. There had been a "Board of Public Schools" as early as 1861, but it had done very little, perhaps because of small resources. Public education began in Kansas City in 1867; classes met in rooms rented by the reorganized school board, which speedily began to acquire land for school purposes. By 1870 several school buildings had been built, over $100,000 in school bonds issued, a staff of teachers hired, and between three and four thousand children were attending classes. Some chinks still remained in the structure, however, and the board's first decade closed in a spirited court battle over the legal status of the school board and its funds.[39] Increasingly, as time passed, the board and indeed the whole system was to find itself involved in the rivalries and confusions of city politics.

Street grading and street improvements in general were urgent matters in postwar Kansas City, built as it was upon the rambling hills and bluffs of the Missouri River's right bank. Soon after the war, city bonds to the amount of $60,000 for street grading were approved and issued. The main north-south streets—Broadway, Wyandotte, Delaware, Main, and Grand—had to be cut through the high bluffs which so many early visitors to the city had described as its most striking physical feature. Some of this work had been begun before the Civil War, and now it was to go on for years as machinery replaced shovels, and blasting powder later came to the aid of machines. Deep into the clay and rocks went the streets; in some cases, cuts eighty feet deep were necessary. In a number of places the materials taken from the

39 *Journal*, January 4, 1868; November 13 and December 18, 1869; January 1, 1870; *Kansas City Directory and Reference Book* (Kansas City: Bulletin Book & Job Office [1870]), pp. 22-33; *Fourteenth Annual Report of the Kansas City Public Schools* (Kansas City: Board of Education, 1885), p. 16; *Thirty-sixth Annual Report of the Board of Education.* . . . (Kansas City: Riley, 1907), p. 205.

cuts were used to fill ravines elsewhere in the neighborhood.[40] Before the work was finished, the original topography of the city's downtown section had been almost completely changed.

Still, the improvement of streets raised political difficulties of a worrisome kind in the growing city. As the city grew, it became a patchwork of neighborhoods, and the inhabitants of these did not agree on where the general interest lay. Special elections for street improvements failed more than once in postwar Kansas City because of neighborhood rivalry. Specifically, this delayed cutting through a good connection between the developing railroad yards in the West Bottoms and the rest of the city. The *Journal* viewed these neighborhood quarrels with alarm: "We have no . . . wish to encourage differences or to stir up strife between different portions of the city. The example of Leavenworth in this regard should be a warning to us." And this was followed by a series of articles on the dangers of neighborhood politics.[41]

Political asperities in general either were becoming sharper in the later 1860's or else were more prominently displayed than had so far been the case. A group of men, headed by one A. L. Harris who was twice elected mayor, were able to delay collection of city taxes for several months in that year by challenging the constitutionality of the charter. They ultimately lost their case, but not before considerable bitterness had developed. At other times Republicans were busy denying charges that Van Horn and others had used bribery to gain political advantage, and Democrats denied that Milton J. Payne had tampered with the registration lists in 1868 to bring about Van Horn's defeat. Political differences, it appeared, were becoming as unmanageable as business interests.[42]

Racial and national distinctions grew in importance as party quarrels and neighborhood differences confused the city's polity.

[40] Conard, *Encyclopedia*, III, 489; Carrie W. Whitney, *Kansas City, Missouri— Its History & Its People, 1808-1908* (Chicago: S. J. Clarke, 1908), I, 109-13; Roy Ellis, *A Civic History of Kansas City* (Springfield, Missouri: By the author, 1930), pp. 77-78.

[41] *Journal*, July 24, 1869.

[42] *Journal*, April 4, September 12, November 14, 1868.

Almost overnight the question arose whether or not Negroes were to participate in public meetings on equal terms with whites. The influence of the Irish and Germans was pointedly described; whether these influences were for better or for worse depended upon one's position. The *Journal*, staunchly Republican, had only praise for the "loyal" Germans in Kansas City, but was less enthusiastic about the Irish. "Although city government belongs to them as a matter of right," wrote the editor about a local Democratic nominating convention,

> and they are entitled to live off of it when the Democratic Party is in power . . . , although "improvements" should be made for their benefit, and contracts let to give them employment, yet just for the look of the thing a single native-born American citizen wouldn't have been out of place upon the ticket. . . .[43]

Meanwhile, other less pleasing urban phenomena forced themselves upon public attention. A large number of people had been attracted to the city by the opportunity for work which the building of the Hannibal Bridge offered. Some of the less desirable characters among them congregated on the north side of the river in an area called Harlem, where by 1869 a vigilante organization had arisen to try to deal with the disorders. Kansas City, too, had "a large number of abandoned characters . . . , as in all other rapidly growing Western towns. . . ." Mayor Harris, in his first message to the council in 1869, referred to the number of thieves in town; gambling flourished, and the police seemed unable or unwilling to do anything to curb it. In 1870 the force consisted of only twenty-four un-uniformed men, counting the marshal; there was no police station and only two small "lock-ups." During the previous winter some of the businessmen had organized and paid their own "merchants' police force," but it had since disappeared. The quality of social life, especially at places of entertainment, was not inspiring, and the *Journal* protested against obstreperous and crude behavior at theaters: "We have now a sufficient number of persons of culture and refinement among us

[43] *Journal,* April 25, February 15, April 4, 1868.

to give tone to public entertainments, and to frown down vulgarity and clownishness."[44]

These matters, however, were just beginning to occupy the attention of responsible Kansas Citians. They signaled a new era in the community's history. The early one—the premetropolitan stage—was properly laid to rest by the opening of the fine new Hannibal Bridge on Saturday, July 3, 1869. Building it had taxed the ingenuity of the great engineer, Octave Chanute, as well as the energy of the carpenters, masons, divers, blacksmiths, and laborers whom he directed. Work had begun February 27, 1866; there was only one small foundry in Kansas City at the time, and the bridge company was forced to make many of its own tools. A steamboat was bought in Wheeling, West Virginia; flatboats, pile drivers, derricks, and dredges were built, and the company set up its own machine shop in an abandoned building near the site.[45]

The local papers reported progress week by week as the builders fought current, ice, and shifting channel. Finally the draw was swung, and late in June, 1869, an engine crossed safely. Great preparations began for appropriate festivities the following week. The Kansas City scene on July 3, according to a reporter from St. Joseph, "was without parallel in Western celebrations." He described the two-mile procession, the gaily decorated train which crossed the bridge, the speeches and the barbecue at a grove just south of the city, the balloon ascension, the firing of cannon, and at night the great banquet at the Broadway Hotel with the inevitable toasts and responses. The *Journal* headline writer was inspired: "LET US ENJOY THE PASS-OVER." Both the *Journal* and its new rival, the *Kansas City Times*, carried long

---

[44] *Journal*, May 1, 1869; January 29 and February 19, 1870; quotations from March 30 and June 5, 1869, issues.

[45] Octave Chanute, *The Kansas City Bridge, With an Account of the Regimen of the Missouri River, & a Description of Methods Used for Founding in that River* (New York: Van Nostrand, 1870), pp. 14-15 *et passim*.

and partly accurate stories of how the bridge had been won by Kansas City, as well as descriptions of the celebration.[46]

The bridge, with its approaches and work on the river channel upstream, had cost just over a million dollars. It was so constructed that teams and wagons could cross when no trains were approaching or on it, but the precious railroads busily used the bridge; in the first eight months of operation, 4,131 trains crossed it. With them came people, goods, wealth—and urbanization.

According to the federal census, the city's population in 1870 was 32,268. But here, too, enthusiastic Kansas Citians had done some promoting, and the figure is much too high. Many years later Daniel Geary, who was city clerk in 1870, recalled how the council, "ambitious to make a good showing," had encouraged census-takers to count one section of the city twice.[47] Data from business directories and the school enumerations bear out Geary's memory, and in 1885 a prominent businessman said that "the census must have been padded to death in 1870. . . ." It was not the first time; a year earlier the city had wanted to issue some railroad bonds for which the law of Missouri required it to have at least 30,000 residents. The city fathers hastily ran a census of their own which came, coincidentally, to just 31,000.[48] It is not possible to say with any real accuracy what Kansas City's population was in 1870, but between 20,000 and 25,000 is a reasonable guess.

Even the revised figures tell a remarkable urban success story. A cynic might suggest that, to 1870, it was a story that began with a fraudulent land sale and ended with a faked census, but there cannot have been many cynics in Kansas City at the close of our period. Too much had been done, and too much was yet to do to allow time for such untoward reflections. A vigorous group of projectors and planners had somehow overseen the birth of a city, and they were by no means done with their labors.

[46] *St. Joseph Weekly Gazette,* July 8, 1869; *Journal,* July 10, 1869, reprinting stories published earlier in the *Daily Journal; Kansas City Times,* July 3, 1869.

[47] Daniel Geary, "Looking Backward," September 6, 1910, typescript in Archives of the Native Sons of Kansas City.

[48] *Kansas City Star,* June 2, 1885; *Journal,* August 28, 1869.

Late in 1869, indeed, a delegation from the Board of Trade left Kansas City for Springfield, Missouri, on a characteristic mission: railroad promotion. For some time a connection with Memphis, via Springfield, had been thought desirable. With confidence derived from past success, Van Horn, Reid, Kearney, and others now set about the project of "the Memphis Road" with all the techniques by now so familiar. This time, however, they were to fail miserably, and before the Memphis dream was liquidated they were quarreling with one another, trying to protect damaged reputations, and leaving the taxpayers of their city and county a heavy bill in useless bond issues.[49]

This did not really matter—but to follow the story of the Memphis Road any further would take this book beyond its chronological limit. Kansas City had seven railroad connections by 1870, and the other roads would seek the city. Five banks made their headquarters there: First National, 1865; Kansas City Savings Association, 1865; J. Q. Watkins and Company, who had bought up the older business of Northrup and Chick, 1865; the Mastin Bank, 1866; and the German Savings Association, 1868.[50] The city's place in the nation's commercial geography was unassailable, and industry was beginning to concentrate. The time for spectacular railroad enterprises was past. Tasks of a different sort faced Kansas Citians as they began to cope with the urban environment which nature, talent, and luck had conspired to create.

[49] Glaab, *Kansas City and the Railroads.*
[50] Conard, *Encyclopedia,* I, 116-17.

Index

231